REPORTAGE PRESS

ABOUT THE AUTHOR

Vitali Vitaliev was born in 1954 in Kharkiv, Ukraine and studied English at Kharkiv University. He then became the first investigative journalist in the Soviet Union. As a result, he was forced to defect from the USSR by the KGB in January 1990. He has become widely known in the West for his regular appearances on TV and radio. Vitaliev has published nine books, written in English and has been translated into a number of languages. He has contributed regularly to the *Guardian*, the *European*, the *Daily Telegraph*, the *Australian* and others, and has also made several TV documentaries. He is currently Features Editor of *E&T* magazine and lives near London.

"Vitali Vitaliev is a star in the making"
TIME Magazine

"Vitaliev has an irrepressible sense of humour"
The Guardian

PASSPORT TO ENCLAVIA

TRAVELS IN SEARCH OF A EUROPEAN IDENTITY

BY VITALI VITALIEV

REPORTAGE PRESS

REPORTAGE PRESS

Reportage Press
26 Richmond Way, London W12 8LY, United Kingdom.
Tel: (0044) (0)7971 461 935
Fax: (0044) (0)20 8749 2867
e-mail: info@reportagepress.com
www.reportagepress.com

Published by Reportage Press, 2008

Produced under the editorial direction of Duncan Barrett

British Library Cataloguing in Publication Data.

A catalogue record for this book is available from the British Library.

ISBN-13: 978-0-9558302-9-7

Cover design by Sheridan Wall
Illustrations by Conrad Steen
Layout by Florence Production Ltd

Printed and bound in Great Britain by Antony Rowe, Chippenham, Wiltshire
www.antonyrowe.co.uk

To Andrei, my London-born half-Ukrainian, half-Australian son – a little traveller and a true European

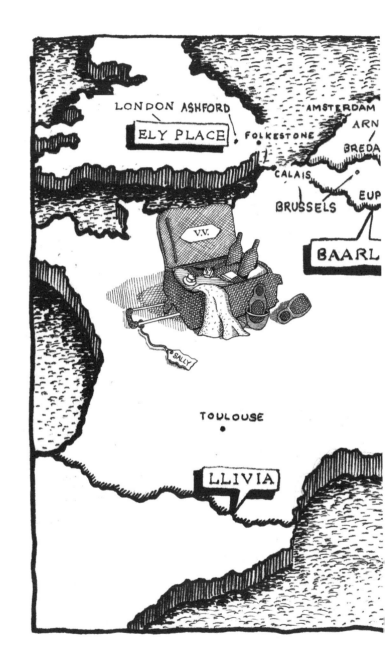

"that misty term 'Europe' "

Geert Mak

"Perchance on your penknife you'll find
A speck of dust from lands afar,
The world will once again arise
Mysterious, wrapped in veil bizarre . . ."

Alexander Blok

CONTENTS

Acknowledgements

I would like to thank, first of all, those who – by their kindness and warmth – have helped me survive during one of the most trying periods of my life, which coincided with researching and writing this book. I cannot possibly name all of them here, but most will know who they are.

I was lucky to have a number of voluntary helpers, without whom *Enclavia* would have never materialised as a book, let alone a country (even if a fictitious one).

The first to be mentioned is Oskar Hinteregger, UK & Ireland Director of the Austrian National Tourist Office, who – selflessly and heroically – ventured to become the project's main enthusiast as well as co-ordinator and organiser, acting as a liaison between myself and various people and organisations – not just in Austria, but all over Europe.

I want to thank Michael Helmerich from the London branch of the German Tourist Board for making arrangements for my visits to Busingen, Schaffhausen and the German-speaking part of Belgium.

I am grateful to the Royal Literary Fund, Inntravel, Julia Spence Public Relations, EasyJet, Internationale Bodensee Tourismus GmbH, the Belgian Tourist Office, the Netherlands Board of Tourism, French Government Tourism Office, Azienda di Promozione Turistica del Comasco, Tourism Promotion Agency of Livigno, InterRail, Eurostar, Hotel Kronenhof in Schaffhausen, Grand Hotel Capoul in Toulouse and many, many others.

My most heartfelt thanks, however, are reserved for the true Europeans – the residents of Western Europe's remaining enclaves and semi-enclaves, who have shared their joys and sorrows, their problems and idiosyncrasies – in short, their everyday lives – with me.

Vitali Vitaliev
London 2008

Introduction: The Road to Enclavia

ELY PLACE

> "If you don't remember anything else I say, remember this: every single fundamental problem of the independent world is rooted in an imperfect sense of identity."
>
> Bill Clinton

There is a place in London where I often go for solace at moments of sadness and indecision. Passing through the ornate iron gates separating Ely Place, a quiet little cul-de-sac off Holborn Circus, from the hustle and bustle of the City, is like entering a mysterious fourth dimension, the name of which is "dislocation".

Very few people know that the straight tree-less lane, the former residence of the Bishops of Ely, is not geographically a part of London. It is a little corner of Cambridgeshire, still enjoying freedom from entry by the London Police, except by the invitation of the Commissioners of Ely Place – its own elected governing body. (The results of the latest elections, dated and certified by "J. Franks, Esq., Clerk to the Commissioners", are duly displayed on the noticeboard of the magnificent St. Etheldreda Chapel – the oldest Roman Catholic church in Britain – halfway up the street.)

One of London's best-kept secrets, Ely Place is a living anachronism from medieval times when the influential Bishops were determined to remain in their Cambridgeshire diocese even while on ministerial missions in the capital. In the local pub, one can view a stack of recent letters addressed to "Ye Olde Mitre Tavern, Ely Place, Holborn Circus, Cambridgeshire".

Why does this stranded street, situated simultaneously in London and outside it, agree with me so well? Why does it evoke in me the peculiar feeling of being elsewhere – a sensation both calming and disturbing? Is it due to the fact that as a Ukrainian-born Russian, with Australian and British passports, I am a thoroughly "dislocated" person myself?

Or is it also because "ee-ly" means "or" in Russian – an ideal association for a place that is neither here nor there, or either here *or* there, if you wish?

Perhaps, part of its attraction lies in the fact that Ely Place, this little chunk of Cambridgeshire in the centre of London, is a model of a full-scale geopolitical *enclave*, of which there are still a handful left on the map of Europe.

According to a widely accepted scholarly definition, "enclaves" are parts of one country totally surrounded and landlocked by the territory of another. This excludes self-governing mini-states, surrounded by foreign territory – San Marino, Andorra, Vatican City, etc. – or isolated parts of a country that are accessible by sea and hence have a direct link to their motherland: Alaska, Kaliningrad (Russia) and the disputed Spanish towns of Ceuta and Melilla on the Mediterranean coast of Morocco, which are often incorrectly referred to as enclaves.

To me the most fascinating quality of the remaining West European enclaves is that each of them combines characteristics of two or more separate European nations, making them an ideal natural laboratory for isolating – as in chemical experiments – a common substance (trait) that makes them tick.

Of the two hundred and fifty-five proper enclaves currently existing in the world, almost ninety percent are located in the small corner of Asia between India and Bangladesh. I dug this figure out from an extremely rare book *The Exclave Problem of Western Europe*[1], penned by Honore M. Catudal, Jr. and published in 1979

---

1. *An exclave is an enclave when viewed from its mother nation. For example, Campione (an Italian town within Switzerland) is an enclave to the Swiss, and an exclave to Italy.*

by the University of Alabama Press in the USA – so far the only printed work on the West European enclaves in the English language.

"The possession of an uninterrupted territory is one of the principal requisites for the smooth functioning of a political entity," wrote the honourable Honore M. Catudal in the Introduction to his engaging monograph. "Enclaves, though, disturb this tranquillity by creating numerous administrative problems for both home and host states, increasing the variety of social groups and physical environments, adding to the difficulties of travel and communication and, more important, lengthening the political and economic boundaries to be guarded." In other – less scholastic – words, one might characterise enclaves as peculiar geopolitical troublemakers and mavericks – which may be one of the main reasons for my enduring passion for them.

Most of the remaining West European enclaves appeared in the Middle Ages – after the treaties of Madrid (1526) and Westphalia (1648), the latter ending the Thirty Years War and creating diverse and independent principalities which made the map of Europe resemble a sloppily manufactured patchwork quilt. Others resulted from land ownership disputes, or plain mistakes. With the advent of capitalism, the Napoleonic wars, the creation of the German and Italian states and the Swiss Confederation, most of the enclaves were eventually re-attached to their mother countries or swallowed up by host-states. Verenahof, a small patch of German farmland inside Switzerland, was the last European enclave to lose its status, as recently as in 1964, when it was happily absorbed by the Swiss.

Apart from Vennbahn, a Belgian railway cutting into German territory south of Aachen to form five Belgian "pockets" inside Germany, and several Alpine villages that can only be accessed from neighbouring countries (Samnaun, Jungholz and Kleinwalsertal Valley, the so-called "semi-enclaves"), only four "full-scale" outliers can now be found in Western Europe. They are: Campione d'Italia – an Italian town in Switzerland; Llivia – a Spanish (or rather Catalan) town in the French Pyrenees; Busingen – a German village in Switzerland; and Baarle/Baarle-Hertog – a unique Dutch/Belgian municipality comprising twenty-two pieces of Belgium and eight of Holland. Like children of mixed marriages, torn between two different cultures and ways of life, they combine the traits of their mother countries with those of their host states – which makes them wonderfully uncertain, idiosyncratic and ambivalent. By their very nature, they defy chauvinism in all its ugly forms in our epoch of ethnic cleansing, racial prejudice and rampant nationalism.

To locate the enclaves on even the most detailed maps of Europe takes a powerful magnifying glass. But even armed with a microscope, it is easy to overlook such places as Busingen – effectively a German suburb of the Swiss canton centre of Schaffhausen, or Samnaun – formerly a smugglers' haven and now the "duty-free" Swiss semi-enclave of a village, lost in the Austrian Alps. Often, even residents of neighbouring towns and villages have no knowledge of the piece of a foreign country on their doorstep.

To make matters worse, it is not uncommon for the authorities of a mother country (a state to which an enclave belongs politically, but not territorially) to claim no responsibility over a "prodigal" bit of their own land. Their counterparts in a host country, by whose territory an enclave is surrounded, are often equally uninterested in the problems of a foreign "intruder".

One could be forgiven for thinking that these obscure geopolitical anomalies in the heart of Europe – whose status, in my view, should be protected by a special European Parliament Act – do not actually exist.

My undying interest in enclosed spaces (by borders, bars, fences, stone walls, etc.) goes back to my childhood. I spent the first three years of my life in a so-called "closed town" near Moscow, to which my parents, young scientists (Mum was a chemical engineer, Dad a nuclear physicist) and newly-married graduates of Kharkiv University, were dispatched to work at a top-secret Soviet government facility, developing nuclear and hydrogen bombs in the early 1950s. The town of forty thousand people was both unmapped and unnamed (it was referred to as "Military Unit

BA/48764", or something similar). It was enclosed by a tall concrete fence, with barbed wire on top, and no-one could enter or leave without a special pass.

Times were tough. Stalin wanted to develop nuclear weapons by hook or by crook to achieve military parity, and then, ultimately, superiority over the West. My parents had to work for twelve hours a day and there was practically no protection against the excessive radiation. My mother told me how skin peeled off her palms when she was pregnant with me (so I must have got my share of the stuff too). Some of her colleagues literally died before her eyes from overdoses, and my father was particularly affected, since he dealt directly with radioactive substances. He died at the early age of fifty-six of the long-term irradiation effects.

Of course, I don't remember much from these distant years; I was too young. But strangely enough I did recall some smells, vague impressions and feelings (claustrophobia being one of them) when I visited the town with my mother shortly before my defection from the USSR – in 1989, after thirty-three years of absence.

The devilish "facility" was still there. It was still located in the grounds of the old monastery, only instead of crosses, the factory buildings had faded metallic red stars mounted on their onion domes.

The town was still surrounded by the thick concrete wall with barbed wire. You could only get in through a couple of checkpoints, provided you had an invitation from someone living inside the compound. We were invited by a woman who had worked with my parents many years before.

At the checkpoint, a young military guard, having carefully scrutinised our credentials, gave us a one-day pass into my childhood and my Mum's youth – equally constrained and repressed. "The place hasn't changed a bit," my Mother noted sadly.

Childhood impressions are extremely potent. And could it be that having been literally "encaged" for the first three years of my existence, I have spent the rest of my life trying to escape the constraints of borders and dogmas, but at the same time having a strange (possibly even dark) fascination, or nostalgia, for little pockets of life, separated – in one way or another – from the rest of the world?

Like Billy Liar in PG Wodehouse's novel, who invented Ambrosia – a fictitious land, to which he could escape from the gloomy reality of his provincial town in the North of England – as a youngster in the Soviet Union I used to entertain the idea of having my own mini-state – an "autocratic democracy", populated and ruled by just one person – myself. In this fluid and moveable "nation", with no stable borders, I could stop being a permanent outcast – both ethnically and spiritually. Even living in the West, I often try to visualise my imaginary "country" ("Vitalia"?) which would comfortably accommodate all the duplicities and uncertainties of my peripatetic existence – the land where no one would regard me, its only citizen, as a foreigner, which in turn would provide me with some sense of stability and national awareness.

Vitalia's biggest flaw, however, is that it doesn't quite correspond to the generally accepted definition of a country as "a territory, distinguished by its people, culture and geography". Travelling around the globe, I am always on the look-out for a real-life, not fictitious land, where I would experience that obscure (to me) sensation of belonging, and my discovery of the West European enclaves, the places where I felt more at home than anywhere else in the world, made me think that I had found one.

Indeed, the remaining enclaves of Western Europe share the never-ending dichotomy of their people – permanently torn between two (or more) different cultures. They also share "displacement" as a common feature of their geography. But what's more important, as I have established while visiting them, is that they all have similar achievements and similar problems which determine their shared common mentality – a peculiar ingenuity of the enclaves' dwellers, shaped by centuries of having to deal with not one but two state bureaucracies at a time. Strewn around Europe – from the Pyrenees to the Austrian Alps – these orphaned and stateless villages and small towns, unwanted by both their mother countries and their host states, have all the credentials to be regarded as a separate entity – the Federation of Disunited European Enclaves (FDEE), or simply Enclavia.

I don't remember exactly when I first had the idea to visit all remaining West European enclaves and semi-enclaves. Was it while researching my book on the mini-states of Europe, *Little is the Light* in 1993–94, when, for the first time, I heard of the special status of Campione d'Italia – economically Swiss, yet politically and geographically Italian? Or was it during my spells in Australia and in the USA, when, tormented by nostalgia, I sometimes saw myself as a stranded one-person Euro-enclave, torn between my constantly changing whereabouts and my roots? It was then that I first thought of the enclaves not just as a geopolitical reality but as a category of the human soul. No man is an island, according to John Donne. This may be true, but some, like myself, are enclaves.

I thought therefore that travelling to all the enclaves of Western Europe was my best opportunity to pin down an elusive European identity – and perhaps my own as well.

If "true Europeans" are to be found anywhere at all, the enclaves should be the places. Yet, visiting all of them, I saw the extent to which officials in Brussels and Strasbourg stubbornly refused to notice (or even to acknowledge the existence of) the enclaves, where cross-cultural harmony, cross-border co-operation and "European integration" have been happening *naturally* for hundreds of years. The reason for such ostracism is simple: by their very existence, the enclaves perfectly epitomise the "unified Europe" ideal, achieved without any assistance and/or interference from the EC, and therefore constitute a direct challenge to the very existence of arrogant and overpaid Euro-bureaucrats. "They don't know about us, and they don't want to know," was the mantra I heard in every single enclave and semi-enclave on my route. Why? The answer was no less repetitive: "Because – through centuries of living together – we have managed to create our own little EU – without any instructions from Brussels!"

It was the end of 2001, and the continent held its breath awaiting the introduction of its new common currency – the Euro, the most momentous change in modern European history. I thought that early 2002 would therefore be the perfect time for my quest.

Shortly after my research was completed, I was hit by a massive personal crisis that incapacitated me as writer for over five years. Having recovered (I always do), I looked at the copious notes of my Enclavia travels and – ten years since the idea of the Euro was first put forward – I decided there was no need to update them: the book would work best as a retro journey chronicling, among other things, the first days and months of the Euro – a historic period when a European identity (if there is such a thing), European values and Europe itself were undergoing the biggest shake-up since WWII.

But what is identity? *Collins Concise Dictionary* defines it as "the individual characteristics by which a person or thing is recognised". This means effectively that one has no control over his or her own identity, which – like beauty – is very much "in the eyes of the beholder", in how others see us rather than in how we see ourselves – a fact so perversely and so cannibalistically substantiated by the Holocaust and, more recently, by "ethnic cleansings" in the former Yugoslavia and in Rwanda, as well as by the September 11 terrorist attacks. One particular detail from media reports about the atrocity haunts me: nearly three thousand people of more than eighty different nationalities were murdered solely for being "American" – in the terrorists' eyes that is. Brits and Arabs, Germans and Australians – all became Americans at the moment of their violent deaths. This makes one ponder over the true meaning of national, ethnic, cultural and other human identities. Where do they start and where do they finish? And what (or who) exactly is it that determines them?

My own gruesome experience prompts me to agree with Scottish writer A.L. Kennedy, who once wrote in the *Guardian* that "national identity rests on bigotry and self-absorption – and the (preferably televised) humiliation by others". If so, then the best way to pin down one's identity is by spending some time in a hostile, not necessarily foreign, environment.

It is important to understand that identity and nationality are two different things, the latter being one of the many components of the former. Identity is permanent and unchangeable, whereas nationality is rather arbitrary and fluid. Unlike identity, which, as we have just established, is largely beyond one's control, nationality can be gained by naturalisation (like my British citizenship), denied (like the same citizenship in the case of Muhammad Al Fayed), altered, withdrawn or even acquired for a bribe – a fairly common occurrence in the former Soviet Union. Identity is for life, and life is sometimes the price for adhering to it.

So is there such thing as a Pan-European identity?

Anthony Sampson in his book *The New Europeans* noted that "in spite of all the interactions with America, there is still not much difficulty in distinguishing Europeans from Americans. Americans have paradoxically helped to unite Europe in two opposite senses: first, by regarding the ... continent as a whole; secondly, by showing Europeans that they have at least one thing in common – that they are not American".

And although I would find it hard to say exactly what "European-ness" involves, I know that I felt profoundly European while living in Australia, where my nostalgia for Europe – not for any particular country, but for Europe as a whole: for its trees and smells, for its low satin skies, for its old stones – became almost obsessive. I also felt European in America, whose loud, hooray-patriotic and often megalomaniac attitudes were a sharp contrast to quieter Europeans ways. And whereas an American President can easily get away with (and even earn some political capital by) repeatedly calling America "the greatest nation on the face of the earth", a similar pronouncement from any European head of state is likely to trigger a prompt election.

It is not just Americans who are helping Europeans to unite by regarding our continent "as a whole" (*pace* Sampson) and thus implying that a Greek, a Swede and a Belgian share some common identity, at least in the outsiders' eyes. It's true that in the USA I often came across ads and signs where "European" was a euphem-ism for "quality" or "classy": "European Leather", "European

Lights", "European Kitchens", and even "European Skin-Care" in Newport, Rhode Island. (The latter made me wonder what particular "skin-care" was implied: Italian, French or, maybe, Estonian?) But it was in Australia that I saw the most striking manifestation of this curious inferiority complex (or was it a post-colonial hangover?), when a mediocre and permanently empty Turkish restaurant in the Melbourne suburb of South Caulfield tried to attract customers by installing a huge brightly painted banner above its entrance: "European women in the kitchen!".

* * *

Contrary to my intentions, it was in Australia that I found myself on "E-Day" – 1 January, 2002. In the weeks to come, I would painstakingly sift through Australian newspapers in search of news from Europe, where – for the second time in its troubled history – a single currency had come into circulation. (The first failed attempt was undertaken by Napoleon III, who created the short-lived Latin Monetary Union in 1863.)

"There is no subtler, no surer means of overturning the existing basis of society than to debauch the currency – the process engages all the hidden forces of economic law on the side of destruction." Who said this? No, not Maggie Thatcher, although she would probable agree. It was written by Vladimir Ilyich Lenin, the great leader and teacher of workers, peasants and executioners, the founder of the Soviet state and an undisputed expert in "overturning the bases" of democratic societies.

For reasons purely emotional, I regretted the passing-away of different European currencies. For years, I used to take pleasure in changing my familiar pounds sterling or Aussie dollars into foreign money first thing on arriving in a new European country. Hunched over a cuppa at the nearest café, I would scrutinise the alien-looking banknotes trying to learn something about the nation's history and culture which they were supposed to reflect. This little ritual was an integral part of travelling and one of its little delights.

I deplored the demise of deutschemarks, especially of the banknote with the portrait of the brothers Grimm; of colourful and crispy – like freshly-baked baguettes – French francs, which I am told started in 1360 as ransom money to bale out King John II of France from English captivity ("franc" meant "free"); of rumpled and near-worthless Italian lire, smelling of sunshine and olive oil; of Greek drachmas going back to the sixth century BC, when they circulated as silver coins in Athens; of substantive Austrian shillings, on which – only several years earlier – women's faces were allowed to be printed for the first time by a special government decree. They were all to be replaced with uniform, badly designed and lifeless Euros. Perhaps, it is a life-long passionate stamp collector speaking in me too: postage stamps, these colourful tiny bits of unknown and unreachable foreign lands, provided me with one of the few little windows to a life outside the world's largest cage of the USSR in which I had been imprisoned for thirty-five years. For the same reason, a couple of my childhood friends collected old foreign banknotes.

On the eve of the E-Day (when the new pan-European currency first went into circulation), the Belgian Foreign Minister, called the Euro "the first important symbol of the European identity". Utter nonsense. On the contrary, it felt as if a chunk of that very "identity" had been forcefully taken away.

What will go next, I was wondering? Postage stamps (indeed, who needs separate national stamps when the currency is the same)? Flags? Anthems? Languages? A new cross-national Pan-European Esperanto?

I thought it was not by chance that immediately after the "E-Day", the EC functionaries – in a sinister thrust towards a European superstate with Brussels as capital – began relentlessly campaigning for the EU president, the EU army, the EU joint police force, the EU arrest warrant, the EU air traffic control, etc. Having grown up in a totalitarian state, I am instinctively frightened of this unstoppable push, for I know only too well that all superpowers are sooner or later bound to show dictatorial traits. Confronted with Brussels' almighty propaganda machine (450 million dollars of European taxpayers' money was spent on the Euro campaign alone), the people of Europe had little choice. The feeling of being out of control was similar to the one I had when calling for a taxi in Melbourne and hearing a recorded voice message: "Hello, we already know your name and address."

In the meantime, Australia was living its normal undisturbed life. January there – like August in Europe – was the start of the "silly season", and everyone was heading for the beach. Possums, whose own endemically Australian "identity" was – unlike mine – totally above suspicion, were climbing up and down gum trees and running along the wires. Some snippets of Euro news made it into the habitual "silly season" media trash.

Melbourne's *Herald-Sun* tabloid reported that "eating more than four hundred new Euro notes can make you ill". The *Melbourne Metro*, a free daily rag, whose "international coverage" was limited to a minuscule "Important but Boring" section, gleefully mentioned an Austrian bank cashier who gave a customer "$A98,000 instead of $A7000" by mistake, because he was "confused about the Euro". The lucky customer had disappeared of course.

I read about the flood of the first fake Euro notes in Germany and in France – some printed from home computers and cut out of magazines; about counterfeiters in Ireland who had left out the "o" on a forged one-Euro ("Eur"?) coin; about the wrath of the Canary Islanders – the territory that was mistakenly left out on the maps of Europe printed on the back of new Euro banknotes; about a peculiar quality of the one-Euro coin that, allegedly, made it always fall face down when dropped and thus rendered it ideal for betting; about the debate in the German media as to what to do with the demised Deutschemarks – burn them (the Greens were opposed to this out of fear of toxic fumes), make bricks out of them or build a monument out of them in Berlin? I also heard my first Euro-joke: Tony Blair, in his pro-Euro crusade, decreeing that from now on the Brits, instead of spending a penny, were officially required to "Euro-inate". Ha-ha.

On a more disturbing note (I don't mean a "banknote" in this case!), there were reports of creeping price-rises under the guise of the changeover to the Euro from almost every Euro-zone country. These were particularly distressing for me on the eve of my potentially expensive journey to the West European enclaves.

Shortly before my departure from Melbourne, my (then Amsterdam-based) eldest son came to Australia for a holiday. He brought me a glittery, freshly minted, one-Euro coin – my first glimpse of the new European currency – as a souvenir. Before putting it in my wallet, I tossed it up in the air, and it fell onto the soft sun-soaked asphalt facing down – towards Europe.

*   *   *

Travels in Enclavia

EUROSTAR

The morning was bright and crispy, like a brand-new Euro banknote. Seagulls were barking happily behind the window of my temporary writing abode in Folkestone, Kent. For the first time in weeks, it wasn't raining. And whereas the British part of my schizophrenic identity was rejoicing at the uncommon February sunlight, its Russian component was not at all happy: Russians view rain as a good omen for a journey, and I was about to start my long-awaited sojourn to Enclavia.

I couldn't wait to leave Folkestone – an unlikely writer's retreat where even the prolific Charles Dickens suffered writer's block.

The red-painted "black cab" (vehicles can also have a mixed identity!) taking me to Ashford was overtaken by two long and suspiciously clean Giraud trucks, carrying loads of fresh asylum seekers from Calais, so I thought. Only two days before, another party of them had been detained while escaping from under a shuttle train at Folkestone station. The sight of the trucks made me feel in Europe already.

The cab soon turned off the M20 motorway and rolled into the suburbs of Ashford – a formerly unremarkable and sleepy Kentish town, whose illusions of grandeur had been limited to a huge mayoral badge – the size of Big Ben – worn by its corpulent Lady Mayor (I once met her at a function in London). Since the Eurostar International Terminal was built there in the early 1990s, the town had experienced an unprecedented boom and now boasted its own smallish business centre and a couple of coffee shops, frequented by a dozen or so latte-slurping City-of-London types. I could understand why my four-year-old son Andrei, after our quick visit to the town centre, started calling it "Cashford".

Unlike other British railway stations at that time, Ashford Eurostar Terminal was clean and fully non-smoking which spoke of a certain European influence. But here I am going to beat the temptation to refer to the station as "an enclave of the Continent inside Britain", or something of that sort. The reason is simple: the toilets there were filthy and out of order – a sure sign of Britishness. On my first visit to Britain in 1988, I was so impressed by the shining cleanliness of my first British toilet on board the *Queen Beatrix* ferry from the Hook of Holland that I thought I had wandered into a barber's shop by mistake. It took me a while to realise that the toilet (as well as the ferry) was actually Dutch.

With about half an hour to spare I headed for the "Grancaffe" under the eye-catching sign: "Try the Italian Coffee Experience". The "experience" was watery.

The moment the Eurostar dived out of the Tunnel, the carriage was awash with the mosquito-like high-pitched beeps of mobile phones. The City types, who constituted the majority of passengers, answered them simultaneously and informed their invisible interlocutors in chorus that they were "already in France".

I stood (or shall I say "sat"?) out among them – both in my principled lack of a mobile phone and in my attire: a fake "Enrico Benetti" shoulder bag, bought for a fiver in Leather Lane Street Market next to Ely Place; an imitation "Salisbury" suitcase (or "Sally", as I shall refer to it from now on) from an Indian luggage shop in Folkestone; a pretend Italian "suede" jacket, forced on me by a bogus "fashion designer from Milan" as an alleged left-over from his recent "show" – a well-known London scam – in a Mayfair street. All three items were phoney, but also smart, cheap and good quality – a perfect Euro-outfit.

For me, leaving the Channel Tunnel was more than simply finding myself "already in France". It was also entering the as yet unexplored domain of "Greater Enclavia", for France was the host country for the Spanish enclave of Llivia, which I planned to visit later in the trip. My first destination was Baarle – a cluster of Dutch and Belgian enclaves and sub-enclaves (i.e. enclaves within enclaves), south of the Dutch town of Breda.

If I had a mobile phone, I would have been pleased to surprise my business-suited fellow passengers by declaring into it loudly that I was "already in Enclavia".

*   *   *

The Eurostar was flying through the vast empty fields of Northern France. After the crammed English landscape, reminiscent of an over-stocked antiques shop, it was nice to feast my eyes on uninterrupted stretches of flatness, restricted only by the horizon.

After a brief stop at Lille, we soon reached the dull redbrick suburbs of Brussels, from where I was to catch a connecting train to Amsterdam – a short stopover on the way to the first enclave on my route – Baarle/Baarle-Hertog.

There, at Bruxelles Midi station, I had my first real encounter with the Euro. As Belgian francs were due to go out of circulation within a couple of weeks, all shops inside the terminal building (as well as all over Belgium, no doubt) were accepting both them and the Euros. Queuing for an early edition of *Le Soir* at a station news-agent, I noticed that most of the customers were still paying in francs (only one of them – a Pakistani girl – chose to cash out Euros for a packet of Kleenex tissues). Not that they were deliberately snubbing the Euro. Renowned for their open-mindedness (otherwise known as practicality), the Belgians were simply getting rid of the coins and notes soon to be branded null and void.

As a good European, I paid in Euros for a newspaper and a pouch of Samson roll-up tobacco, which, incidentally, cost me five times less than it would have in Britain. I then spotted a stack of "Facilitating the Euro" brochures in a cardboard box in the corner, and sure they were free, picked one up before leaving the shop. An ear-piercing siren was activated the moment I passed through the turnstile. It felt as if the whole station came to a stop, and everyone was staring at me clutching the useless "stolen" brochure. In the end, I had to cough up two Euros for it.

I could be forgiven for thinking that the brochure was a giveaway. Travelling in Europe in 2001, I saw heaps of "complimentary" Euro-propaganda material – from free Euro brochures, calendars and rulers in Germany to Austrian coffee biscuits in imitation Euro-banknote wrappings and "New Euro-size lollies" in Holland. Even in Britain – a Euro-zone outsider – every bank branch had piles of free leaflets and pamphlets explaining the Euro to their customers. The embarrassing incident at Bruxelles Midi station proved again that any generalisations about Europe as a whole were potentially dangerous.

Like many other people inside the Euro-zone, my first experience of the Euro was unnerving.

My cheeks still flushed with discomfiture, I took a seat in a smoking carriage of the Brussels-Amsterdam train. My only travel companions were a group of English football fans on the way to the next day's England-Holland friendly in Amsterdam. They were easily identifiable, as if bending over backwards to correspond to the hooligan stereotype. They all had clean-shaven heads and unshaven cheeks, which gave the upper parts of their bodies the look of cacti. They had regulation beer-bellies, as if each of them had swallowed a football. They were tirelessly pumping up these intestinal footballs through their mouths with cans of Stella Artois. Their red hairy hands were covered with pale tattoos of unclear message and origins. I overheard a snippet of conversation (if one could call it conversation) between the two sitting closest to me:

"I am fucked! This is the worst station in Europe!" [He must have meant Bruxelles Midi]

"Yeah . . . And the fucking chocolates everywhere . . . Poisoning our children . . ."

He didn't explain how the Belgian chocolates on sale at a Belgian station could poison unsuspecting English children.

It was clear that these two were not going to queue for the Van Gogh Museum while in Amsterdam.

Suddenly, there was a commotion among the soccer fans. They all sprang up from their seats and glued their beer-sodden faces to the nicotine-soaked windows. The remaining population of our one hundred percent male carriage followed in their stead. Women in different stages of undress were sitting in the windows of shabby low-built houses, lining the railway track around Bruxelles Nord station. Some of them were pointing their bare buttocks at passing trains, whose passengers they were obviously targeting – a futile task by any standards. What did they expect? That some desperately horny males would press emergency brakes and jump out of the train windows straight into theirs? Or were they just trying to prepare Amsterdam-bound passengers for the pleasures of the Dutch capital's famous red-light district? Whatever it was, the presence of this mini-Amsterdam in superficially purist and straight laced Belgium, where a special law banned erotic shops from the vicinity of public buildings, made one think of a new ERO-Union (or a common ERO-identity?) in the making.

At Mechelen our train was boarded by two sullen Al Pacino types in Harley Davidson bomber jackets. One – stocky, pot-bellied, with red beefy face – was obviously in charge; the other – bony and dark-skinned, with brown eyes and unintended "designer" stubble – had the look of a Mafia minion: frightened and threatening in equal measure. In Russian criminal jargon, which I had learned while investigating the Soviet Mafia, the bossy type is known as *pakhan* – "big daddy", and underlings as *shestiorki* – "little sixes" – meaning "gofers", a term whose origin remains unclear.

I knew the men were Russians even before they opened their mouths. After many years in the West, I had learnt to identify my former compatriots from a mile away, with zero error margin. No matter what chic Western clothes they were sporting, there was something in their gait, bearing and body language that made them immediately recognisable. That "something" was a complex mixture of bad haircuts, stilted movements and over-defensive I-am-waiting-to-be-hurt behaviour, multiplied by a peculiar facial expression that I came to call "the seal of oppression" – a haunted and permanently worried look, moulded by years of queuing, fear and repressed emotions – as if constantly expecting a blow from behind. Interestingly, the same genetically transferred look is characteristic of all people living under totalitarian regimes, no matter which part of the globe they come from – Cuba, the former USSR or North Korea. This means that social identity often overshadows ethnic and racial ones. As in the case of Russia, it does not automatically go away with the demise of the system itself, for human psyche and behaviour – identity's main components – are resistant to change. It takes several consecutive generations to alter them significantly. I suspect that at times I myself still carry this "seal of oppression" on my face.

There is a huge advantage in being able to understand your travel companions' language when they themselves are sure that you don't. There's no need to ask them questions, for they are bound to spill out everything anyway.

The Russians installed themselves across the aisle. Pretending to be immersed in the obituaries page of *Le Soir*, I could hear every word they said.

For a while they were chain-smoking silently. Then Gofer said:

"I saw that nice old paperweight on sale in Brussels for two grand."

"Why don't you call Andriusha and offer it to him for three?" asked Pakhan.

Gofer took out a mobile phone and dialled a long multi-digital number, which sounded like a musical overture: "Andriusha, how are you? We are fine, on the train to Antwerp . . . Listen, I've got a lovely paperweight – exactly like you wanted. Yes, with a beetle – very cute . . . I could deliver it for three plus our ten percent commission. (Pause) Well, think about it . . . Also, I saw a chandelier – the authentic art deco stuff, about 1910 . . . Don't know how to carry it – very bulky . . . Shall be sending you a photo by e-mail, just in case, OK? Anyway, I'll call you back about the paperweight, bye!"

He pressed the end-call button and asked Pakhan: "If he buys this chandelier for a fiver, could you throw in the paperweight?"

"No way! For six, maybe . . . Andriusha is a bloody millionaire. Whatever costs six, he sells for ten. Whatever costs ten, he sells for thirty." There was a good deal of admiration in his voice.

They went quiet for a while, only swearing occasionally under their breath.

"Look at these beautiful villas!" Pakhan exclaimed all of a sudden, pointing at the window. The train was passing through some slum-like suburbs of Antwerp.

"I know this area well," he carried on. "There's one spot here where girls undress in the street and then come to sleep with you in your car . . ."

The train arrived at Antwerp, but, despite what had been said to the mysterious millionaire Andriusha, my travel companions did not get off there. They obviously had their own secret agenda and kept carrying on about how to dupe other contacts of theirs: Sasha, Kostya, Petya, etc. – but I was no longer listening. By then, I was profoundly bored with these two shining (or rather swindling) examples of the relatively new breed of my former compatriots, the so-called New Russians – the most peculiar product of Russian "hyena capitalism" – who had invaded the Western world. Their command of foreign tongues was limited to two words: "buy" and "sell". Their unwritten business code allowed anything – from chicanery to murder. Their favourite colour was pink.

I remembered how a couple of years earlier I was introduced to a ten-year-old Russian boy from Samara who came to visit my London friends on an exchange scheme. "How much do you earn?" he asked me instead of saying hello, and, without waiting for me to react, continued: "My dad makes fifty million roubles. A week. He owns a fur-making business, the greedy old man. Just imagine: he has given me some miserable three thousand pound pocket money for all ten days of my stay in Britain!"

What was he going to do with such a fortune, I wondered. He waved his plump cherubic hand: "Dunno . . . Will probably buy myself another DVD player."

"Have you . . . Have you already got a DVD player? 'cause I haven't: can't afford it."

"Yeah, I've got three!" replied the horrible brat, showing me his wallet, bursting with crunchy Liz-headed pounds sterling.

And let me tell you: although we were speaking the same language and, in the eyes of the Brits, were supposed to share the same "Russian identity", for me this young rep of the new capitalist Russia was a creature no less alien and mystifying than some misanthropic pygmy from the jungles of Equatorial Africa.

The two Russians finally left the train at Rotterdam Centraal. With relief, I thought that, all things considered, I very much preferred the company of the increasingly tipsy British football fans, who were now discussing shepherd pies and their undisputed advantages over Belgian chocolates.

More passengers got on the train in Holland. Some were openly smoking cannabis. The closer we came to Amsterdam, the more colourful, cosmopolitan and multi-lingual our carriage became. I counted at least five languages spoken: Dutch, German, Turkish, English and the soccer fans' slurred patois. By the time the train came to a halt at Amsterdam Centraal, it could be easily mistaken for a little dope-smelling chunk of Europe on wheels.

"Have a good game!" one of the soccer fans blurted out to me as he was staggering towards the exit.

*   *   *

AMSTERDAM

I don't know why, but Amsterdam always evokes in me childhood associations – not just the memories of my own early years, but rather the joyful feeling of being a child again, similar to that experienced by adults in Disneyland or in Venice, that medieval playground of doges and spice merchants.

Is it the characteristic smell of canal water mixed with odours of tar and tulips? Or, maybe, it is the soothing shuffle of bicycle tyres against the cobbles? Or the sight of Amsterdam's old ladies – "God's dandelions" (a good Russian expression) with mischievous twinkles of past indiscretions in their fading eyes? Or clusters of narrow-façade gabled houses (in the Middle Ages, Amsterdam landlords were taxed per square inch of their house façades) huddling around the canals, looking like tower-chambers from a Russian fairly tale?

But, most likely, it is the trams – these moving wrinkles on Amsterdam's face that, curiously, make it look younger. Trams were the main (and pretty much the only) vehicles of the city of my childhood, and no noise is more familiar to me than the sound of an old tram, squeakily turning the corner. As a little boy, I used to wake up to it every morning.

For me, Amsterdam begins and ends with tram number one – running from the Central Station to Overtoom, where my eldest son Mitya once lived. Chatty, smiley, multilingual and multi-racial, this tram is a microcosm of the Dutch capital itself. It is a stark contrast to a taciturn and stuck-up London bus, or to a Tube train carriage with its strict mind-the-gap attitude.

The people on Amsterdam's tram number one make a lot of noise. They laugh out loud; they read Kafka and Umberto Eco as the tram freezes for what feels like an eternity at the permanently red traffic lights. Its progress along the congested narrow streets is so slow that at times it gives the impression of sliding backwards in space and in time – towards the melting pot of medieval Amsterdam, and its passengers get miraculously transformed into diamond-cutters from Antwerp, Jews fleeing the Spanish Inquisition, Huguenots from France and dissenters from England – all of whom found refuge in the most tolerant and accommodating city in the world, the "people's" capital of Europe.

Amsterdam's main distinctive feature has always been that – unlike London – it never pigeonholes people according to their origins, occupations and addictions. It accepts them as humans first and only then – as politicians, junkies, academics, beggars, plumbers or prostitutes. It embraces humans in all their complexity: with their merits and sins, peculiarities and idiosyncrasies, passions and peccadilloes. It invites them all, without exception, to the never-ending party celebrating tolerance, if not temperance: the twenty-four-hour-a-day bash called Amsterdam.

Overtaken by cars, cyclists and some disabled pedestrians in wheelchairs, tram number one is crawling towards the city centre – past canals and across bridges – a seemingly endless journey. On this bridge over Keizergraht, bike-junkies – the addicts maintaining their habit by stealing and quick-selling bicycles – congregate. In pre-Euro times one could acquire a stolen bike from them for as little as twenty guilders (seven pounds). It is not common knowledge though that the bike-junkies have their own website, where a potential buyer can view a stolen bicycle before agreeing a pickup point. Old bikes and those that do not sell fast enough are routinely dumped into the canals, from which a special city council dredger fishes them out once a month.

From the tram window, I spot the smallish Die Port Van Kleve Hotel, where I stayed during my first ever visit to Amsterdam in August 1991. My KLM flight Melbourne-London included a free stopover in Amsterdam which I decided to use walking off my jet-lag and preparing for a week of interviews and public talks in the UK. For the first two days, I was staggering along the canals as if drunk, overwhelmed by the half-forgotten smells of European summer. Of course, I committed a first-time visitor's boo-boo by asking for a cup of espresso (and nothing else!) in a seedy coffee shop next to my hotel, and the barman eyed me with scornful disbelief, as if I had ordered a cup of sulphuric acid. On the second night, I went – alone! – on a candle-lit dinner cruise along the canals. Surrounded by snogging homo- and hetero- couples, I wouldn't have been surprised to discover that going on such a "romantic" cruise on one's own constituted a minor offence in Holland. But I didn't mind my loneliness in the least. The boat was sliding noiselessly under the bridges, and the reflections of burning candles were wriggling in the water like restless fiery serpents.

I remember feeling such indescribable happiness at being back in Europe after many months down under, at being re-united with the smells and sounds of my childhood, that I couldn't help thinking: this simply cannot last. From experience, I knew that one could only feel such bliss on the eve of a disaster.

The next morning, the military coup took place in Moscow, where my mother was still living. Barred from returning to the Soviet Union as a recent defector, I spent the following days trying – in vain – to get through to her by phone, from Amsterdam, from Brussels and then from London. Persistent crackles at the other end of malfunctioning lines were like muffled screeches of tank caterpillars against the old stones of the Red Square. I was only able to speak to her after the *putsch* was defeated. Having given up smoking six months earlier, I lit up again on the first day of the coup and have been unable to quit ever since.

So Amsterdam has a somewhat sinister touch for me. It was there too that I learnt about the 9/11 terrorist attacks on America. The night before, Mitya and a bunch of his cosmopolitan Amsterdam mates had dragged me into a disco – my first disco experience in my entire life. I tried to resist, saying I was too old for it, but they persevered, and, fuelled by a couple of Amstels, I soon found myself twitching and shaking next to my son in the middle of a crowded hall. Contrary to my expectations, I was enjoying it all: the music, the open and civilised faces of my fellow-dancers, amongst whom – I was pleased to note – I was far from the oldest. Everyone in the disco was bouncing strictly within his or her imaginary little square, never trespassing into someone else's space. At one point, a young Dutch woman came up to Mitya and whispered something in his ear, pointing at me. "What did she say?" I yelled, trying to outcry the deafening techno beat. "Have I done something wrong?" "No!" my son screamed back. "She told me that looking at the two of us she had guessed we were father and son and that it was very nice to see us dancing together . . ." In short, the experience was profoundly *gezellig*, to use a popular Dutch colloquialism[2].

---

2. *The closest English word to* gezellig *(pronounced heh-ZEL-ick) I can think of is "cool", although its meaning is much broader. A* gezellig *environment is one that allows good times to happen. It is almost like a vibe, and it is contagious. As a Dutch friend once explained, a* gezellig *place is cosy and inviting and full of* gezellig *things that make it so* gezellig*. A two-hour leisurely meal with friends is* gezellig*, whereas gobbling up a Big Mac on your lap in the car is not. He said that the constant pursuit of* gezellig*-ness is the key to the Dutch psyche.*

It was early morning on 11 September 2001 – Mitya's twenty-first birthday.

Past my favourite café "Chaos", with its wonderfully eclectic interior and friendly informality (patrons are encouraged to dump pistachio-nut shells on the floor), tram number one enters the fringes of the red-light district, which I have always found not much raunchier than London's Carnaby Street. If you overlook the occasional drug-peddlers, the tax-paying law-abiding women in the windows (the District police brochures warn repeatedly – and somewhat intriguingly – that "they are not always women") and the confused British louts haggling with bouncers over the price of those women (or whoever they may be), it can be a very interesting place. I once overheard a bouncer trying to extract a payment for two consecutive visits to a "window woman" by a British man of soccer-hooligan appearance. The man was only prepared to pay for one visit, his argument being: "I was on my way out, but she just pushed me back in!"

Where else in Europe can you see establishments like "Cannabis Connoisseurs Club"? Or a thought-provoking exhibition of conceptual "Media Art" under the motto "Are You Experienced?" (one of the exhibits – "Disinformation" – allows visitors to inscribe a huge painting with images created by their own shadows)? Where else are tourists desperate for a pee officially invited to relieve themselves at the district police station? But the thing that strikes me most about this little "enclave" of super-tolerance in the midst of tolerant Amsterdam is how strict its boundaries are: three metres away, there's no sign of it whatsoever. You can literally brush past it without spotting anything unusual. Like the Cheshire Cat's smile, the red-light district is visible only to those who want to see it.

The tram screeches to a long, seemingly endless, stop in Laidseplein – a small square in the hub of Amsterdam. Here, after 11pm each night, one can watch an amazing street performer – a slightly built young man with a sad Mediterranean face. Dressed in a soiled tracksuit, ridden with holes, he attracts crowds by climbing lamp posts and trees while kicking a football in the air and never dropping it onto the ground. His technique being second to none, I think that the only reason this "feet juggler" (as I came to call him) hasn't yet been recruited by Ajax, Eindhoven or some other Dutch premier-league football club is the anxiety that he would start climbing goalposts in the middle of a match. I often wonder what he does during the day: sleeps in some dodgy vermin-infested room pressing the ball to his chest – like a piece of his sultry childhood somewhere in Turkey or Macedonia?

In a lane off Laidseplein, there's a small cinema showing obscure foreign movies that never hit the big screen. I once went there with Mitya. They were running an American film, with Dutch subtitles. At some point, a protagonist said: "I don't like wogs", which was subtitled "I don't like Italians" in Dutch. "They don't have derogatory words for Italians or any other nations in Dutch," explained Mitya, who had just come back from a live-in crash-course in Dutch in a suburban convent (!) paid for by the company for which he worked. A player for an amateur soccer team, he also assured me that the worst curse he had ever heard on a Dutch football pitch was "Goddamn!"

What a gentle nation, I thought.

Gentleness and tolerance have their limits though. The Dutch will be quite happy to chat to a visitor in colloquial English, or in a number of other European languages which most of them can speak after secondary school. But if you have lived in Holland for a year and still do not make an effort to learn Dutch, they are likely to start ostracising you. I don't blame them.

The tram turns into Overtoom – a long traffic artery connecting the city centre with the melodiously alliterated suburb of Lelyllaan. Halfway along it, hidden from idle tourist eyes by massive wooden gates, is an establishment, which – for me – represents the spirit of Amsterdam better than anything else. It is the city's oldest and most prestigious (sic) squat – yes, a "wrongfully and unlawfully" tenanted premises (by both British and Dutch legal standards), known to the Amsterdam police and happily tolerated by them, despite its obvious illegality. Getting a place in The Squat is almost as hard as finding a reasonably priced apartment in London's Mayfair. Only in The Squat accommodation is free. Its residents – tramps, buskers, travellers, recovering drug-addicts and impoverished students, often with small children – also enjoy free Internet access, free charity-supplied meals, free in-house concerts from leading Amsterdam pop groups, and so on. In its basement, The Squat houses Radio Patapoe – Amsterdam's oldest pirate radio station, also illegal, yet tolerated, because, as my son explained, its signal is rather weak and does not reach outside central Amsterdam.

Mitya certainly knew what he was talking about, for, on top of his other Amsterdam occupations he was a DJ for Radio Patapoe – the world's only radio station whose casually vetted (by squatters) "anchors" were not just unpaid but had themselves to contribute 5 Euros a month towards the equipment maintenance in order to be allowed on air. He once invited me to his basement "studio" to take part in a program on music in poetry, or poetry in music – we couldn't quite sort that out. As a regular visitor to The Squat he was entrusted with a coveted key to the wooden gates.

I felt at ease in the tiny cubicle of a "studio", lit by an antique lamp in the shape of Patapoe – the dog in whose memory the station was named. Sitting on a battered leather sofa, so deep and soft that it negatively affected one's self-esteem, I spoke with relish into an old-fashioned, heavy (and, no doubt, extremely "tolerant") microphone, and read out poems in English and in Russian, while Mitya introduced musical pieces with a peculiar – estranged and almost robotic – radio DJ's voice.

The basement studio reminded me of my writing closet in Moscow. When Mitya was a baby, we occupied a single room in a communal flat, and I had to type away in an extended wall cupboard so as not to wake him up. By ironic coincidence, the room's previous occupant had been a radio pirate, using the cupboard for illegal broadcasts at considerable risk to himself: the word "tolerance" was not in the police lexicon in Brezhnev's USSR. So, in a way, I was an old-timer in radio pirates' dens.

Meanwhile, The Squat was living its normal life. Children were playing with crude homemade toys in a small walled courtyard. A dishevelled man in ragged clothes was browsing the Internet. An invisible young woman, with a good London accent, was loudly complaining about going "cold turkey": "I can hardly walk, and I've got a splitting headache . . ."

On shutting the wooden gates behind me, I suddenly realised that I had fallen head over heels in love with Amsterdam.

I hop off the tram at Overtoomsesluis, and pop into Ter Brugge – a pub where Mitya always leaves a set of house keys for me. The staff know me and fish out the keys from under the cash register. Before moving on, I drink a cup of tepid wishy-washy Amsterdam espresso tasting and smelling of unclean canal water, with "Sally", my obnoxious Salisbury suitcase, parked at my feet. It is late afternoon, and the city canals are slowly releasing the sunlight they had accumulated during the day, although many patrons were still having their breakfasts. Amsterdam wakes up late. At midday, it often feels like London at six am, and in late afternoon like London at nine o'clock in the morning. This peculiar Amsterdam time loop makes lunch there feel like breakfast, and dinner like lunch. Sometimes, it is hard to believe that anyone works in this permanently partying city. But some people do, and my son was once one of them.

I wait for a drawbridge across the canal to join together after letting a barge called *Marianne* and a flock of carefree Amsterdam ducks pass through a small lock. The skipper waves to me from the cockpit. From here, it is just a hundred yards to my son's flat. In a couple of minutes I am looking up at a handwritten plate underneath the doorbell – "M. de Boer; R. Stewart; D. Vitaliev".

I could stare at it for hours rejoicing at the lucky fortune of my Moscow-born and Melbourne-educated, yet thoroughly European boy, for there are few better things in this life than being young and living in Amsterdam.

*　*　*

1. Holgium (Holland and Belgium)

BAARLE

The Mother of All Enclaves

Forty-eight hours after my arrival in Amsterdam, I was sitting outside a Brasserie on Platform One of Amsterdam Centraal station, sipping an espresso and waiting for a train to Breda, the nearest station to the first enclave on my route – Baarle. From time to time, I had to fend off pale-faced – yet invariably polite, neatly dressed and multilingual – Amsterdam beggars, who were now – less than a month since the Netherlands' currency demise – habitually asking for "one Euro" (pronouncing it as "u-ee-rou"), as if guilders, or florins, had never existed.

It was not long before I spotted my recent travel companions, the football fans, sleepwalking to their train, heads down, their snappy verbal exchanges limited to just one short English word and its derivatives. They looked awful: sullen, bruised and unshaven, yet with a satisfied "mission-accomplished" expression on their faces. The England-Holland friendly had ended in a seemingly peaceful draw, which, reportedly, hadn't stopped the pugnacious England supporters from scuffling with their Dutch counterparts inside and outside the watering holes off Dam Square.

Having observed aggressive and dead-drunk English "holiday-makers" in Greece, Spain, Portugal, Florida and elsewhere on numerous occasions, I often wondered what it was that made the English so belligerent and foolhardy while abroad. Was it the inherent need to throw away barriers the moment they left their claustrophobic and strictly regulated (not to say oppressive) home environment?

In the introduction to the 1857 edition of his *Handbook for Travellers in France*, John Murray, the acclaimed London-based guidebook publisher, bravely attempted to pin down "the causes which render the English unpopular in many countries of the Continent". Among these, he listed such traits as "the morose sullenness . . . arising from the Englishman's ignorance of foreign languages, or at least from his want of sufficient fluency to make himself readily understood, which thus prevents his enjoying society" – as well as "inattention, unguardedness, wanton expenditure in some cases, niggardly parsimony in others, but above all . . . an unwillingness to accommodate themselves to the feelings of the people they are among".

Significantly, a survey conducted in the resorts of continental Europe almost 150 years later established that the English were the rudest, the least welcome, the least willing to speak a foreign language and the most tight-fisted holidaymakers abroad – followed by . . . the Russians. The best visitors, according to the same survey, were the Germans and the Japanese.

"Our countrymen," continued John Murray in 1857, "have a reputation for pugnacity in France: let them therefore be especially cautious not to make use of their fists, however great the provocation, otherwise they will rue it."

Well, it is good to know that, while modernity and changing realities have touched all traditional British institutions, including the Royal family and the Mother of Parliaments, at least one old

English practice has been kept absolutely intact through centuries. Even Dutch patience has its limits. In early 2002, Amsterdam city council – in an unprecedented gesture – moved to ban British stag parties, for which the Dutch capital, due to its relative proximity, had become a popular venue. "All these British people want to do is drink for a weekend and make a lot of noise," in the words of the Mayor of Amsterdam's spokeswoman.

My Breda-bound double-decker train left the station at 14:11 *on the dot*. Having installed myself comfortably on the upper floor of a clean and warm carriage, I took out my Baarle folder, planning to do some background reading. Twenty minutes into the journey, however, I was distracted by the sight of a huge glass dome, crowning a large circular building near Haarlem station, where the train made a brief stop. The temple-like domed structure was familiar. It housed the town's main landmark – a "normal security" prison, inside which I had found myself one Christmas Eve several years earlier. Don't hold your breath: not as an inmate, but as a journalist, researching a series of features on "Dutch tolerance" for the now-defunct *European* newspaper. The Haarlem prison struck me then as an epitome of the Dutch psyche and way of life, much more so than Amsterdam's "coffee shops" and the red-light district. Memories came flooding back . . .

Inside the prison, right under the dome, jailbirds and warders were playing football on an artificial pitch. It was not an inmates versus prison officers match: the captives and their guards were evenly distributed between the teams, and the only way to tell one player from another was the colour of their jerseys. It was almost Christmas time, and the mood underneath the dome was nothing short of festive. Numerous Christmas trees illuminated the corridors, decorated with original paintings and sculptures: according to Dutch regulations, one percent of a prison budget was to be spent on works of art. The governor led me through the immaculate prison kitchen, through a gym, where a handful of muscled inmates were pumping iron, through empty computer-equipped classrooms and two well-stocked prison libraries. He told me that only once had he had to ban a book from the libraries' stock: it was called

How to Make a Bomb. "The librarian never forgave me for that," he added.

With amazement bordering on disbelief, I learnt that prisoners were allowed to keep pets (birds and fish, not German Shepherds) in their cells. They were entitled to make unlimited phone calls, and to take six seventy-two-hour home leaves during the last year of their sentence. They participated in prison affairs and could even vote out the governor himself. Members of the prison staff were not allowed to enter the cells, which the governor diplomatically referred to as "residential quarters", unless invited in. And indeed, each cell looked more like a hotel room, with a bathroom, a tiny kitchen, a TV set and the occasional birdcage or aquarium. In stark contrast to the chronically overcrowded British penitentiaries, the "one prisoner per cell" rule was observed to the letter in Haarlem, which had no communal canteen: each inmate had food delivered to his room.

"You don't improve people by locking them up," said the governor as we sat down in his office for a glass of prison-bottled wine (yes, bottling wine was one of the inmates' paid-for activities). "The construction of new prisons must stop."

Later, I learned that, despite a relatively high crime rate, the Netherlands locked up fewer people than almost any other country in the world – and the rate of re-offending was very low. Instead of treating the offenders like animals and thus pushing them further towards the brink, in Holland they chose to remind them that they were human. Despite all those little prison "luxuries", the inmates were still bereft of their main human asset – freedom – and that in itself was enough of a punishment to make them suffer.

The football game under the dome came to a halt, and the prisoners moved to the assembly hall for a charity concert by a well-known Amsterdam rock group. Muffled sounds of rock music floated over the empty pitch . . . I raised my head and saw a bright-yellow canary, an escapee from a cell, beating desperately against the dome, trying to break through the glass. But prison walls, even transparent ones, are thick – and there was no escape.

The Haarlem prison was a good illustration of Richard Hill's characterisation of the Dutch as "democratic dogmatists" rather than over-tolerant sissies: their lenience to criminals, as well as to drug-addicts, prostitutes, radio-pirates, squatters, etc., has always been based not so much on compassion as on a practical assessment of the effects on society.

My previous flying visit to Baarle (or Baarle-Hertog, as the Belgian parts of the town are known in Flemish) had left me in little doubt that this small Dutch-Belgian settlement was one of the world's most amazing places. In his book *European Detours*, Nino Lo Bello, a rare American visitor, branded it "Splittsville" and a "hermaphroditic [*sic*] homogenous hamlet". As you must have guessed, Lo Bello visited Baarle in the year 1980, BPC (Before Political Correctness). Indeed, in its history, geography and in its schizophrenic reality, Baarle – a cluster of Belgian and Dutch enclaves to the south of Breda – was, and still is, a direct challenge to the American concept of uniform unity (*e pluribus unum*), better known as patriotism.

Baarle/Baarle-Hertog can be safely described as insane. The border there resembles an ECG of a patient on the brink of a heart attack. Like a hank of wool thread chased by a playful kitten, it thoughtlessly leaps across streets and squares, cutting through houses, offices and shops. The confusion is such that every single building in town has to be marked not just with a number, but also with a tiny Dutch or Belgian flag underneath it. Out of three houses standing next to each other on the same side of the same street, one can be in Belgium, the next in Holland, and the third one split between the two.

The existing twenty-two Belgian and eight Dutch enclaves that constitute modern Baarle are a huge improvement on the situation in 1843, when, in the aftermath of the Treaty of Maastricht, five thousand, seven hundred and thirty-two parcels of land between just two border posts – 214 and 215 – had their nationalities laid down separately. This "duplicate" 214/215 border post now stands in the town centre – on the very spot where, in the Middle Ages, the enclaves' joint Court of Justice would convene under a huge lime tree – as evidence of Baarle's ongoing split personality crisis.

45

It all started in 1203, when the Duke of Brabant – in a gesture of gratitude and appeasement – lent a chunk of his territory to Godfrid of Schoten, the powerful Lord of Breda, but cleverly kept all inhabited – and hence tax-paying – bits (houses with their land allotments, farms, etc.) for himself. Over the centuries, most dwellings either moved or disappeared altogether, but the patches of land on which they stood retained their original "nationhood". To confuse the situation even further, the 1648 Treaty of Westphalia ceded the land that belonged to the Lord of Breda to the northern province of the Greater Netherlands, whereas the pockets owned by the Duke of Brabant went to the southern province. Eventually, these provinces became Holland and Belgium respectively, but the "nationality" of all five thousand, seven hundred and thirty-two disputed parcels of land had to be established separately over the years.

Even the major conflicts of the twentieth century failed to alter the town's ambiguous status quo: during World War I, Holland's neutrality allowed Baarle's Belgian enclaves the distinction of being the only bits of Belgian territory not occupied by Germany. The World War II *blitzkrieg* barely affected the town. When the Belgians surrendered, the Nazis assumed the civil administration of Baarle-Hertog – the town's annexed Belgian bits – whereas its Dutch outliers were administered by the German military because Holland did not capitulate and was therefore regarded as occupied enemy territory. When, after the town's liberation, the Dutch town hall was destroyed by gunfire, the Belgian Mayor of Baarle-Hertog temporarily permitted his Dutch counterpart to share the Belgian Town Hall across the road – an impressive example of the pre-EU cross-border cooperation.

It has to be said that the residents of Baarle – both Dutch and Belgian – have staunchly resisted attempts to normalise the situation by clearly defining the borders. With inherent common sense as one of the very few shared Belgian-Dutch character traits, they realised that the town's dubious status was its main (and probably only) selling point. "The people got so accustomed to this situation that if it took an end, our village would become a dead-alive place. We like to keep Baarle as it is, a precious inheritance we shall defend against every attack!" states a no-nonsense community leaflet, the only piece of printed material in English I was able to pick up at the local (joint) tourism office during my short "reconnaissance" visit to Baarle six months earlier. In its aggressive, almost threatening tone, it reminded me of an American mid-West road sign "Don't Mess with Texas!"

During my short first visit I had learned that this small international town – of fewer than eight thousand, five hundred people – had two Mayors, two sets of political parties, two town councils, two town emblems, two telephone networks, two currencies (until the Euro that is), two fire brigades trying to beat each other to conflagration sites, two post offices, two refuse collection services, two Roman Catholic parishes, two different income tax rates, two separate sets of street traffic and military service regulations and so on. It was the only town in the world where police forces of two different countries shared not just the same building, but the same room (the only one in this international police mini-station) and the same desk. I visited Baarle in the company of two friends, armed with mobile phones, one of which showed "Belgium", and the other "Holland", while the operator's messages on both, for some obscure reason, switched into French.

I also discovered that, alongside (or rather inside) "normal" Dutch and Belgian enclaves/exclaves, Baarle was the world's only place to possess sub-enclaves – seven Dutch outliers within Belgian enclaves inside Holland – a true Matrioshka-doll scenario!

A Baarle tourism official, with whom I then had a brief chat, assured me that the locals did not look upon themselves as either Dutch or Belgian. "We all think of ourselves as Baarlenaars," she said.

"The strangely entangled exclaves of Baarle-Duc and Baarle are an administrative quagmire for Holland and Belgium," noted Honore M. Catudal, Jr. in his groundbreaking book. He was right of course, although my first sketchy impressions of that schizophrenic town could be best summed up by a peculiar food item I saw on sale in an Amsterdam supermarket. "*Nieuw-Zeeland Lambbiefstuck*" was printed on its price tag, which, even with my non-existent Dutch, I was able to translate correctly. A geopolitical "lamb beefsteak" could pass for a good description of that little chunk of *Holgium* (or *Belland*?).

*   *   *

In relative terms, my two-and-a-half-hour train journey from Amsterdam to Breda – one of Holland's longest routes – could probably be compared to London–Fort William overnight train ride in Britain, or to Moscow–Vladivostok seven-day-long Trans-Siberian ordeal in Russia.

At Breda station, I boarded bus number 132 for a forty-five-minute-long trip to Baarle. The bus puffed through a burning sunset along the winding lanes of neat, manure-smelling Dutch countryside – past windmills, irrigation canals and grazing cows. Every now and then, it would bounce over a *drempel* (ramp) before making a sharp rollercoaster-like turn in the manner of a black London cab trying to beat the rush-hour traffic. The houses in countless villages we rode through were generously decorated with Dutch flags – a fact that could be easily mistaken for an American-style display of patriotism, so uncharacteristic of Europe. Only here, in the Dutch-Belgian border province of North Brabant, the flags were rather objects of convenience. In the absence of other markings, they assumed the role of border posts, preventing unwary travellers from stumbling into a wrong country.

As the bus was approaching Baarle, I had a peculiar butterfly-ish feeling in my tummy, like before a long-awaited tryst with a sweetheart. Or rather like one feels on returning home after many years of globetrotting. Enclavia felt like "home" to me, and Baarle, with its thoroughly messed up "identity", particularly so.

The bus driver dumped me at the edge of the town, having waved his hand in the general direction of my hotel. It was already dark. For lack of pavements, I had to push my "Sally" along a cycling path, lining a surprisingly busy road, with cars flowing in both directions and blinding me with their flashing headlights. I could see, or rather feel, the drivers throwing startled looks at me – a solitary hiker in this headlight-pierced tsardom of vehicles. But I couldn't care less, for I was already in the magically displaced little world of Baarle: most of the houses on my side of the road had their numbers set against a background of painted red, white and blue horizontal bands – the colours of the Dutch national flag, whereas on the opposite side, most of them had number plates with vertical stripes of black, yellow and red showing that they were in Belgium.

The bicycle path soon ended, and I had to keep walking along the edge of the busy road at considerable peril to "Sally" and to myself. Dutch (or Belgian?) country roads were obviously not meant for pedestrians. The feeling of discomfort was similar to what I once experienced in the USA during a heroic attempt to go for a stroll outside the town of Woodstock, Vermont. I remember eliciting outrage from the couple who owned the small B&B where I stayed, by announcing that I was going out for an evening walk. "What?" they yelled in chorus. "A walk? Tell us where you want to go, and we'll give you a lift." "No, thanks, I want to walk," I insisted. "But where are you going to walk to? No one walks anywhere here. It's dangerous . . ."

They were right: the B&B stood on a grassy knoll overlooking a roaring highway with no "sidewalks" in sight. Blinded by headlights every five seconds, I had to trudge along a slippery muddy track during that bizarre evening stroll, which I still undertook – mostly out of principle, better known as obstinacy.

"Americans' legs will atrophy soon and will be replaced with special gadgets for pressing pedals," predicted the Russian satirist Ilya Ilf in his American notebooks, as far back as 1935. Nearly seventy years later, as I could see, the same evolutionary change was about to affect European bodies too – at least those in rural Holland (and/or Belgium), where everyone either drove or cycled.

It was probably for those who wanted to keep their legs intact that Sporthotel Bruurs, where I was put up, had been constructed. The oblong modern building, surrounded by farmland, housed a huge gym with an adjoining swimming pool and a "health centre" – a modern euphemism for a sauna. Swimming goggles and bathrobes were dispensed at the reception. "Do I have a telephone in my room?" I asked a lean, track-suited young woman, who looked more like a swimming instructor than a concierge. "No, but you can take a sauna for free," she replied, with a peculiar Dutch (or Belgian?) logic. The incongruous eighteen-room residential appendix, advertised in the hotel's glossy brochure as "comfortable lodging at interesting prices", was totally "uninteresting" in all other respects and looked like the ailing, sallow and thoroughly unwanted child of a body builder.

Having dropped "Sally" in my small Spartan room, which looked and smelled rather like a gym locker, I went down to the hotel's restaurant only to make sure that – like most eating places inside "health-centres" all over the world – it only had hamburgers and chips on the menu. With weight loss through near-hysterical exercise viewed as a twenty-first century Klondike by many crafty entrepreneurs, a vicious circle was created whereby a famished patron was bound to restore every single calorie lost painstakingly in the gym (and to gain many more on top of that) by gobbling up a couple of hamburgers at the in-house buffet on the way out – the best guarantee of further custom. I once witnessed the extreme of such cynicism in a private cardiological hospital in Australia which operated a busy junk-food outlet in its lobby, so that it could successfully clog human arteries and thus supply potential clients for expensive bypasses.

I decided to walk back to the town centre for a more salubrious dinner alternative.

Next to the hotel stood a traditional Dutch farmhouse, looking uninhabited and deserted except for a couple of horses grazing under the moon in its vast fenced garden. A large pink billboard above the mansion gates depicted a shadowy, yet clearly naked, female figure under the lettering "Sans Limites". It was a rural Dutch brothel, many of which adorn the border with Holland's sexually repressed, and at the same time sex-obsessed neighbour Belgium, the country where, according to a 2001 survey, the most popular car number plate was SEX 001, closely followed by TIT 001 and GAY 001. At the same time, a sexually explicit book about the youthful escapades of King Albert was publicly branded by Belgian prime minister Guy Verhofstadt "an assault on the dignity of our nation and its people". Brothels were still illegal in Belgium, whereas in Holland they were all *sans limites*, so to speak, although from the forlorn look of that particular Baarle establishment, I thought it should have been renamed "Sans Clientes".

Had there been a single living person inside, I could have advised him or her to follow the example of Daily Planet, one of Melbourne's sixty-nine legal brothels (not to be confused with Lonely Planet – a guide-book publisher whose head office is also in Melbourne) which used to conduct regular media briefings. I was once invited, but was too busy to attend (I mean, honestly!) and gave my invitation to a fellow hack. In return, he brought me back a twenty percent discount voucher, with kissing doves in the corner, entitling the holder to visit the establishment during "off peak" hours – from 2 to 5pm.

I retraced my footsteps to the town centre along the Dutch side of the same road, past the Dutch Fire Station next to a Belgian border sign. Having crossed the frontier, I was puzzled to note that most houses in what was supposed to be Belgium stubbornly continued to show Dutch flag colours on their number plates. A meticulous foreign visitor once calculated that any pedestrian was bound to cross borders no fewer than fifty-five times during a twenty minute walk around Baarle.

The first catering establishment on my way was the Belgian Toerist Snackbar. I deduced it was Belgian because all menu prices were in Belgian francs. It was two weeks since guilders stopped circulating in Holland, now operating solely in Euros, whereas Belgium had another fortnight of optional Euro- or franc-paying ahead of it. The prices in the "snackbar" were all in hundreds of francs, and although I knew that the exchange rate was over forty Belgian francs to one Euro, and that the Euros, which I had in my wallet, were to be accepted alongside the outgoing Belgian currency, which I didn't have, all those three-figure price tags looked intimidating. I made up my mind to stock up with food – to be consumed in the discomfort of my own hotel room – at the nearest supermarket.

The only open supermarket in the town centre was the Dutch C 100 store. During my previous visit to Baarle, I had noted that it had two separate bays for shopping trolley hire: one accepted guilder coins, the other francs. The francs bay was still unchanged, whereas the ex-one-guilder slots were now reshaped into one-Euro ones, meaning that, with the exchange rate of 2.2 guilders per one Euro, the relative cost of hiring a trolley had risen more than two-fold – my first experience of creeping price rises on the Euro bandwagon. In an ironic, if temporary, twist, this Dutch store was now accepting Belgian currency, but not its native Dutch one, which was no more.

I bought some Dutch Gouda cheese, a German *grillworst* sausage, Italian *roma* tomatoes and French *lait battu* for dessert and was very much looking forward to unifying these tasty bits of Europe inside my stomach – the sort of European integration I am ardently in favour of.

An agreeable blonde salesgirl at the till kindly provided me with a free knife and fork set for my impromptu pan-European dinner. Before heading back to the hotel, I decided to buy some more loose tobacco. Another pleasant Dutch girl at the supermarket's tobacco stall, however, advised me to buy it at the Belgian shop next door, where a fifty-gram pouch of Dutch-blended Samson was forty

Euro-cents cheaper than in Holland. "We always buy tobacco, petrol and chocolates in Belgium," she said.

Baarle was immersed in darkness as I trudged back to my hotel with shopping bags in both hands. The only brightly-lit windows in Neusstraat were those of a massive Simply the Best Sex Shop – or rather Sex Superstore judging by the sheer size of it. From my previous visit, I knew that the most thriving trade in the Belgian parts of Baarle was in fireworks (I had counted half a dozen fireworks shops in the town centre), which could be legitimately sold all year round in Belgium, but only on Christmas eve in Holland. The Dutch had responded with numerous sex shops, strictly regulated and not allowed anywhere near public buildings in Belgium, yet both *sans limites* and "simply the best" in Holland. Simply the Best, by the way, with its door wide ajar and not a single customer inside (*sans clientes* again?), was across the road from Baarle's Belgian Town Hall, albeit on Dutch territory of course.

The next morning, Anne-Miek Smit-Rygersberg, my main and – so far only – contact in Baarle, picked me up at my hotel. A native Baarlenaar of Dutch descent, with appropriately double-barrelled first and last names, she was tall, middle-aged, energetic and extremely practical, if not to say calculating: living in Baarle, one had to be. Born in a house on the Dutch edge of the town, to which, in her own words, "smugglers often popped in for a cup of tea", she had gone to a Belgian school "because it was closer". During our previous brief encounter six months earlier, she had shown me her two purses – one with Dutch guilders, the other with Belgian francs. "I buy medicines at the Belgian pharmacy where they are less strict with prescriptions, but flowers, cheese and spirits at Dutch shops, where they are cheaper." I also remembered her matter-of-fact comment to the effect that if the border ran through a house, it was better for a baby to be born on the Belgian side, because child benefits were higher in Belgium (in rural Holland, as in rural Belgium, many women still gave birth at home with the help of a midwife).

"No more two purses!" she announced triumphantly after greeting me in the lobby. Later she conceded that, alongside Euros, she still kept some Belgian franc coins for cheaper trolley hire in the Dutch supermarket in the next couple of weeks.

European currencies were disappearing one by one, and with each of them a part of a national identity was vanishing into the thin winter air. It was the day when France was saying *au revoir* to its good old franc – despite an arduous and vociferous anti-Euro campaign. On the news that morning I heard a reporter asking a Paris shopper whether he felt "a bit sorry for the francs". "*Oui*, but not a lot," was the reply. In the meantime, the Euro itself was in a sorry state: due to the mounting economic problems in Germany, its value against the US dollar kept dropping.

Ahead of us was a half day of official visits; Anne-Miek had arranged for me to meet both Mayors of Baarle, one after the other.

We started with the Dutch Town Hall. Why? "Because it was closer."

Unlike his Belgian counterpart, who was an elected politician, Dr. J.P.M.M. Hendrikx, the youngish Dutch Mayor of Baarle, was an appointee of the Crown. A sociologist by education, he described himself as a "town manager". From behind a massive oak desk in his modernistic and strictly non-smoking office, stylised to look like a hall of an old Dutch country house, he was telling me about some of the problems of administering Baarle, with its never-ending dichotomy. They could be roughly reduced to the following issues:

1. Traffic accidents. With the deviant state border criss-crossing town squares, roads and car-parks, it was not unusual to have a car parked with its bumper in Belgium and its boot in Holland, or vice versa. Thus it was hard – at times impossible – to determine on whose territory an accident had occurred. This in turn led to problems of responsibility, insurance, police investigation (which police force should be entrusted with it – Dutch or Belgian?). On top of this, because car insurance premiums were more expensive in Belgium than in Holland, although cars and petrol were cheaper, Belgian car mechanics were reluctant to serve Dutch customers. My only conclusion was: when in Baarle, drive carefully.

2. Trespassing. With both Dutch and Belgian policemen strictly banned from operating on a foreign territory, Baarle cops had to be sure (literally) where they stood at any particular moment. Theoretically, if a Dutch policeman saw a woman attacked on the Belgian side of a street across the road, he could watch and register the assault but had no right to intervene. I made a mental note to pop into the local police station to find out how they got around this bizarre situation in reality.

3. Draft-dodging. This problem became a thing of the past when the armies in both Belgium and the Netherlands were made professional. Prior to that, Baarle was a paradise for both Dutch and Belgian draft-dodgers and deserters, who were able to avoid conscription indefinitely by changing their residential addresses from one country to another, in most cases easily achieved by moving to the house next door.

4. Ambulance and health services. Although Baarle's nearest ambulance station was in Belgium (about five miles from the town centre), its paramedics were not allowed to answer calls from foreign nationals, and all Dutch emergencies had to be dealt with by the nearest Dutch ambulance station in Breda – over thirty miles away. As the Mayor assured me, they had been trying to alter this ridiculous situation since the 1980s by directly appealing to the relevant authorities both in Brussels and in the Hague, but had received no help from either. The officials in both capitals have thus demonstrated international bureaucratic unity by ignoring the needs of enclave dwellers. Remembering the sad example of Mijnheer Theo Bloem, local GPs are careful where they have their surgeries. Dr. Bloem was qualified to practice in Holland, but not in Belgium. His surgery was attached to his house, which was in Belgium, next to the border, and one day Belgian local authorities decided he could no longer practice from their territory. The surgery had to be closed down, and Dr Bloem had to build a new one on Dutch soil thirty feet away – at considerable cost to himself. A recent incident, however, inspired hope that this bureaucratic cross-border madness could one day be overcome. Until several years ago,

Baarle's Dutch psychiatric nursing home – an establishment that was probably in great demand due to the constant lunacy of the town's everyday life – wasn't allowed to accept Belgians. It so happened that a Belgian old lady, who lived fifty metres away from it, had to be urgently admitted to a psychiatric institution, but the hospital next door refused to accommodate her, and she had to be taken to the nearest Dutch one – fifty miles away. The absurdity of this was such that the two Mayors, no longer willing to rely on assistance from their respective capitals, decided to resolve it between themselves, and by mutual agreement, the Dutch nursing home in question now has five beds permanently reserved for Baarle's Belgian residents.

5. Law enforcement. Some time ago, a Dutch citizen was arrested by the Belgian police in Baarle-Hertog (i.e. on Belgian territory) and taken to a remand prison in the nearest Belgian town of Turnhout. In order to transport the offender there, the police had to go over Dutch territory: there was simply no other way out of the enclave. The detainee later argued in Court that his transportation across his native Holland, which did not result in his extradition to the Dutch authorities, was illegal from the point of view of international law – and he was acquitted. In 1997, when some European countries had a pig pest epidemic, the Dutch authorities banned transportation of pigs through their country. Belgium had no such ban, but when a Belgian farmer from Baarle tried to take his pigs to a slaughterhouse in "mainland" Belgium and therefore had to cross through Dutch territory, he was turned back by Dutch police. A similar scenario took place in 2001, during the foot-and-mouth epidemic, which was taken much more seriously by the Dutch authorities than it was by the Belgian ones – to the detriment of Baarle's long-suffering Belgian farmers who – again – found themselves locked up inside their exclaves with all the produce they were unable to sell.

It was not all black and schizophrenic, however, and Dr. Hendrikx was able to quote numerous examples of the two communities' successful cooperation: a joint Dutch-Belgian public library and cultural centre, a joint school of music, a shared rubbish dump (or "waste park" – as he called it in politically correct terminology) and "the Common Organ" – a non-governmental and non-executive consultative body, comprising representatives of both town councils and sitting three times a year. These achievements, insignificant by pan-European standards, were small, yet shining, examples of a united Europe in action – without any assistance (read intervention) from Brussels and Strasbourg. I was particularly interested in the rubbish dump – sorry, waste park – and asked Anne-Miek to take me there that very afternoon.

"We shall never change. It is our duplicity that makes us interesting. We need tourists. We need to eat!" recapitulated Dr. Hendrikx on the same slightly aggressive "don't mess with us" note I had felt in the community leaflet.

"What would be the single most important off-the-record question you would ask your Belgian opposite number, if you bumped into him in the street or in a pub?" I asked the Mayor. He hesitated before answering.

"We don't socialise together, you see," he said with a smile. As the Crown-appointed "manager" of this extraordinary community, he was of course a consummate diplomat.

The only analogy I could think of for Baarle's peculiar double rule was San Marino in Italy, a mini-monarchy ruled simultaneously by two Captains-Regent – a unique governing push-pull. But at least they ruled over the same territory and shared the same office, whereas Baarle's second – Belgian (or rather Flemish) – hub of power was a hundred yards away from the first. Walking from one to the other involved at least fifteen border-crossings. Baarle's cobbled streets were covered with snow-like patches of confetti – the remains of the previous week's joint (Dutch and Belgian) town carnival.

The office of the Belgian Mayor could not have been more different from that of the Dutch. To start with, on entering the Belgian Town Hall, I could immediately smell the beloved titillating stench of stale tobacco smoke, and Mr. Alfons Cornelissen, the Belgian Mayor – an avuncular, even grandfatherly, figure, started our conversation by offering me a cigar. Much less of a diplomat than Dr. Hendrikx, he didn't even have a business card and didn't speak a word of English. Since my Flemish was even less fluent that my non-existent Dutch (they are basically the same language) we had to speak through an interpreter – which gave our encounter something of the feeling of an important international summit. A professional politician, Mr. Cornelissen had been the elected Mayor of Baarle-Hertog for the last thirteen years. Unlike Dr. Hendrikx's, his job was both unpaid and part-time – a vivid illustration of the difference between the two countries' political cultures.

"We have travelled a long way from barely tolerating each other to living with each other quite happily," he said, pointing at a huge map of Baarle behind his back. The map was covered with differently coloured spots – each denoting an enclave or a sub-enclave – and resembled a daltonism-testing ophthalmological chart. Interestingly, he listed roughly the same set of problems and achievements as his Dutch colleague, adding only "different taxation levels resulting in slightly different prices for certain goods" (I immediately remembered my Samson tobacco experience of yesterday), which, in his view, was rather advantageous for the community, for it brought about "petrol and tobacco tourism".

"The biggest obstacle to better cooperation is that the bureaucrats in both countries are reluctant to give our area an exemption from some of their equally binding, yet mutually exclusive, regulations. We have to use a lot of ingenuity trying to get around them."

He led me to the office window.

"Here's a living example," he said pointing to the opposite side of the road, where a small sex shop was nestling comfortably and inconspicuously among clusters of residential cottages. "That part of Kerkstraat is all Dutch, except for one square metre which is Belgian. If you look carefully, you will see that the doors of as many as four houses are facing that particular bit. These houses are Belgian. By international law, the "nationality" of a house is determined by the location of its front door. By placing their doors in Belgium, the house owners have managed to avoid the complicated

Dutch planning regulations, by which they would have had to abide had their doors been set in Holland."

"For the most part, national authorities have no idea the enclaves exist at all," the Mayor continued, having returned to his desk. He recounted a recent reception in Brussels during which he was introduced to King Albert of Belgium, who, as it turned out, had no notion of Baarle. When the Mayor described it as a set of Dutch and Belgian enclaves and exclaves, the King – perhaps preoccupied with the published revelations of his tempestuous youth – admitted: "I had no idea we had exclaves." Belgium's Minister of the Interior, who stood nearby and overheard the exchange, hastened to support his King by saying: "Neither did I, your Majesty!"

"The same prideful ignorance about us and the reluctance to learn is often demonstrated by the regional Flemish authorities and by those of the neighbouring villages and towns."

He gave out a deep sigh.

"National governments were responsible for our dubious status in the first place. It is therefore their duty to support us, but instead they fake lack of knowledge and don't even want to recognise our problems, fearing they would be too complicated to deal with. It is a shame really, for here we have a natural laboratory of united Europe. Rather than creating meaningless models of cross-border co-operation, the functionaries from Brussels should come here and see how we live."

One recent example of such blatant lack of co-operation was the Belgian government's point-blank refusal of financial help to update Baarle-Hertog's Dutch sewage system to Belgian standards, which they had themselves requested.

Having despaired of getting national or European authorities to understand, they were trying elsewhere. The Mayor introduced me to his full-time Secretary, Mr. Jan Vervoort, who had been working at creating an Assembly of all West European enclaves, which were bound to share lots of similar grievances. The project was still at an early stage, he said.

I was absolutely delighted to hear about it. My imaginary Enclavia was being made real!

I said I was planning to visit all West European enclaves and offered to act as a travelling ambassador of the would-be Assembly of West European enclaves – an offer that was gratefully accepted.

"I think it would be logical if we had lunch first and then head for the rubbish dump," Anne-Miek said ponderously. She liked having things planned in advance – a typically Dutch character trait, I am tempted to add (Belgians, allegedly, are more flexible and make plans as they go). I had to agree that the order she had suggested made sense. The reverse one – rubbish dump and then lunch – could spoil our appetites.

Den Engel restaurant – Baarle's plushest Dutch eating establishment – had an unmistakable Belgian touch to it. The interior was reminiscent of an upscale Paris (or Brussels) café – with *al fresco* furniture and a spacious conservatory facing the street. The waiters – all male, middle-aged and white-aproned – were sporting long cockroach-like moustaches. Den Engel served mussels with Belgian beer and offered a French/Belgian-style *plat du jour*. Portraits of both Dutch and Belgian royal families – next to each other – adorned the walls, and spotty maps of Baarle served as place mats.

Anne-Miek was talking about the practicalities of everyday life in Baarle. The town had two different postcodes – Belgian and Dutch. "There is one Belgian house in my otherwise Dutch street, which allows me to avoid international mailing fees by using the Belgian postcode in my return address when sending a letter to Belgium and the Dutch one when corresponding with Holland."

"How about foreign correspondence?" I asked and immediately regretted the way I had formulated the question: the word "foreign" had no real meaning in Baarle, where every short walk was a trip abroad and almost every purchase constituted an international transaction. But my lunch companion was probably used to such slips, made by careless "foreign" visitors.

"I can use either of the postcodes," she replied calmly and went on to explain Baarle's complicated system of phone dialling. To avoid paying international rates when calling a neighbour or ordering a take-away meal from one of the town's two Chinese restaurants, locally known as "Dutch Chinese" and "Belgian Chinese"(!), a universal local dialling code for Baarle's internal use only had been introduced by mutual agreement several years before. I thought this was a promising example of mutually beneficial cross-border cooperation, triggered by necessity.

In the course of our conversation, it also turned out that Anna-Miek, the umpteenth-generation Baarlenaar, was distantly related to Hugo Grotius, a seventeenth-century dissident Dutch lawyer and theologian, imprisoned by Dutch Prince Maurice for his support of the Remonstrants. Having escaped from jail, Grotius came to Baarle and found refuge in the Belgian half of a house, divided by the border, thus placing himself outside his Dutch persecutors' jurisdiction.

There was no end to the little – and big – discoveries an inquisitive visitor could make in Baarle.

Baarle's international "waste park" was in the outskirts of the town, a fifteen-minute walk from the centre, but Anne-Miek insisted on driving us there. I have noticed that residents of small towns all over the world (and not just in the USA) love driving their guests around, which probably helps feed their provincial delusions of grandeur. In Port Stanley, the miniature capital of the Falklands, my hosts never allowed me to walk a mere hundred yards separating my hotel (one of two in town) from a restaurant (one of two in town) where I had my meals, and were always out there in force, opening the doors of their jeeps to lure me into accepting an unwanted lift.

On the way to the waste park, we drove past Bakkerei Onder de Torren – a bakery where bread is baked in Holland but sold in Belgium; past Utility Automation – a small office, which had just closed down, unable to cope with dual taxation; past a Dutch Rabobank branch, divided into *Belgische Relaties* and *Nederlandse Relaties*; past the Artists Agency Roelen, which once used to house a branch of the Dutch Femisbank, with secret basement doors and underground passages to access Belgian vaults several metres away (it was closed down by the Dutch Treasury after a raid which uncovered massive cross-border wheeler-dealing); past the border-dissected Baarle's Print Works, the town's biggest employer, registered and licensed both in Holland and in Belgium.

Rubbish dumps have always struck me as highly philosophical places. Humans, after all, are similar to cows, who for one litre of fresh milk produce tons of manure. Mountains of refuse surround every hillock of human achievement, and waste disposal has become one of the most burning problems of our times. I often try to visualise how the proverbial scrap heap of history would appear. I see it as a larger version of a standard "waste park" where heaps of rust-eaten swords, bullet-ridden helmets and dog-eared folios are mixed with disintegrating dogmas, moss-covered political ambitions and rotten military doctrines.

My favourite London rubbish dump, where I used to go with various girlfriends to dispose of bulky household items (I feared – prophetically – that one day they might dump me there, too) was quite civilised, if naturally filthy. Like a distorting mirror, it accurately reflected everyday life, on the seamy side of which it was conveniently located. To begin with, just like in Baarle, one could no longer call it a rubbish dump. A large sign at its entrance announced that it was now a "Civic Amenity" under the North London Waste Authority, no less. Political correctness had finally come to the rubbish dump, the place where it organically belonged.

"The public may enter this site only for the purpose of depositing rubbish and do so on their own risk" read another authoritative sign, probably installed by the mysterious "Waste Authority". Its wording used to strike me as arrogantly British: had it not been for the warning, the dull-witted "general public" would undoubtedly start coming to the rubbish dump in droves to play snooker or to have a Malaysian meal.

Depositing rubbish can indeed be a risky business: we express ourselves not only in what we create, but also in what (or whom), and how, we dump, and disposing of rubbish is often the first step towards creative self-manifestation – of a person or even of a nation. The place that struck me once as the epitome of Switzerland was a communal rubbish dump near the town of Sargans. At first sight, it could easily have been mistaken for a deserted Legoland playground. Variously coloured and freshly-painted boxes stood inside a geometrically correct rectangular enclosure. Each of them had a tag: "Paper", "Cardboard", "Metal", "Glass", "Clothes", even "Old Furniture Pieces". The ground inside was evenly covered with unpolluted gravel: not a single microscopic piece of paper could be spotted on it. And towering above this amazing receptacle of neatness was a placard in German: "Littering the territory of this rubbish dump is punishable by law!"

I thought one could safely eat from the gravel surface – and one morning I saw a uniformed attendant hosing it clean with soapy water. Tables in many restaurants in London were a lot dirtier than the territory of that small Swiss rubbish dump.

In its cleanliness, Baarle's new Dutch-Belgian waste park was closer to the Swiss rubbish dump than to my favourite London "civic amenity". A soft music from hidden loudspeakers floated above rows of containers, marked "Plastic", "Asbestos", "Bottles", "Building Materials", all of one colour – light green. There were also special wooden crates, neatly packed with old radio parts, transistors, computer panels and electric appliances. The dump's most interesting feature, however, was that it had been deliberately laid out to allow the Dutch-Belgian frontier to run straight through its middle.

Why? I addressed this question to Ludovik Glassen, or Ludo as he insisted on being called informally. Ludo's politically correct job title was probably a "collateral matter co-ordinator" or something similar, and he proudly informed me that he was the Dutch Mayor's brother-in-law. Obviously, there was no stigma attached to being a worker at the rubbish dump in Baarle.

"The reason is that certain substances – like asbestos and cement, say – which are banned from being dumped in Holland can be disposed of on the Belgian side of the waste park a couple of metres away, and vice versa," said Ludo in his near-perfect English, which didn't quite agree with his bulbous violet nose resembling a badly printed map of the London Underground. We were standing on the

Dutch side of the rubbish dump, and as we spoke I had a clear view of the "near-abroad", where a red Belgian tractor was pushing around containers with some mixed Dutch-Belgian waste in them.

Working at a place like that, Ludo could not help being a philosopher, of course. "In the end, it all comes to waste," he concluded, with the omniscient grin common to gravediggers and rubbish-collectors.

I always felt that cemeteries and rubbish dumps had a lot in common: a cemetery, after all, is a well-kept rubbish dump, where our worn-out remains are bound to be left one day; and a rubbish dump is, in a way, a cemetery, where all by-products of our messy lives – from the headless teddy-bears of childhood to the wasted opportunities of youth and the unfulfilled aspirations of maturity – are buried.

I warned you: rubbish dumps never fail to put me in a philosophical frame of mind. Baarle's "waste park", however, was special. Not just because it was the world's only international rubbish dump, with a border running through it. It also symbolised a small triumph of human ingenuity over the shenanigans of international bureaucracy.

"Ingenuity born out of necessity" was definitely one character trait shared by both Dutch and Belgian residents of Baarle. I marked it in my notebook as the first possibly common European feature that I was able to "isolate" in Enclavia.

*   *   *

How was Baarle coping with the Euro? To find out, I decided to pay a quick visit to local banks – Dutch and Belgian. At the branch of Dutch *Rabobank*, I suffered a fiasco. A neatly dressed manager staunchly refused to talk to me about the Euro, or anything else, due to the bank's "privacy policy". Instead he asked for my e-mail address, promising to send me the information after it was cleared with his regional bosses – a polite twenty-first-century euphemism for "get off my back", or "get off my bank" in this particular instance (he never bothered to do it of course). Anne-Miek, however, thought that we might be luckier at a Belgian bank branch, where she herself was a client. "We Dutch are so secretive and dogmatic," she lamented.

And – as usual – she was right.

John Nemsdael, the KBC Bank branch manager, was busy. Hunched over the desk in his little cubicle of an office, he was packaging Belgian franc coins, bearing the puzzled profile of the embattled King Albert, into long snake-like sausages. "They will all go to somewhere in England to be recycled," he explained.

I thought it was symbolic that Britain, which was far behind the Continent both on the Euro and on recycling, was nevertheless involved in reprocessing the old "Continental" currencies.

A stack of completed neat "sausages" on the desk looked forlorn and somewhat disturbing, as if decades of turbulent Belgian history were being wrapped up in front of my eyes. For some reason, this scene brought back a popular Fleet Street April Fool's Day spoof that the United Nations had decided to abolish Belgium. We once printed it in the news section of the *European* newspaper.

"The Euro is a godsend for a community like ours," continued the manager. "The majority of our customers are Dutch. Because the whole town's cable TV comes from Belgium, it is cheaper for the Dutch residents to pay for it through a Belgian bank and thus save on transfer fees. Also, it is cheaper for them to buy a house in Belgium. Living in Belgium and working in Holland is Baarle's ideal scenario."

He was much more relaxed and informal than his Dutch counterpart.

"When I need something, I go to Belgium. I don't like Holland," concluded my Dutch escort Anne-Miek as we were leaving her Belgian bank branch.

It was late afternoon and already dark. Before leaving me to my own devices, Anne-Miek took me to a Dutch pharmacy at 31 Niewstraat, owned and run by Desire Doornbos, who lived next door – at 33 Niewstraat, a house dissected by the border.

"I can cross the border without leaving my living room," said Mr. Doornbos – a tall quiet man with kind brown eyes. "My son's room is in Belgium, my daughter's in Holland," he carried on in the resigned fashion of a person who had to answer the same questions several times a day. "In my own bedroom, I sleep with my head in Belgium and my feet in Holland."

With the front door in Holland, his house was technically Dutch, although twenty percent of it was in Belgium. He had to pay taxes in both countries in proportion to the size of their "territories" he occupied.

I questioned Mr. Doornbos about the effects Baarle's reality had on his children.

"It is better for a kid to grow up in Belgium, with its higher child benefits and traditionally good schools, but for an adult it is more lucrative to live in Holland, which has better healthcare schemes and is generally cheaper and neater: a special Dutch law requires home-owners to keep their properties clean. So, on reaching adulthood, a child could profit from swapping countries, which is not a big deal in Baarle."

I thought that Mr. Doornbos' own son could achieve this by simply relocating to his sister's room across the corridor.

On the way back to my hotel, I paused to admire the horses grazing in the moonlight next to the gabled country mansion of the Sans Limites brothel. Some time ago, the Dutch Tourism Board commissioned the University of Aachen to undertake a survey to conjure up a single image that would represent Holland to foreign visitors. After months of painstaking research, the academics produced the following impression: two moustached Dutch men, with tulips in their buttonholes, getting married to each other inside a windmill. Had the researchers consulted me, however, I would have rather suggested this one: horses grazing in the field under the moon, next to a gabled mansion housing a brothel.

Tired of the day's unending ambiguity, I was relieved to observe such an archetypally Dutch scene. The crisp night air reeked of manure.

From the breakfast room of my Sporthotel Bruurs, one had a full view of the hotel's outdoor tennis court, with sweaty middle-aged players trying (unsuccessfully, for the most part) to hit the ball. This clever layout worked in two ways: it made the people inside wary of stuffing themselves with too much food, thus they consumed less of the all-inclusive breakfast buffet. On the other hand, it could not fail to make the podgy tennis-players even hungrier than they were already, so that they were bound to leave the court and join the breakfasters long before their pre-paid game slot had expired, thus generating even more takings for this peculiar gym-cum-hotel.

On the way to the police station, I spotted Mr. Hendrikx, the Dutch Mayor and my acquaintance from yesterday, coming out of a Belgian bakery with a baguette under his arm. Seeing familiar faces in the street is one sure sign of coming to grips with a place – an adjustment that did not take long in Baarle.

The world's only international police station was not quite a station. It was just one room inside the Belgian Town Hall. Or, to be even more precise, it was just one desk, albeit a large one, shared by two visiting constables – Paul En Hilde Dierckx-Folders (I am talking about one person here!), Belgian, and F.W. Keulen, Dutch. Neither of them was permanently based in Baarle: the former came from Turnhout, the nearest Belgian town with a proper police station, the latter from Breda. The border (in this particular case, an imaginary one) ran through the middle of the desk, at which they both sat staring at their respective computer screens, discreetly turned away from one another to underline the fact that neither of them was allowed to access (or even to glimpse at) his foreign counterpart's files. The desk frontier was clearly marked by two sets of mail trays: red, white and blue on the Dutch side; red, yellow and black on the Belgian.

Policing Baarle was probably one of the safest, yet also one of the trickiest, law enforcement jobs in existence.

"Before detaining an offender, I must first make sure he is on Dutch territory," said Constable Keulen – a dark-skinned young man with thick black hair, a long moustache and a goatee. "If I see someone committing an offence on Belgian territory, I can only carry out a citizen's arrest and then call my Belgian colleague. It is even harder with traffic accidents."

He told me that the speed limit in the Belgian parts of Baarle was sixty kilometres an hour, whereas in the Dutch bits it was fifty. With the border running across every other road cobble, the absurdity of the situation was such that the Dutch police had to ignore the speeders staying within sixty kilometres an hour.

It was the same with different licensing hours – a paradox that used to be blatantly exploited by the landlords of several of Baarle's pubs dissected by the frontier: they simply installed two sets of doors – one in each country. When they stopped selling alcohol in Holland, the patrons hastily left through the Dutch doors only to re-enter immediately through the Belgian ones to carry on boozing. This practice was eventually curtailed, and the two countries' licensing laws were now fairly similar. But a slight discrepancy remained: in Holland they stopped selling alcohol at 2am, in Belgium – at 3am. So, come 2am, all locals, who wanted to carry on partying, had to relocate to Belgian pubs, provided they could still drive or cycle. (Remember: Baarlenaars do not walk, even when sober.)

"With my Dutch colleague, we have to keep reaching little compromises all the time," said Constable Dierckx-Folders. "For example, we are not allowed to carry arms on foreign territory, but in Baarle we do of course." In appearance, he was the direct opposite of Constable Keulen: middle-aged, clean-shaven and round-faced, with a neat blonde hairstyle starting to go threadbare above the forehead. Unlike his Dutch counterpart, he was not wearing a police uniform, but was sporting a "civilian" collarless sweater.

"Theoretically, I am now on Belgian territory, where – officially – I am not allowed to carry out my policeman's duties," added Constable Keulen. "I cannot question anyone here, not in this station inside the Belgian Town Hall. If I want to write an official statement, I have to leave my desk and walk across the road, to Holland, to do it in the nearest Dutch pub, say. But I am sure that if I preferred to write it here, my Belgian colleague would not report me," he chuckled. "For lack of official regulations relating specifically to Baarle, our success rests on mutual understanding and respect. All Euro-bureaucrats should come here to see how we practise cross-border co-operation."

I thought that these two cops would make an ideal "windmill" couple, for weren't the strongest marriages (between people and between countries, too) based on mutual respect and lots of little compromises?

And wasn't the ability to compromise on smaller things and to overlook irrelevant, overly-forbidding regulations for the sake of a larger aim another truly European quality?

Although only nine hundred Baarlenaars were Belgian citizens, and despite the fact that even in the town's Belgian parts forty percent of the residents were Dutch, its Belgian bits looked and felt different from the Dutch ones. Belgacom public phone cabins; open-plan cafes; numerous tobacconists, chocolatiers and fireworks shops; newsagents, with *Gazet van Antwerpen* banners above the windows; a Brusselshot restaurant and queues (albeit short) for baguettes at bakeries – all these spelled out Belgium. On that Saturday morning, all Belgian establishments, with the exception of bakeries (and public phone cabins, no doubt), were firmly shut and looked as if they were never going to function again. The joint Belgian-Dutch local library, however, was open. With very few language barriers between Dutch and Flemish, the library's only visibly distinctive feature was the different keyboards of its two public-use computers: in Belgium they use the French key lay-out, in Holland – the English. It was there that Mr. Jan Vervoort, the Secretary to the Belgian Mayor, had arranged for me to meet several "interesting" locals from both communities.

The first to arrive – with military precision – was Arie P. de Jong, a retired Colonel of the Royal Netherlands Air Force and now an amateur local historian. Tall, loud-voiced and avuncular, he spoke almost unaccented "posh" English, although he had only visited Britain twice.

"I live on Dutch soil, two hundred yards from Belgium," he shouted amicably, with a broad smile on his face. "My daughter and her children live in Belgium. My doctor is Belgian, but my insurance bills go to a company in the Netherlands where they ask me every time why I have gone for treatment abroad. To which I reply: I just happen to live in this funny mixed community of Baarle where we have played unified Europe for many years."

His wartime stories were truly amazing. "Do you know that Baarle saved London from being bombed in 1916?" he demanded vociferously and, without waiting for me to reply, recounted the following little-known episode:

During the First World War, all twenty-two Belgian enclaves of Baarle were occupied, whereas the town's Dutch enclaves remained neutral. Inside one of those Dutch enclaves, there was (and still is) a tiny forty-square-metre Belgian sub-enclave, which the German army, for obvious reasons, was unable to access without violating Dutch neutrality. It was there, in that tiny unoccupied bit of Belgium, that the people of Baarle built a wireless tower, which was able to intercept German radio communications. Among those was an early warning of the impending bombardment of London by three German airships (dirigibles). As a result, all three were shot down en route by the British artillery, and the bombing never took place. It was one of the first air-defence operations in British military history. The wireless station continued to forewarn the British about impending air raids throughout 1917, when the first bomber-planes came into existence.

"Do you know that during World War II it took twenty-eight days to liberate Baarle – the longest liberation time for any Dutch municipality, whereas Breda and the whole of North Brabant were liberated in a single afternoon?" he thundered. Needless to say, I didn't.

He told me how Maria, the wife of a local postman and the mother of Alfons Cornelissen, Baarle's Belgian Mayor, had helped the allied pilots shot down over Baarle to find refuge in Dutch enclaves and be re-united with their troops. Three weeks before the liberation she was captured by the Gestapo and executed. A small monument to that brave lady, erected by Baarle's joint Dutch-Belgian War Victims Commemoration Society, now stood in the town centre. (It must have been very small indeed, for I had failed to notice it so far.)

With every hour spent in Baarle, I liked it more and more, and its confusion of borders and cultures was making more and more sense to me. It made me feel in my element. Almost at home.

Three members of PLUS – Baarle's joint Dutch-Belgian Youth Club, none of whom looked much younger than thirty-five – were next to arrive.

"Our organisation's age bracket is from sixteen to fifty," said Jan, one of the newcomers, having registered my unspoken surprise, which promptly turned into a contented smile: it was nice to know that I could still qualify for youth club membership, if only in Baarle.

According to Jan, the Club had been started twenty-five years ago, "when there wasn't much to do for younger people in Baarle". Belgian and Dutch kids used to fight each other, and the Club tried to stop this by "organising rallies of protest".

An opponent of all sorts of rallies, most of which are staged solely for the self-expression of the demonstrators rather than for the cause they claim to highlight (or to protest against), I immediately lost interest in PLUS (if not my respect for its liberal membership criteria). The personal story of Jan himself, however, was much more engaging.

A native Baarlenaar, he was Dutch, but because his family lived "on Belgian territory", he had been to a Belgian primary school. His parents thought that the Belgian education system was better due to stricter discipline, whereas Dutch schools had always been "more relaxed". In Belgian schools, for instance, it was considered rude for a pupil to make eye contact with a teacher – behaviour that in Dutch schools was actually encouraged. After several years of strict Belgian schooling, Jan acquired a "slight Flemish accent" and got so "Belgianised" that, when it came to scuffles, he always fought with Belgian kids against Dutch ones (being Dutch himself that is). No wonder that when he started attending a Dutch secondary school, the only secondary school in Baarle, they branded him *Belske* – a mildly derogatory Dutch nickname for Belgians.

The bullying was so consistent that he had to swap the Dutch school for another Belgian one, outside Baarle, only to earn himself another moniker – *Kees*, a Belgian insult for the Dutch.

"This is what they call Dutch Baarlenaars in the rest of Holland – *Belske*, and in Belgium, they brand us *Kees* or 'Hollanders'," Jan concluded sadly.

His story rang the whole belfry of bells to me and evoked memories of my own stigmatised childhood and youth in Ukraine and Russia. Like myself, Jan was programmed to become a permanent outcast and a "rootless cosmopolitan", although, unlike myself, he had probably never heard of this last cliché, coined by Joseph Stalin.

Both my parents were branded "Jewish" – a fact that I never fully realised until at the age of sixteen I was given my first Soviet passport, where in the section five, the notorious "nationality" column, it was written in black and white *Yevrei* – Jew. Did it mean that I was a follower of Judaism? Not in the least. No one in my family, not my parents or grandparents, knew a single word of Yiddish or Hebrew or had ever been inside a synagogue. My Mum and Dad were the products of two cultures: Russian and Ukrainian. I was also – even then – deeply influenced by English culture: I had started learning English as a small child, and by sixteen was able to read and speak it quite easily.

Of course we couldn't have practised Judaism (or any other faith, for that matter), even if we had wanted to. In the USSR, atheism was the only official ideology in the realm of religion ("the opium of the people", according to Karl Marx), and every university student was subjected to a compulsory course in Scientific Atheism! The only synagogue in my native East Ukrainian city of Kharkiv had been turned into a gym in the early forties.

As I proudly received my brand-new passport from the smiling militia officer, I could not possibly have realised that with this hammer-and-sickled little book I, despite being the son of a communist and the grandson of committed Old Bolsheviks and revolutionaries, was acquiring an official lifetime stigma, for one's "nationality" in the Soviet Union was asked everywhere – in libraries, hospitals and schools.

Shortly after receiving my passport, I first came to realise that life could also be the price of one's identity as perceived by others.

I had just turned sixteen and was finishing at a secondary school which – in normal Soviet Empire fashion – was multi-ethnic to the extreme: among both pupils and teachers there were Russians, Ukrainians, Greeks, Georgians, Armenians, Tartars and so-called *polukrovki* (half-bloods) – the children of mixed marriages. I liked Ukrainian language and literature. Studying them was not compulsory, but I chose to attend all the lessons and was first in my class in these subjects. Not that I felt particularly "Ukrainian" at the age of seven, but I was already interested in languages and was painstakingly learning English with a private tutor. Had I then lived in Estonia, say, I would have no doubt picked up some Estonian. It is interesting, however, that all the Jewish kids attended the optional Ukrainian lessons, whereas many ethnically Ukrainian ones didn't. Some of the latter could not speak and read Ukrainian and did not want to. This shows how bound up in conventions the very concept of national identity is.

The whole episode was in many ways my own fault. I had just acquired a taste for alcohol, and had persuaded myself that I had an unusual tolerance for alcoholic drinks. Indeed, I seldom seemed to get drunk at parties and even earned myself the nickname "the guy without a lid". With a lot of youthful bravado, I had been flaunting my ability to hold alcohol – until four of my classmates decided to prove me wrong. They lured me into going on a booze trip with them.

Having packed up our rucksacks full of vodka and cheap plonk, we took a train to a forest in the outskirts of Kharkiv, where they started – literally – pouring drinks down my throat. Convinced of my extraordinary drinking skills, I did not show a lot of resistance. My classmates were drinking too, but in moderation, whereas I was soon totally plastered and lay supine on the grass in an alcoholic stupor – to their obvious delight at having deconstructed the myth.

Semi-conscious, I could see through the alcoholic fog a group of local lads – much older than we were – materialising from nowhere. They had the merciless faces of juvenile delinquents. And they probably were hardened felons. They carried knives. They oozed cruelty and blunt force. They were swearing nastily. They were all deadly drunk (not as much as I was though). My friends were rather frightened (who wouldn't be?) and offered them some booze as a camouflaged bribe for leaving us alone. At this point, one of the newcomers staggered up to me lying on the ground. He grabbed me by the hair, lifted my head and said: "Here's a Jew, and I am going to kill him." From his pocket he produced a flick-knife and slowly moved it towards my throat. His fish-like eyes – empty and cold – left no doubt of the seriousness of his intentions. I could not move. It was the end.

"Are you blind, or what?" I suddenly heard a familiar voice shouting. It belonged to one of my class-mates, Sergei Svezhentsev, a hopeless student and a dunce. We had never been close to each other.

"Are you blind?" Sergei was screaming at my would-be killer, who was rather taken aback by such unexpected cheek – and I could see his sinewy tattooed hand, clutching the knife within an inch of my face, tremble slightly. "Where did you see a Jew with blue eyes and blonde hair? Look at him!" Sergei grabbed my poor limp head from the back. "Does he look like a Jew? And his last name is Ivanenko! Have you ever heard a Jewish name like that?"

The name was one hundred percent Ukrainian of course. The rest of our party froze at such an obvious lie.

Sergei's impromptu tactics were successful. The hoodlums did not expect this turn of events and chose to soften up and let me live. We ended up finishing the remaining booze together.

Thirty-six years later, sorting out my mother's papers, I came across my old school album. From one of the faded photos, a lop-eared teenager in a worn-out jacket smiled sheepishly. It was Sergei Svezhentsev, who once preserved my human identity by challenging my ethnic one – or, in plain words, saved my life.

This is how the Jewish part of my identity was moulded – through "humiliation by others" (*pace* A.L. Kennedy), through years and years of unfair treatment and the resulting inferiority complex. Apart from this, however, I have never felt particularly Jewish.

On the 10 June, 2002, after twelve and a half years of living and working in Britain, I was naturalised as a British citizen. From that moment, I was an official carrier of "Britishness" as perceived by the outside world – a complex phenomenon comprised of the royal family, football hooliganism, Margaret Thatcher, picture-postcard villages, drab council estates, etc., etc.

My "Britishisation" was gradual and at times painful. Some time ago, for instance, I started noticing – to my own consternation – that, irrespective of my mood, my lips would instinctively curve into a smile at the sight of a dog or a baby, and that I was abusing the words "lovely" and "cheers", especially while abroad. You won't believe it, but despite my strong Russian accent, I have been mistaken for a Brit a couple of times during my travels (not that I particularly wanted to be): once in Tasmania, by a sleepy and not particularly bright waiter in a Chinese restaurant in the town of Longford; and once in Alaska, where a young Kodiak girl assured me that she "loved" my "beautiful British accent" and my aftershave (which, in her words, made me "smell like a gentleman"). To my surprise, in both cases I felt proud, although even now, with a British passport in my pocket, I would rather refer to myself – in the manner of nineteenth-century guidebook writers – as a "Britisher".

I was once taken for a German on the Scilly Islands, and confused for a Scot in Dublin by an elderly Irish lady who must have been not simply deaf, but blind, too.

Despite intermittent cases of mistaken identity, I had plenty of reasons to be pleased with my newly acquired "Britishness". The qualities that I love most about this country are that patriotism here is quiet and unobtrusive and that it is a culture that instinctively dislikes rapid change, without being slow and retrospective. I tend to agree with the inimitable Julie Burchill, who once wrote that "the major reason to admire the British is our refusal to be corralled, controlled and cowed by those who seek to impose their rules on us".

"Tony George Ruggles, Patriot, lived in this house in 1764–1774". I spotted this memorial plate in Cambridge, Massachusetts, while looking for the house of H.W. Longfellow, my favourite American poet. "Patriot" was obviously regarded as an occupation, a lifetime achievement, or an honorary title in the USA – on a par with a knighthood in Britain perhaps. While in America, I watched these "professional" patriots spontaneously spring up from their seats to burst into renditions of "God Bless America", with their hands on their hearts and tears in their eyes, at the end of many a raunchy "country show", with cross-dressing, topless dancing, poor imitations of The Beatles and a regulation "Stars 'n' Stripes" proudly waved from the stage. To my astonishment, they normally constituted a hundred percent of the audience.

"Britishness" for me is a complicated feeling which includes hating the country's chilliness (both human and climatic), its claustrophobia, its dirtiness, its inefficiency, its increasingly hypocritical governments, its persistent imperial psyche and the snobbishness of its elite – but also missing it painfully, almost to tears, during my travels. Responsible citizenship, to my mind, is not a passionate love affair with a land whose passport you carry, but rather a love-hate relationship – a mature marriage, in which you can see your spouse with all his/her warts and eventually learn to accept, possibly even to like, the very qualities you have hated. It is a difficult liaison – at times romantic and at times oppressive.

My many years in Britain were not all milk and honey. Here I experienced elation, creative fulfillment, near-fame and personal happiness – but also loneliness, betrayal, extreme poverty, near-homelessness and despair bordering on depression. I came to regard London as a chameleon city – a place with a unique ability to adjust to my changing moods: bright and radiant when I am joyful, grey and dismal when I feel miserable. I think one can fully affiliate with a country (or with a city) only if one has suffered in it.

As for the inevitable irritations, well, at the end of the day, even the proverbial inefficiency of British public transport has a positive side: it makes any October (or, say, July) revolution in Britain utterly impossible, because the rusty British equivalent of the *Aurora* cruiser (whose blank salvo signalled the start of the armed Bolshevik uprising in Russia in 1917) will be indefinitely delayed, due to "signal problems", somewhere near Greenwich.

And when, finally, the cruiser's gaping guns are somehow aimed at Westminster, it will be too late, for, by that time, all rebellious sailors and soldiers, together with workers, motorists and soccer fans – in festive, yet orderly, formations and with a song: *God Save the Queen* – will have long been gone for lunch.

In short, having been born in the wrong country, if I do belong anywhere at all, Britain comes closest to being home.

Naively, until coming to live in Britain I used, like many a foreigner, to regard Britishness and Englishness as almost synonymous. After my first BBC TV documentary (1990), in which I stupidly chose to use them interchangeably, I received a pile of angry letters from Wales and Scotland urging me to be more careful with my choice of words. By now, I am well aware of the fact that referring to Scotland as England is as ignorant and tactless as calling my native Ukraine "Russia".

Until my temporary move from London to Edinburgh, I had never imagined the strength of the anti-English feeling in Scotland, which seems to be on the increase since devolution. In a way, I can understand it: just as *glasnost* in the Soviet Union was never meant to imply "freedom of speech", but was rather a clever euphemism for the lack of it, the very term "devolution" does not imply "independence", or even "semi-independence" (although being semi-independent is like being half-pregnant: you are either free or subservient, *tertium non datur)*, but underlines the persisting English domination in all spheres of life. Indeed, what independence can we talk about when the new-born Scottish parliament only controls ten percent of Scotland's budget? But finding myself, Vitali Vitaliev, on the receiving end of anti-English racism (an "official" term used by Scottish media) was more than bizarre. This happened due to my two London-born children, Andrei, four and a half years old, and Anya, two and half (at the time we moved), both of whom spoke with "posh" English accents. It was painful to watch how my two gorgeous and extremely outgoing kids were openly snubbed by some adult Scots because of the way they spoke. (Several months on, they were speaking English with a strong Scottish accent, of course – not out of a desire to fit in, but simply due to children's natural adjustability.) When, confronted with this near-hostility, my half-Russian, half-Australian London-born little boy would proudly say "I am English," I would start feeling English too!

Another proof of one's identity being solely in the beholder's eyes.

"My nationality is the language I write in," said Joseph Conrad, a fellow scribe and a fellow cosmopolitan. One more reason for me to feel English. If only when I am writing.

How about my Russian-ness, you may ask? Paradoxically, having never felt particularly Russian in the Soviet Union, where I was officially stigmatised as a *Yevrei*, I was made to feel oppressively and stereotypically Russian when in Britain. The *Times* magazine, for example, once branded me "a typical Russian soul" and explained what – in its view – that implied: "Sometimes I am happy." Long pause. "Sometimes I am sad." Even longer pause. 'How . . . can . . . this . . . BE?' "

And why is it that if you have a Russian-sounding name, everybody in Britain thinks you must know for sure who is going to be the new Russian President?

"Hello, is this Vassili Vassilieff? This is the *Daily Annual* calling. Who do you think will become the next ruler of Russia? And what should the West do about it – disarm or dig a bomb shelter?"

"Well, as to who is going to be the next Russian President, I can tell you exactly – I have no idea! My advice is this: disarm while sitting in a bomb shelter. And leave your poor cows alone. And the foxes. And me, too. I want to sleep."

This lively conversation took place at 2am.

And at 5am, my phone rings again.

"Hello, is this Vivaldi Vitara? I am calling from Gay-Lussac radio station for sexual minorities. What political developments do you expect in Russia and what effect will they have on the plight of Russian homosexuals?"

At this point, I lose my temper. "Any other questions?" I shout. "Do you want a quick briefing on the shaky balance of power in the Diet – the Parliament of Liechtenstein? Or maybe you are interested in my views of the ongoing conflict between the warring tribes of Papua New Guinea? Or of Papua New Zealand? Or of Papua New York? I'd be much happier to comment on these than on any developments in Russia, where I haven't been for donkey's years. And, by the way, don't you know that I am Australian? Yes, a fair dinkum Aussie! I can show you my passport over the phone ..."

Outside, the car is honking impatiently to take me to a TV studio, where the somnambulant presenter of a breakfast show is already opening his omniscient mouth – either in an irrepressible yawn or in an attempt to ask me the same unanswerable question: "What is going to happen in Russia?"

Well, there's no denying the fact: the British love labelling and pigeonholing, especially people with foreign names. And if you were once branded "a former Soviet expert", "an ex-Soviet journalist" or "a Russian Clive James", you are expected to carry this burden until the end of your days – no matter how many articles, books and films on utterly non-Russian subjects you have produced. You join the sullen ranks of the eternal "professional foreigners", whose only use is in how-they-see-us media slots.

Stereotyping Russians goes back a long way. "The theory of right conduct universally accepted and acted upon in Russia may be truly affirmed to be on a level with the egotistic principles or instincts which determine the unheroic actions of the average man and woman – which is another way of declaring it devoid of ideals," E.B. Lanin ("the collective signature of several writers") stated unequivocally in his (their?) book *Russian Traits and Terrors*, published in 1891. The chapter titles of this poorly-written folio speak for themselves: "I. Lying; II. Fatalism; III. Sloth; IV. Dishonesty," and so on ... At least, "Arrogance" and "Narrow-Mindedness" did not feature among all those despicable "Russian traits".

Luckily, I didn't experience similar problems with my Ukraine-ness, simply because the British public – not unlike the imperialist Soviet *apparatchiks* of the not-so-distant past – persist in their thinking that Ukraine and Russia are synonyms. As a native Ukrainian (well, I was born and grew up there, after all), I was often a victim of this geopolitical ignorance. When I made a television documentary about Ukraine for Channel 4, most reviewers labelled it "a film about Russia". Even the Queen, to whom I was once introduced at a press reception, in response to my "I was born in Ukraine" (a reply to her perfunctory, almost rhetorical "Where are you from?"), concluded: "So you were born in Russia." One could be forgiven for thinking that Ukraine was a figment of someone's wild imagination – rather than an independent country with a territory larger than France and a population of more than fifty million.

On the other hand, I used to make a similar mistake about Britain and England.

"Don't you miss Russia or Ukraine at all?" my British friends often ask me. My answer is "No". Had you been born and spent half of your adult life in a prison cell (even if it were the largest prison cell in the world), would you miss it when you finally broke free? I forget who it was who said that true motherland is not necessarily the place where you were born, but rather the country where you started developing as a free human being – another argument in favour of regarding the UK as the land of my birth. "Where freedom dwells, there's your country," Benjamin Franklin once wrote to his son.

And then there is the last component of my schizophrenic and hard-to-pin-down identity – my Australian-ness.

So who am I, after all? The answer is I don't know. A former Fleet Street colleague of mine once noted that generalising about nations is a tricky and not entirely respectable business, even though whole careers are built on it. The same can be said about separate individuals. It is "tricky and not entirely respectable" to pigeonhole and to label others on the grounds of where they were born, what name they have or what language they speak. National characteristics, to my mind, can only work as a jest. Or as a children's game. The moment they get one hundred percent serious, they become xenophobic and capable of triggering all sorts of disasters – from pub brawls to wars and terrorist attacks.

To cut a long story short, I am more than happy to repeat after my late friend Sir Peter Ustinov: "Ethnically, I am filthy." When people are bewildered by my name, or my accent, or both, and ask me what nationality I am, I normally answer: "I am Vitalian!"

No wonder that Jan's experiences rang so many bells!

Driek, Jan's fellow Dutch Baarlenaar and PLUS member, told a familiar story: of being called a "wannabe Belgian" and "a fake Belgian" both at his Dutch University and at his workplace near Eindhoven, and of being often addressed by his work colleagues in a mock "Belgian" accent.

Among their Youth Club's "internationalist" achievements, both men quoted joint – Belgian/Dutch – football and tennis classes and jointly attended rock concerts at the Club's own venue, with the border running across its stage, so that visiting rock musicians often quarrelled jokingly as to which band members would play in Holland, and which in Belgium.

I somehow thought that Baarle-based youngsters (particularly those in their late forties) did not really need a formal "inter-nationalist" education, as this was provided by their environment itself. It was the name-calling bullies from outside the town who would have benefited greatly from learning more about Baarle.

Interestingly, the third member of the Youth Club "delegation" – a middle-aged Indonesian lady called Ellen – admitted that she wasn't often subjected to racist chanting in Baarle's streets, but when she was, it mostly happened on Belgian territory. "There are very few immigrants living in Baarle: one Afghan, a handful of Chinese and some Italians – that's all," she concluded meekly, almost apologetically. Her calculations clearly did not include the forty percent of Belgian Baarlenaars who resided on Dutch territory – and the same proportion of the town's Dutch residents who lived in Belgium. All those hundreds of people were immigrants, too, if only by definition.

* * *

It was my last evening in Baarle. Walking back to my hotel, I could hear the muffled sounds of religious hymns from the Dutch Roman Catholic church of St. Mary (Baarle had two separate Roman Catholic parishes), built by Belgian architects with Belgian red bricks, next door to an Erotic Sex Shop.

In the dark, one could easily tell Dutch houses from Belgian ones, even without consulting their "nationalized" numberplates. Whereas windows in Belgian houses were mostly curtained or shuttered, Dutch ones were wide-open for inspection by every (non-existent) pedestrian – an admirable sort of exhibitionism underlining the greater openness of Dutch society. In one of the Dutch windows, I saw an elderly couple reading newspapers in armchairs. In another, a much younger couple were canoodling on the floor: it was not hard to guess what they were planning to do next – without bothering to draw the (non-existent) curtains, no doubt. The Amsterdam red-light district principle applied here: if you don't want to see it – don't look.

Both the Dutch fire station and Club Sans Limites next to my hotel were immersed in darkness; the horses grazing silently in the surrounding fields were the only sign of life. It was plain that neither fires nor sex romps were happening in Baarle that night.

* * *

On Sunday morning, Baarle's streets were blocked with bumper-to-bumper traffic. With all shops closed for the day in the rest of Holland and Belgium, it looked as if the entire population of both countries had flocked to Baarle to take advantage of the special inter-governmental provision authorising Sunday trade within the limits of the town. Cars with Belgian and Dutch number plates were parked on every square inch of Baarle's territory – apart from the spacious and totally empty car park of Club Sans Limites, which could have been named Car Park Sans Voitures.

Observing the merrily shopping crowds, I noticed that Belgians were mostly bulk-buying Dutch butter, whereas the Dutch were mostly after cheap Belgian petrol: the queue to Baarle's Belgian petrol station stretched for several hundred yards. I also spotted a group of East European shoppers – Czechs or Slovaks – bulk-buying everything they could lay their hands upon.

It was a far cry from twenty years before, when Baarle was a real haven for smugglers. The cleverest of them knew that the notoriously strict Dutch customs office, where all the goods were assiduously checked, had a tiny bit of Belgian territory in one of its corners. The moment any forbidden item was exposed, a smuggler quickly walked to the Belgian bit of the room, together with all his goodies. As long as he stood there he was officially on the Belgian territory – out of reach of Dutch customs. One local lady tried to smuggle some Belgian curtains from Turnhout (she was obviously Belgian, for the Dutch, as we have established, do not use curtains), having wrapped them around her body. When exposed, she proceeded to the Belgian corner, where she remained for almost twenty-four hours, until – driven by a call of nature – she dropped the curtains on the Belgian floor and walked off unhindered into Holland, with no strings (or contraband) attached!

Before leaving Baarle, I had one last appointment to keep. Jack Haagen, a part-time chief of Baarle's voluntary Dutch fire brigade, had kindly agreed to show me around his station that afternoon.

It was the neatest fire station I had ever seen: helmets, suits and gear, stacked evenly on specially designated open shelves, to be grabbed and used as soon as the necessity arose. All looked brand-new, and they probably were. From the look of them, they had not been either grabbed or used for many months, if ever. Mr. Haagen showed me a "crisis cellar" – a large well-equipped bomb shelter in the station's basement, where all residents of Baarle could find refuge.

"In case of what?" I asked. "A sudden Belgian invasion?"

He laughed: "I think this is highly improbable. We are on excellent terms with our Belgian neighbours. We even have a common emergency phone number – 112. If dialled from a Belgian patch of Baarle, the call first goes to the switchboard in Antwerp, then to Baarle's Belgian fire station. Sometimes, if we are not sure of where exactly a call came from, we travel to the fire together with the town's Belgian fire brigade. If it turns out to be a Dutch fire I am the boss; if the fire is in Belgium my Belgian counterpart is. If we are there together, no matter whose fire it is, we split it into two parts and deal with one each."

"There is only one little problem," he went on. "Our Belgian colleagues have methods and training of their own. Also, their French-standard fire hoses are thicker than our German-standard ones and do not fit Dutch fire-hydrants, while ours do not fit theirs."

"How do you get around it?" I enquired.

The chief's kind face was beaming. From one of his desk drawers, he produced a round stainless-steel object, the size and the shape of a telescopic lens. Hollow inside, the object had two differently shaped ends.

"What do you think this is?" he demanded cheerfully. I said that I honestly didn't have a clue.

"This is a unique fire-hose connector, designed and made in Baarle, with one end fitting Belgian fire-hoses and the other – Dutch ones! All Belgian and Dutch fire-engines in town carry it."

He was clearly relishing the effect he had.

I handled the weighty, gleaming adaptor, cold to the touch. It was the most vivid practical symbol of the inventiveness and mutual adjustability of enclave dwellers. If I were to choose a national emblem for Enclavia, there couldn't have been a better one than a double-edged fire-hose connector to suit the needs of two diverse communities in case of emergency. It was also the perfect metaphor for Baarle, this small bi-national municipality of Belgian and Dutch enclaves fitting each other nicely, despite their different ways and standards. This "mother of all enclaves" – to use Saddam Hussein's favourite figure of speech – had all the credentials to be nominated the Capital of Enclavia.

In my notebook, I jotted down "adjustability" and "flexibility" as two more possible character traits of the elusive "European identity".

A couple of hours later, my new friend Colonel de Jong (the military historian) drove me back to Breda, from where I was to catch a train to Arnhem to board a sleeper for an eleven-hour overnight ride to Basel. After that, another five hours by train to Como, my base for visiting Campione d'Italia – an Italian exclave inside Switzerland. The Colonel's driving was fast and daring. A pilot is always a pilot.

With a couple of hours to kill in Breda I went to see an international exhibition of political posters in the town's modernistic art gallery. To enter the exhibition hall, I had to leave "Sally" in a cloakroom locker, for which the attendant required a one-Euro deposit. In exchange for a shiny Euro coin, he gave me a battered one-guilder piece and told me to insert it into the locker's slot. (With Dutch coins and banknotes out of circulation for over two weeks, it was probably one of the last guilders in existence.) "We have failed to adjust our lockers to Euros," apologised the attendant.

And I suddenly realised very clearly that I was no longer in Baarle – the place where constant, unfailing and timely "adjustment" was the main rule of life.

*　*　*

2. Switaly (Switzerland and Italy)

COMO

The second-class sleeper carriage of my Basel-bound train greeted me with a distinctive "Soviet" smell of unwashed bodies and dirty socks. The Soviet associations were further enhanced by the absence of any water – hot or cold – in the toilet and by a sloppily dressed attendant, who took away my passport "for the Swiss border". My hopes of having a decent sleep were shattered the moment I entered my compartment and met my travel companions – a Dutch family of five: four teenage children and their mother travelling to Rome. The kids all looked roughly the same age – she must have had them in a very quick succession.

Packed like sardines, we rattled through the pitch-black darkness of Germany, occasionally interrupted by blazing station lights and muffled *Meine Damen und Herren* announcements, which sounded both soporiphic and somewhat raunchy. By morning, I felt so shattered that when at 5am the attendant brought in tepid coffee, some stale rolls and my passport – all on the same breakfast tray

– I nearly gobbled up the passport. (It couldn't have tasted much worse than the rolls anyway.)

At least, the train arrived in Basel on time (they always do in Europe). I had ten minutes to run across the platform and to jump into a smoking carriage of the SBB (Swiss Railways) Basel–Milan express.

I knew that Basel had two railway terminals – Swiss and German. From the Swiss-franc prices in the windows of the still closed platform kiosks, I deduced that it was the Swiss one. It was nice to find myself outside the Euro zone again – if only in transit.

The moment the train started, a uniformed attendant sporting a bow tie pushed in a trolley with food and drinks (it must feel peculiar to wear a bow tie at six o'clock in the morning: not dissimilar to having a glass of champagne – and nothing else – for breakfast, I assume). I bought a coffee and a croissant to suppress the taste of the breakfast rolls (or was it the passport?) and was given change in Swiss francs. I said I didn't need them, because I was going to Italy, but the trolley man staunchly refused to replace them with Euros, of which he, allegedly, was short. "Buy something else," he suggested and I bought a packet of chewing gum, which I immediately offered to a bespectacled young man sitting opposite me. We started chatting.

He was Dutch and came from Utrecht. Having just finished school, he was going to Rome for a short holiday. In fact, he had been on the same overnight train as I had, only in a different carriage. He told me that during the night he had been repeatedly "searched and whisked" by German policemen. "I always get searched and checked," he shrugged. "They think that if you are young and Dutch, you must be carrying drugs."

He dug into his backpack, and I was half-expecting him to come up with a spliff (the power of stereotypes!), but he produced a natural oat bar and started munching on it ponderously. He told me he spoke four languages, disapproved of any drugs – hard or soft – and wanted to be a journalist. At seventeen, he had already hitchhiked across Europe and was finding it hard to believe that

I had first been allowed outside the Soviet Union at the age of thirty-four.

Near Lucerne, the snow-capped Alps first came into view. My next couple of weeks would be spent in their constant shadow. The Swiss Alps looked symmetrically picturesque as if recycled and then neatly packaged. They resembled tidy haystacks, wrapped in snow-white tarpaulins, floating past the train windows. I wouldn't have been particularly surprised if the mountains were indeed pre-packaged. Nothing was impossible in Switzerland – a country where one could be fined for "littering a rubbish dump".

We rolled across Ticino – an Italian-speaking Swiss canton[3]. All new passengers on the train were well groomed, cashmere-dressed and spoke some guttural version of Italian.

At Chiasso, Italian frontier guards in red berets boarded the train. They pounced on my neighbour, the goody-goody Dutch youngster, and *pronto* ransacked his possessions. He accepted the inspection with quiet stoicism. "I always carry my passport with me, even when travelling in Schengen countries," he sighed, when the search was over, and added sombrely: "Borderless Europe is not for everyone."

He was right: stereotypes were obviously much sturdier than some European frontiers.

Apparently, it was not only Germans who were infected with the false stereotype of the Dutch. "In Holland, all women are whores, and all men either drug-addicts or drug-pushers, or both," as a pseudo-omniscient Australian once told me. My young travel companion was the most unlikely victim of this groundless and vicious generalisation.

The moment we crossed the frontier, I spotted washing put out to dry on the balconies of otherwise plush and tidy Swiss-style chalets. There could be no mistake: we were in Italy.

The first thing I did in Como was buy a ten thousand-lira (5.2-Euro) international phone card at a station souvenir kiosk. "We not like the Euro . . . Coins too small . . . *lire* was better," said

---

3. *The cantons are Switzerland's semi-autonomous administrative units.*

a bored and fat salesman. Lira (or rather *lire*) were still in circulation for another ten days or so, but most prices were already in Euros. Having to switch from a small to a large denomination currency, Italy was the most apprehensive Eurozone member, and that was probably why it insisted that the plural of the Euro would be "Euri", whereas the rest of the zone would use Euros. The "Euri" must have been intended to give the emotionally charged Italians the impression of preserving their habitual, albeit delusional monetary multitude.

Several hours later, I found out that the phone card was well past its expiry date. Remembering a straightforward Italian proverb *fidarsi e bene, non fidarsi e meglio* (to trust is good, not to trust is better), I made a mental note to check my future Italian purchases – be they in lires, in Euros, or indeed in "Euri" – more thoroughly, and *before*, not after, paying for them.

At the same kiosk, I also acquired a pair of sunglasses: it was warm, sunny and almost spring-like in Como – a stark contrast to drab and wintry Holland. Unlike the phone card, the sunglasses proved genuine and good quality: they helped me to beat snow blindness in my subsequent travels in the Alps.

I thought it was a good sign that my hotel on the lakefront was called Metropole Swisse. Having come to explore the Italian exclave in Switzerland, it felt appropriate to stay at a Swiss hotel in Italy. Why couldn't I stay in Campione itself, you might ask. The answer is simple: there wasn't a single hotel there.

The Metropole Swisse was tired and in need of renovation. Or at least of a good clean up. It smelled of dust and cheap decadence. Half of the lights in my two-room suite, with touches of battered *belle époque* luxury, did not work, and – just like on my overnight train – there was no water of any kind.

"A plumber is coming any minute," a bored and fat male receptionist assured me. I knew the country well enough not to rely on the punctuality of an Italian plumber and washed myself with a couple of bottles of still mineral water that I found in my bedroom.

On the positive side, my little suite had a stunning view of Lake Como and a telephone, which I used to phone Campione's tourism office. Unlike with all the other enclaves, I hadn't been able to organise anything in advance, despite numerous faxes, e-mails and phone calls from London. "Not possible," was the tourism office's favourite reply. Their second favourite was not replying at all.

To call Campione from Como, I had to dial an international code for Switzerland, although the town itself was Italian. I was lucky, for a lady called Paola promised to pick me up at Lugano station the following morning. Campione could not be accessed by public transport outside of the summer season, when there was a boat service across Lake Lugano.

My conversation with Paola was not all positive, however: many weeks before I had requested an audience with Campione's Mayor and a visit to the Casino – not a big deal by any standards. "The Mayor is busy and the Casino is not possible," Paola now told me. I had also asked to trace down Fedra – my guide during my previous visit to Campione five years earlier. "Fedra is now a police woman and she is not on duty tomorrow," I was told.

It was useless. One could be forgiven for thinking that I was trying to arrange a private audience with the Pope or a short-notice in-depth tour of a top-security US defence facility, not one day's research in a small Italian town of three thousand people. The key word here was "Italian" of course. "It is impossible to govern Italians. It is merely useless," Benito Mussolini once snapped. "It is even harder to organise them," I could add. And weren't these two national impossibilities – to govern on the one hand, and to organise on the other – to blame for the quick collapse of each of the fifty-odd Italian governments (on average, one new government a year) since World War II – every one more incompetent and more corrupt than its predecessor?

To calm down, I had a cup of excellent espresso while basking in bright sunlight at an open-air café in Piazza Cavour. The waitress was struggling with my Euros (as well as with her English). "New money . . . Too soon to remove the *liri* . . . Many people profiteer . . ." she mumbled while counting my change. Her confusion was understandable: I soon discovered that all public phones in Como were still accepting only lira coins, whereas most cashpoints dispensed Euros, US dollars, lira and Swiss francs – all at the same time!

I then retraced my footsteps to the station to check train times to Lugano and was baffled to discover that they did not feature in the timetable at all. A bored and fat male cashier, however, promised that trains to Lugano did exist. Reassured, I walked back to the lakefront.

The cashier (another fat and bored male) who sold me a €4.20 ticket for the boat cruise of Lake Como "forgot" to give me change from ten Euros. "New money," he shrugged when I asked for it. He was probably still thinking in lira, and some five-odd lira indeed did not make a lot of difference – like five pence in Britain. But five Euros certainly did.

The most amazing thing about Lake Lugano was its water – sweet smelling, full of sunlight and mica-like at the surface. At the height of off-peak season, there were just two other passengers on the boat: a local girl (I guessed she was a local, for she didn't throw a single look at the dishevelled lake-side mountains and stunning medieval villas on the shores, but kept talking on her mobile phone) and a dark-skinned hook-nosed woman, who wore so much make up that her head was constantly bent forward under its weight, making her look like a carnivorous predator-bird ready to swoop at its prey. She turned out to be a tourist from Washington, DC spending a week in Italy on her own. Her profession? A make-up artist! She asked me what she should visit in the remaining three days of her holidays – Rome, Venice or Verona? I suggested she "did" all three in one day and flew back to the States forty-eight hours ahead of schedule. She was American, used to "doing the world" rather than travelling it, and I was sure she was going to follow my advice.

The sun was setting over Lake Como, and the water was aflame. Like a giant madman's dagger, our boat was cutting this liquid fire into shreds.

To get a better perspective on the area, and hopefully a glimpse of Campione too, I took a hydraulic and driver-less *funicolare* to

Brunate, a suburban village at seven hundred and twenty metres above the sea level. The idea was doomed from the start, for it got dark before I started my ascent. I decided to proceed anyway. At the *funicolare* station, I saw a dark-eyed young man literally carrying his disabled old father to the toilet – an emotional scene one was unlikely to observe anywhere else in Europe but in Italy, a country so family-oriented that an astounding one third of all Italian men over thirty still reside with their parents.

It was cold and snowy up the mountain. Como, and possibly Campione too, lay somewhere beneath, totally obscured by clouds. A tiny "enclave" of unnaturally pink wintry sunset, as if from a Barbie-doll "Nature" play set, lingered in the black sky above the Lake before being absorbed by its vast "host country" of darkness.

I descended back to Como alone in the same *funicolare* carriage – so compact and cold that it felt like a mountain-crawling freezer compartment. A Euro familiarisation poster was the only decoration on its frostbitten walls.

Cold and ravenous, I popped into a pizzeria next to the *funicolare* station. Unsurprisingly, it was called Funicolare Pizzeria. Having settled down at a table, I realised I was the only customer – a fact that, under different circumstances, would have made me suspicious. But as it was, I couldn't care less.

Desperate to get warm, I asked for the wine list. Two wines immediately grabbed my attention: "Nino Negri Inferno" and "Sassella Valtellina Negri". "Negri" was the surname of my Australian-Italian ex-wife Jacinta, whose ancestors originated from the nearby Northern Italian province of Sondrio, or, more precisely, from around its main town Tirano, where – for centuries – they had been making wine and running the renowned Negri Vineyards.

Several years earlier, Jacinta and I had undertaken an emotional journey to trace down her Italian roots. The trip had a practical purpose too: we needed to find birth and baptismal records for her great-great-grandfather Giacomo Negri, who had emigrated to Australia in 1864. In accordance with some peculiar Italian descendancy laws, if we were successful Jacinta, who spoke some Italian but had never been to Italy, could apply for an Italian (i.e. European) passport which would facilitate her employment in Britain.

All we knew was that Giacomo Negri had been born in Villa di Tirano in 1838. Driven by extreme poverty, he had moved to England at the age of twenty-five, from where – attracted by the prospect of securing a quick fortune as a gold miner – he had set off for Victoria on board the *Empress of the Sea* three years later. He had been the only Italian among the passengers during the hundred and forty-day journey.

After numerous painstaking enquiries at the Italian Consulate in Melbourne, we were assured that Giacomo's birth and baptismal records – like all other registration documents prior to the proclamation of the United Italian Kingdom in 1861 – should have been kept at a local church. In fact, the over-loquacious and fidgety Consulate officials kept hinting that there could be an "easier" (a quick wink) and a "much faster" ("you know what I mean" plus another quick wink) way of obtaining the passport ("you help me – I help you, *capisce?*"), but we decided to go through legitimate channels – a route that, in the words of the same officials, was *difficile*, in fact nearly *impossibile*.

After several initial setbacks, we were about ready to believe that the compulsively twitching and winking Italian officials – who looked as if they were all suffering from St. Vitus' dance, aggravated by a severe eye-tic – had been right. Firstly, the Tirano priest whom we tried to track down had been taken to hospital for a prostate operation two hours prior to our arrival. Secondly, after a good deal of door-knocking (my Soviet experience as an investigative hack came in handy), we discovered that the records, if they even existed, had been kept not in Tirano itself, but in Villa di Tirano – a suburban hamlet, where Giacomo had been born.

Father Roberto, the village priest, was a short-tempered charac-ter. His response to all our queries was an angry *"impossibile"*. He didn't even wink. Instead, to show how infuriated he was by our intrusion, he resorted to storming out of his office periodically – his black robes flowing – and slamming the door behind him. During one such outburst (in the true sense of the word) we spotted a row of old dusty folios in the cupboard next to his desk. Having stealthily opened one of them at random, we almost immediately came across the sought-after *nascita* entry, made in black ink which had gone pink with time (or, possibly, with shame for the priest's stubborn lack of co-operation). According to the entry, Giacomo Negri had been born on the twenty-first of October 1838 and baptised a year later. The most amazing thing, however, was that the next entry, directly underneath Giacomo's, was that of a certain Giovanna Vitali – born and baptised on the same day.

The following morning we learnt that Jacinta was pregnant with our first child – Andrei.

The bottle of Nino Negri Inferno had a big letter "N" printed on its label. Fruity, full-bodied and pleasantly intoxicating, it warmed me up and made me feel less lonely.

I was still the only person in the pizzeria, if you didn't count a good half-a-dozen managerial-looking waiters, with the sullen, almost tragic, faces of remorseful crooks and gold rings on every finger (I was sure they had rings on their toes too). As they made a typically Italian *bacciare* ("yummy") gesture, touching their thumbs with index fingers and straightening the remaining three, to describe the taste of every dish on the menu, the rings on their hairy fingers rubbed against each other with a soft clanking sound – like the buffers of model railway carriages when coupled.

The radio was at full volume, broadcasting something noisy that sounded like a quiz show. At one point, I overheard the word "Campione", which triggered loud laughter from the audience.

Halfway through the meal, a rectangular piece of cardboard and three cheap cigarette lighters landed on my table without warning. "I am deaf. Please accept this for €2.60" was printed on the card in English. I looked up. A tall, smartly dressed man was towering above me. For some reason he avoided eye contact and was staring in the direction of the restaurant till, which had a small icon of the Virgin Mary above it. It was hard to say whether he was indeed deaf or just pretending. But even if he was, I still wondered how proclaiming his disability could help him sell the lighters.

My first impulse was to return the card, having written on it: "Sorry, but I am blind and I don't need your lighters anyway." Then I thought that as a travelling smoker I could always do with a couple of extra lighters, which – alongside hair-combs and socks – have a tendency to disappear without a trace never to be seen again. I counted out three one-Euro coins and put them on the table expecting change. But the "deaf" man was not happy. With his expressive Italian fingers, he indicated that he wanted two more Euros. I didn't feel like arguing with someone who was deaf, even less so with someone who pretended to be deaf, so I gave him two more Euros.

My bill amounted to the suspicious sum of €29.99. I gave the waiter a fifty Euro note and patiently waited for my change for about forty minutes. The ringed waiters were fluttering past aimlessly, without as much as a look in my direction, as if I were no longer there. When I eventually stopped one of them in his pointless flutter and asked for my change from fifty Euros, he apologised, mumbling something about his "*mamma malata*" (sick mother), as if that justified his forgetfulness, and gave me back €10. I realised that if I demanded the rest, he would probably blame me for his mother's alleged illness, possibly even for her premature demise.

Walking back to my hotel, I wondered why I always got robbed in Italy? My only consolation was that I was definitely not the sole victim of Italy's age-long tradition of good-natured cheating. According to some impressive statistics quoted by the *Wall Street Journal*, forty percent of Italians regularly fiddle their tax returns. For a number of years, I had entertained a tongue-in-cheek "theory" as to the possible origins of this cheerful chicanery. My observations showed that the level of corruption in this or that part of the world was in direct proportion to its climate: the higher the average temperature, the more crime-ridden the country. Indeed, Italy was one of Europe's warmest places and by far the most corrupt. The same was true about Queensland in Australia, Brazil in South America, India in Asia and the Central Asian and Caucasian republics of the former Soviet Union. On the other hand, I had never come across a major corruption case in Finland, Sweden or Norway. To say nothing of Greenland.

A possible explanation might be that in the countries with warmer climes, people tended to spend more time outside: in the streets, parks, al fresco cafes, on the beaches, etc. – where contacts, deals, conspiracies and unholy alliances were evidently forged with greater ease than indoors. Also, the residents of warmer countries were usually much more open and outgoing than northerners, who were calm, taciturn, restrained and generally docile (read law-abiding). So, Italy's biggest problems – corruption, deception and even the omnipotent Mafia – were probably direct and objective results of the sultry Mediterranean/Adriatic climate, and the only way of eradicating them would be to move the country further north – somewhere towards Greenland, say, a proposal to which most of the Italians (both honest and corrupt) would have undoubtedly objected.

Thus pacified, I continued my shivery progress towards the hotel. A huge, brightly lit Crucifix was burning on top of a mountain high above the dark and deserted – almost COMAtose – streets of Como.

*   *   *

CAMPIONE D'ITALIA

Italian Boy in Swiss Costume

I don't know whether the memories or the peculiar qualities of Nino Negri Inferno were at fault, but the following morning I was suffering from a truly infernal hangover.

Dragging my bulging "Sally" to the station along the uneven ancient cobbles of Como, I was seriously thinking of renaming her "Elly" or "Nelly' – a suitable diminutive for "elephant".

School kids in their early teens were running cheerfully towards the sixteenth-century *Collegio Galleo* near the station. "Twinkle, twinkle, little star" they sang in chorus, which made me conclude grudgingly that the *Collegio*'s standards of English teaching were not particularly advanced.

Five minutes after departing Como, my Lugano-bound train was stuck on the Swiss border at Chiasso. Two stone-faced Swiss frontier-guards in dark-green uniforms scrutinised my passport photo for so long that I started having doubts as to whether it was indeed my own head-shot and not that of some hardened international fraudster.

The whole border-control fuss in the effectively borderless Western Europe was ridiculous. It brought back memories of my several trips across the Berlin Wall (by train from Moscow to London and back) in 1988–89, although now I was not travelling from East to West (or vice versa), but was simply going from Italy to Italy via Switzerland. Furthermore, had I been visiting Campione in summer, I could have taken a boat and thus avoided any passport controls whatsoever. The whole thing was illogical – like most border controls, or borders in general, for that matter.

I thought that it might not be by chance that "Switzerland" in Russian was "*Shveitsariya*", and *shveitsar* meant "doorman" (or "porter"). The direct English equivalent of the Russian word for "Switzerland" would probably be "Doormania" (or "Porteria"?) – the land of doormen, a name which nicely agreed with the Swiss border guards' behaviour, similar to that of an over-zealous, Cerberus-like doorman guarding the entrance to a luxury hotel.

Having crossed the Italian border, the train screeched to a halt again – this time to allow Italian frontier "doormen" to admire my passport photo. Like their Swiss counterparts, they also carried the peculiar sullen look of people having to do a totally useless job.

I decided to use the delay to refresh my memories of my first visit to Campione several years before by browsing through my old "Campione" files and notes.

"What is Campione?" would probably constitute an unanswerable question on Brain of Britain or Mastermind, let alone The Weakest Link. Answers would be likely to range from "a dry white Italian wine" to "a medieval Venetian sculptor of little renown".

Campione d'Italia was the first European enclave I had learnt of
– about ten years ago, while researching a book on the mini-states
of Europe. In actual fact, until a couple of years later, I had had
no idea it was an enclave and had regarded Campione as a little-
known European curiosity, the true status and location of which
was not easy to establish. The first mention of Campione that came
to my attention was in an ad in the *Economist* magazine promising
some lucrative property bargains to those keen on obtaining a
second passport. Then – unexpectedly – the name popped up in a
chat with my old friend Igor Pomerantsev – an émigré Russian radio
journalist and wine writer, who said he had once spent a couple of
days in that curious "pocket handkerchief" tasting local wines.
Since prior to (and in the course of) our conversation we had tasted
a number of drinks – and not just wines – I failed to drag much
more out of him on that particular subject.

A real breakthrough in my quest for Campione occurred shortly
afterwards, when, browsing the Internet – still a novelty in 1997 –
I came across the *Campione Report* by Dr W.G. Hill, "the world's
leading expert on personal tax havens", subtitled "Switzerland's
secret semi-tropical paradise!" (yes, with an exclamation mark at
the end). The document was written in the punchy style of a cheap
TV commercial: "Live inside Switzerland without having to put up
with heavy Swiss income taxes. In fact, Campione has no income,
property or value-added taxes!" Despite numerous exclamation
marks, most of the *Report*'s statements, as I discovered later, were
pure fibs, and the residents of Campione did have to pay taxes –
not Swiss, but Italian.

The *Report* went on to refer to Campione as a "glorious freak
of history, a geographic oddity and a climatic anomaly" and called
on its readers to "Claim your share of the emerging tax haven. One
of the most unusual locations on Earth!" before informing them –
in small print – that the full text of the 96-page *Campione Report*
was available for "just $100 per copy".

I could not afford the full *Report* – at least not without claiming
(and receiving) my "share of the emerging tax haven" first – and

decided that it would probably be quicker (and cheaper) to go there in person and to claim my share on the spot.

It didn't take me long to establish that Campione was indeed an Italian enclave within Switzerland. Politically Italian, it was economically Swiss. Its residents voted in Italian elections, yet received their salaries in Swiss francs to suit the prices, which were Swiss. Swiss francs were the currency of the budget of the town, where the safeguarding of law and order was entrusted to the Italian police force, with most constables coming from Como. Every time a policeman went back home, he had to leave his weapons in Campione – in accordance with a Swiss law, forbidding foreigners to carry arms while in Switzerland.

The Campionese drove around in cars with "TI" number plates – for Ticino, the Swiss canton by which it was surrounded – but mailed their letters with stamps of the Italian Republic. Like in Baarle, they had a choice of two different postcodes – Swiss or Italian – although most preferred the former, because the Italian post was notoriously slow and unreliable. They shopped for food in Switzerland, to where they had an unhindered passport-free access, and for clothes in Italy, where Italian border guards routinely checked their Italian passports.

Although part of Italy, Campione was nevertheless *not* part of the EU, from which it was excluded by a special protocol. Despite this, Campione's residents – as Italian passport holders – had the right to live and work in any EU member state, but not in Switzerland, on whose territory the town was located.

Campione's striking duality started in the year 777 AD, when a local landowner, Totone, tried to buy himself an indulgence for his sins by donating all his holdings, including the small fishing village of Campione, then part of the diocese of Como, to the Basilica of St. Ambrose in Milan. As a result, Campione fell under the rule of the Milanese ecclesiastical authorities, and not those of nearby Como, as would have been more logical. Throughout the Middle Ages, while the Abbot of St. Ambrose exercised spiritual control over Campione, the village's everyday affairs were greatly influenced by the Swiss region of Lugano. This ambivalence went on until the Swiss obtained full possession of the region comprising the present-day canton of Ticino in 1512. With Campione still remaining an outlier of Milan, it became a full-scale enclave within Switzerland. Since then, the Swiss had undertaken numerous peaceful attempts to gain control of Campione, but to no avail. Shortly after the village (then already a town) was annexed to the brand-new Kingdom of Italy in 1861, an international convention to specify Campione's boundaries came into force, thus sealing the enclave's fate.

During my first visit, this Italian town struck me as "un-Italian", or rather "Swiss-ish" – in its cleanliness, in the absence of washing on balconies, in the quiet demeanour of the locals, who seldom raised their voices. It was as if two seemingly incompatible life-styles and national characters – fire and water; sand and snow? – were recycled and neatly packed, Swiss-hay-stack-like, into one square kilometre of territory. In the words of the Italian writer Giovanni Cenzato, Campione remained "a little Italian boy wearing a Swiss costume".

After a thirty-minute delay on the Swiss side of the border, the train resumed its erratic progress and five minutes later arrived at Lugano.

Waiting to be picked up by Paola, a Campione tourism official, I admired the lake, lined with white-capped mountains and framed by Swiss chalets with Italian (Venetian) blinds on their windows.

My day in Campione had a rather confusing start. Firstly, contrary to my expectations, Paola turned out to be not a tall and bronze-skinned Mediterranean beauty, but a short and rather plain-looking bespectacled young woman. Secondly, her name was Christina. "Paola sends her apologies for nor being able to come and meet you and for having dispatched me – a part-timer – in her stead," she said with a slight, almost unnoticeable, cheek in her excellent and all but unaccented English. Christina proved to be a real godsend: a native Campionese, with a diploma in psychology from Padua University, she had also done a stint at the University of Bristol. Ironic, quick-witted and open-minded, she represented a rare, almost extinct, type – the Campione intellectual.

Driving me to Campione, she kept apologising on Paola's behalf for not having made any appointments for me: no one was available, and the Mayor was busy. "*Tutto impossibile*," she smiled, obviously mocking somebody (I thought I knew who) and added: "*Burocrazia Italiana . . .*"

She told me that Fedra, the "Paola" of my previous visit, was now a police officer and as such could not be approached by the media (?). I wondered whether the relative ease of making contacts five years before had been due to the fact that I came to Campione as a BBC reporter. Then I had represented the BBC, the world's second most recognisable trademark after Coca-Cola (and equally sugary of late, I might add), whereas now I represented no one in particular, apart from myself.

All things considered, Christina was much better value than all my official would-be contacts taken together, including the Mayor (whom I had met during my previous visit): her knowledge of Campione was sound and her views – unorthodox and not uncritical – were unusual for a tourism official, even if a part-timer.

According to her, not many things had changed in Campione since my last visit. The official currency of the enclave was still Swiss francs, the only difference being that now they had to be changed into Euros, not lira, when the locals travelled to their native Italy. They still had to show their passports when crossing the Italian border. "The Italian border guards have no idea what we are," she shrugged. "On the way to Italy, we are checked by the Italians, on the way back by the Swiss . . . We still have quotas on goods we can bring back from our home country: three bottles of wine, limited amounts of meat and tobacco – as if we are Swiss . . ."

Like five years before, there was not a single hotel or single B&B in Campione, which needed them desperately. "All administrative and building regulations are Italian and therefore very bureaucratic – worse than Swiss," Christina explained. The Campionese still paid no VAT, but – contrary to the *Campione* Report by Dr. W.G. Hill – they did pay all other Italian taxes, which were, incidentally, higher than the Swiss ones, and had to comply with Swiss prices, which were higher than the Italian ones. The worst of both worlds, so to speak.

The only slight change was that the Campione authorities were no longer able to grant automatic citizenship to wealthy property buyers from abroad. A new rule, adopted a couple of years before, stipulated that one had to live and work in Campione for at least a year before applying for Italian citizenship. The paradox was that, apart from the Casino, there was practically nowhere in town one could get a job, and to work in Switzerland took a Swiss work permit, which was extremely hard to acquire (even Christina, a native of Campione, had so far been unable to get one). So the prospect of "obtaining a second passport" in Campione was now largely unrealistic, irrespective of one's riches.

Campione's townscape remained equally unchanged: spotlessly clean narrow streets winding up and down the hill; mountains spotted with red-tiled houses, as if suffering from a severe case of the measles. There was one obvious novelty though: the cranes towering above the building site of a new Casino, which was being erected on the spot of the demolished local elementary school. I knew that the "old" and rather capacious modernistic Casino on the lakefront combined its role of a gambling den and the town's main employer (the locals could only work, but not gamble in it) with that of Campione's cultural centre, where conferences, concerts and exhibitions were often held. I also knew that in its main capacity, it was a popular haunt for punters from both Switzerland, where gambling was semi-legal, and from Italy, where it was frowned upon. But to build a new "skyscraper Casino" (as Christina put it) in the extremely compact historic centre of a fragile old town of seven thousand people seemed (literally) over the top.

In line with an old habit of mine, I started my exploration of Campione with a cup of espresso – in Bar Campione on the lakefront. Christina agreed to keep me company.

The bar was noisy, like a normal Italian *trattoria*, yet spotlessly – Swiss-style – clean and neat. Some old men were reading *La Provincia* – a local Italian paper from Como – and calling out to each other across the room. In contrast to the Italian *joie de vivre*, the bar's state-of-the-art – Swiss-style – toilet, with blue urinals and electronic soap dispensers, was spotlessly sterile. "The hygiene regulations in Campione are Swiss," remarked Christina. "Among other things, this means using Swiss recycling and rubbish-collecting services, although the refuse-collecting trucks are Italian."

She went on to say that Campione's gas and water supplies came from Switzerland, but the electricity was Italian, although the Campionese had to pay for it in Swiss francs. The town residents were the only Italians eligible for Swiss medical insurance, similar to the American Medicaid system, even if they did not work in Switzerland. This insurance made them the world's only "foreigners" allowed to use the Swiss ambulance service and to be treated for free in Swiss hospitals. The only resident physician in Campione was Dr. Roberto Salmoiraghi – an Italian GP and the town's Mayor (hearing this made me feel less cheesed off at his apparent lack of time to see me) who was not allowed to practise in Switzerland.

The excellent espresso was taking effect. Christina became a bit more relaxed and more inclined to talk about herself. "I seriously think of going to Italy," she said (we actually *were* in Italy!). "For what on earth can a psychologist do in Campione?" (apart from temping for the local tourism office that is) "You either have to leave or you end up working at the Casino . . ."

I thought it would be a great shame if someone like her ended up as a croupier.

Warmed up by the coffee, we went for a walk around the town. I recognised some of Campione's sights from my previous visit – the tiny Auditorium cinema, which would routinely close down for the summer, when the local library doubled as a video-salon; the house facades, displaying Campione's coat of arms – a shield divided into three sections: the pastoral staff of St. Ambrose, the whip of the same saint, and a snail, which I had initially been tempted to interpret as a symbol of the town's slow pace of life. In actual fact, the snail symbolised a local artistic school, the so-called *Maestri Campionese* – a group of Renaissance artists who eventually left Campione to work in Milan, Rome and even in

St. Petersburg, but left a trace (just like a snail when it moves away) on the town's artistic face. Their magnificent sculptures and frescos could still be found in Campione's parish church of St. Zenone and in the impressive Basilica of the Madonna dei Ghirli, facing the Lake.

There, on the lakefront, I spotted a seemingly new – and unquestionably Swiss – feature: a cluster of brightly-painted recycling bins, clearly marked in three languages (Italian, German and French). The pink one was for cans, the yellow for cardboard (*carta, karton, papier*), the blue for plastic, the green for domestic refuse, the brown for mineral oils, and the red for vegetable oils. With sadness, I remembered trying to dump several cardboard boxes in London a couple of weeks before. Having failed to locate a single properly designated recycling bin, I had stealthily left them next to an overflowing "Newspapers" container (the only one in our area) under cover of darkness.

It was obvious that the Swiss features of Campione were on the increase. But if cleanliness and better recycling were more than welcome, the recent cancellation of the town's colourful – and very Italian – street festivals, probably deemed too messy and too noisy to correspond to countless forbidding Swiss regulations, was regrettable. To me, it felt not dissimilar to the replacement of the variously vibrant banknotes of the twelve EU member countries with dull and uniform Euros.

A red London double-decker bus – a good old Routemaster, with "Cricklewood Garage" on its front – had been part of a Campione carnival procession I had witnessed five years before. Looking incongruous and too big in the streets of miniature Campione, it nevertheless added colour and festivity to the parade. Christina told me it had been scrapped in accordance with the EU regulations that classified all Routemasters as unsafe.

There in Campione, I realised with renewed clarity that, apart from their questionable economic implications, most of the EU directives (including the introduction of the Euro) aimed at homogenising our continent were sapping joy and versatility out of the Europeans' lives. The powerful killjoy factor was one thing they had in common with the numerous restrictive regulations of the non-EU "Doormania", Switzerland.

I recognised her straight away – Frances Coates, the only British resident of Campione, whom I had interviewed for a BBC Radio feature five years earlier. She then worked as a cashier at Campione's boat station. This time, I had her name on my list of contacts submitted to Paola, the *Impossibile*, who assured me that, just like everyone else on that list, Frances was "not available". And here she was walking up the street looking as "available" as anyone could be.

Frances said that she now worked for the town council and therefore had to get clearance from her bosses to talk to me. "*Burocrazia Italiana* . . ." I thought ruefully, while also being pleased for Frances, who seemed to have landed with a much more important job than before. We agreed to meet up after lunch in Bar Campione.

I had a solitary lunch at Taverna, an Italian restaurant with prices – intimidatingly – in Swiss francs. In its menu and in the constant "*bacciare*" (yummy) gestures of the imposing owner-cum-waiter, the restaurant was typically Italian. The same could be said about its décor, which included a regulation Crucifix above the cash register in line with the archetypally Italian spirit of pious commercialism. But it had one thoroughly un-Italian (even anti-Italian, if I may say so) trait. Here I must apologise for reverting to the toilets again, but no one can deny that many dominant features of a culture are reflected in bathroom mirrors. The toilets in Taverna were way out of this (Italian) world: marble, fresh flowers and sophisticated fragrances. So, if you could excuse me for a moment . . . Thank you!

I had an Italian pasta, washed down with Feldsclusschen Original Swiss beer – an ideal Campione combination which could only be matched by a perfect espresso and a glass of cold tap (therefore Swiss) water.

Frances Coates, a native Mancunian, had been living in Campione, where her husband came from, for over ten years.

During this time, as she told me, she had totally integrated into the community. Her three boys – an eight-year-old and a pair of seven-year-old twins – "eat *rosti*, speak Italian and think of themselves as Campionese". Their English was getting far worse than their Italian, and they would rather support Zurich or FC Milan than Manchester United. Frances absolutely loved Campione and was not missing England at all. The only problem she faced was work, for there were not too many job opportunities in Campione. "How about in Switzerland?" I asked her.

"A Swiss work permit is hard to obtain," she said. "And even if you are lucky, they will only grant you the so-called *Permeso Di Lavoro Per Frontiera,* which only gives you the right to work, but not to live in Switzerland, so you have to return to Italy every evening."

"But you do have a good job here in Campione, so you needn't worry," I remarked.

"Yes, but . . ." she lowered her eyes, not willing to continue.

It turned out that she indeed worked for the town council – as a public toilet cleaner. I assured Frances that, with Campione being by far the cleanest town in Italy, she had nothing to be embarrassed about. Having had a chance to check out one of her workplaces, I had seen for myself that she did her job to the highest Swiss standards.

I was finding it hard to fathom that a council employee who had to obtain clearance from her superiors to talk to a visiting writer was, in actual fact, a toilet cleaner. On the other hand, there could have been valid reasons for that: achieving the amazingly high Swiss levels of cleanliness had to involve some carefully guarded technological know-how, which the town council was probably unwilling to disclose.

Gambler or not, no visit to Campione was complete without the Casino – the backbone of the town's economy and culture. Since the new "skyscraper" Casino would not be completed for another couple of years, I had to make do with visiting the old one. Both "Paola" Paola and "Paola" Christina told me there were problems with interviewing any of the Casino's management. But I decided to pop in nevertheless.

I could see from the start that I was not welcome. Three burly male receptionists viewed me with suspicion and took about half an hour to check my name on their computer. What were they checking it against? A list of obsessive gamblers and card tricksters?

Here I must confess that, having visited a number of casinos, including the famous Casino de Paris in Monte Carlo and several "thematic" gambling emporiums in Las Vegas, I had never gambled in any of them, being more interested in punters than in gambling machines. I was always fascinated by the universal seriousness of gamblers' faces as they obsessively fed their tokens into the insatiable bellies of slot-machines, or stared unblinkingly at a dispassionately rotating roulette wheel, with "no memory and no conscience", in the words of Dostoyevsky – himself an obsessive gambler. Having observed the happenings in gambling halls of various countries and continents, I came to a conclusion: seen one, seen them all.

At long last, the receptionists entrusted me to *Le Direttore* – the Casino's Director of Gambling, a middle-aged Italian man with the velvety, constantly darting eyes of a petty crook and a womaniser. Talking to him was hopeless, for he kept either totally ignoring my questions or saying something that had no relevance to them whatsoever. He was the sort of a person, who when asked what time it is answers: "Yes, it is rather warm." He quickly walked me around the main gambling hall, with large opaque mirrors on its ceiling, reflecting a handful of aging gamblers, who looked like human stalagmites, or bats with bald crowns.

One thing that briefly grabbed my attention was an "electronic horse race" – a gambling game in the shape of a functioning model of Royal Ascot racecourse. One could stake money on model horses, their model jockeys sitting astride them. Like Campione itself, the model was unreal yet fully operational.

Le Direttore was clearly uneasy. Mumbling something along the lines of "*grosso business* – new casino . . .", he kept turning his briolined head right and left – like a troubled turkey. I could see he couldn't wait to get rid of me. He refused to give me his name. He was also avoiding my eyes and was constantly told off for something from behind his back by another smooth-looking Italian man, who was following in our footsteps. From time to time, my escort would suddenly disappear leaving me in the middle of a gambling hall, only to come back a minute or so later looking even more frustrated than before. "Is the Casino run by the Mafia?" I was thinking. *Le Direttore*'s erratic behaviour was that of a person who had something to hide.

With mutual relief, we parted at the Casino's ornate doors. Walking up the hill, I passed by the carcass of the New Casino under construction. A plate on the fence around the site explained that Campione's new gambling den was designed "to blend with its surroundings". Did they mean the mountains that surrounded Campione on three sides? Was the New Casino meant to rival the Alps? Having examined the drawing of the modernistic would-be building on the top half of the same plate, I decided that the mountains were not in danger.

Once in the USA I had an interesting conversation on Mount Rushmore – a formerly beautiful uncomplaining mountain, disfigured by Gutzon Borglum, a monumentalist sculptor, who spent many years blowing it up bit by bit to carve the heads of four American Presidents: Washington, Jefferson, Lincoln and Roosevelt. The result is a totalitarian, almost Stalinist, memorial, where the four giant stone-faced (in more than one sense) heads of these truly remarkable men – surrounded by a myriad of plastic American flags and "Shop and Dine with the Presidents" billboards to advertise the adjacent factory outlets and junk-food joints – look down impassively at the unstoppable flow of visitors. Like the Lenin Mausoleum in Moscow, Mount Rushmore has become a place of mass pilgrimage in America.

"I can hardly believe I am actually here," an elderly lady with the quasi-intelligent face of a provincial school headmistress (she actually *was* a school headmistress – or a "school head", as she introduced herself in the modern PC manner) was mumbling to herself reverentially – as if in a trance.

"What's so special about this place?" I asked her.

"They were our great leaders," she gasped, sounding unnaturally elated – almost orgiastic – like a Radio North Korea news reader.

"Do you think this was enough reason to blow up the mountain?" I asked, and reminded her of a remark from Nikolai Gogol's comedy *The Government Inspector*: "Of course Alexander the Great was a hero, but why smash chairs over him?"

Her school obviously did not have Gogol on its curriculum. She got angry: "We Americans are patriotic, we love our country, unlike you Brits [another case of mistaken identity], who are like sheep. You can't stand up for yourselves, and we can. We want our people to be proud of where they live and you Europeans [this time she might have struck it right] are not!"

At this point, I was tempted to quote Samuel Johnson's "Patriotism is the last refuge of a scoundrel", but thought better of it. Instead, I said: "We Europeans are wary of patriotism for one simple reason: too many bloody wars in our long history were launched on the wave of it."

This encounter took place prior to 11 September, 2001. I would have thought twice before making my last remark had it happened after that date.

Having not quite recovered from Mount Rushmore, I soon had to face the nearby Crazy Horse Memorial. If Mount Rushmore struck me as totalitarian, Crazy Horse was clearly dictatorial – both in message and in size. It was there that the descendants of Korczak Ziolkovski, a brazen long-bearded sculptor of Polish descent, who died in 1982, were carrying on with the job of their dad's life – blasting another mountain to create "the world's largest mountain carving" – a statue of an Indian on a horse. The horse's head, when completed, was meant to be the size of a twenty-two-story-building, and a nineteen-story house would fit under the Indian's armpit (I don't envy the residents of that imaginary house) – as they proudly informed me in the enormous Crazy Horse Visitors' Centre.

Korzcak started ruining the mountain – a sacred Indian site, by the way – in 1949, and sired ten children specifically to help him with the massive task, but died without finishing the statue. "Every man has his mountain – I'm carving mine. Only in America could a man carve a mountain," he once remarked.

What are the reasons behind the Americans' ongoing vendetta against their mountains? Maybe, they see them as a natural challenge to their country's greatness? Or do they instinctively subscribe to the opinion of Ostap Bender, the protagonist of a famous Soviet satirical novel, who described mountains as "Too showy. Weird kind of beauty. An idiot's imagination . . ."? Whatever it is, blowing up mountains to build patriotic memorials in their stead strikes me as a distinctively un-European character trait. (The only European analogy I can think of comes from the Faroe Islands – a football-crazy little country, with no flat surface whatsoever, so a mountain or a hill has to be excavated every time they want to build a football pitch there.)

I walked up the street past the *magazino communale* – the Swiss/Italian equivalent of a corner shop – one of the two remaining in Campione; past a mysterious sign reading *"Carabinieri Control. Zona Militaria. Commando Nucleo"* (as far as I knew, neither Italy nor neutral Switzerland were nuclear powers – could it be that tiny Campione had its own secret nuclear arsenal?); past the familiar Auditorium Cinema, now showing – to my disappointment – *A Beautiful Mind* with Russell Crowe (every night at 8pm). Five years before, it had advertised *The Lost World*, which I thought suited Campione better.

The sight of the cinema evoked more memories of that previous visit, especially of my last evening in Campione, when my guide Fedra invited me for dinner at the Casino. Its brightly-lit building on the lakefront was lined with casually parked, or rather abandoned, Ferraris and Rolls Royces – many of them with open tops, as if inviting hijackers. "Don't worry," said Fedra. "Campione is entirely crime-free."

I had never seen so many Ferraris in one place. Fedra explained that Campione was the venue for the annual gathering of the European Ferrari Owners Club. "We call them Ferrarists," she added.

On top of a set dinner, the Casino's enormous restaurant offered a compulsory selection of Strauss' waltzes, performed by a live orchestra on a stage decorated with portraits of dancers *à la Matisse*.

We were sitting among men in tail-coats and bow-ties, women in evening dresses and bored-looking "Ferrarists" in T-shirts: the latter were obviously so rich that they could afford to ignore dress codes. Having looked around, I was able to spot almost everyone I had met in Campione during the previous couple of days: tourism officials, clerks from the Mayor's office, even a friendly rubbish-collector whom I had seen emptying colourful Italian refuse into his sterile Swiss rubbish-collecting cart the day before. He was now dressed in what I had always thought of as the working outfit of an Italian Mafioso – a snow-white double-breasted jacket with a black shirt and a white tie underneath.

Fedra was nervously smoking a cigarette, hiding it under the table. "I don't want my younger brother, who works here, to see me smoke," the twenty-nine-year-old former Miss Campione (and future police officer) whispered to me conspiratorially. The Casino, where one quarter of the enclave's population worked and the other three quarters routinely dined, was not the best place for a local girl to hide from her numerous family members.

Fedra told me that her brother wanted to be a pilot, but had ended up working in the Casino. Indeed, spreading one's wings in the miniscule and somewhat claustrophobic enclave was much harder than playing roulette.

After dinner, Fedra insisted that we entered the gambling hall, from which she – as a local – was strictly banned, unless she was accompanying a foreign guest in line with her job as a guide. Visiting journalists were rare in Campione, my only predecessor being a writer for some obscure Uruguay tabloid.

"I want to surprise my father, who works there as a croupier," she said innocently.

Fedra's Dad, wearing an impressive mane of long grey hair, looked both scholarly and artistic – a cross between an Oxford don and an orchestra conductor. He was busily moving chips up and

111

down the table with something that resembled a small garden rake, under the unyielding gazes of chain-smoking punters, mesmerised by his dexterous movements. Having noticed Fedra, he lifted his thick grey eyebrows slightly in a momentary expression of disapproval. "He was impressed!" concluded Fedra, pleased as punch.

Mission accomplished, we elbowed our way towards the exit, through a joyless crowd of frantically puffing punters. One could get the impression that smoking was as compulsory inside the Casino as showing one's ID card to the security guard at the entrance.

The round, clean (as if freshly painted) and geometrically correct Swiss moon lay like a winning chip on the black cloth of the Italian sky. Reflected in the dark waters of the Lugano Lake, it resembled a brand new yellow Ferrari, waiting for its jackpot-winning owner to emerge from the Casino.

"I don't know who I am," said Christina while driving me back to Lugano station. "In Switzerland, they take me for an Italian, whereas in Italy they dismiss me as a Swiss . . ."

"Haven't I heard something similar in Baarle?" I thought. The similarities of life-styles, idiosyncrasies and mentality between the two were undeniable – another argument in favour of my decision to treat them as parts of the same imaginary country, Enclavia.

At a station kiosk at Lugano, I bought myself a tiny Swiss penknife to replace my old one, which had been confiscated at Melbourne's Tullamarine airport several weeks before. "Fifteen Swiss francs, or ten Euros," a smiling saleswoman said in English. It was only on the train that I remembered that one Euro was equal not to 1.5 but to 2.2 Swiss francs. Thus I was robbed of four Euros – literally at knifepoint! The Italian tradition of good-natured cheating was obviously out in force in this part of Switzerland.

At the border station of Chiasso, where the train was again delayed for over thirty minutes, I was subjected to a double interrogation – first by Swiss frontier guards, then by Italian *carabinieri* in black uniforms, with brass pendants hanging from them, like sets of saucepans from a kitchen shelf. "Business? Holiday? Have you got something to declare?" they kept asking.

I wanted to say: "Yes! I declare: Something!" but decided not to test their sense of humour.

There were no checks in my hotel room in Como, where I dined on exquisite salami and mascarpone cheese, bought at a delicatessen not far from the station. To celebrate one week on the road, I washed the food down with a somewhat plebeian Cabernet from Breschia (sweety-sweety, fruity-fruity, but lacking in depth – like a provincial beauty) and spent the rest of the evening looking at the map of Europe through a magnifying glass and trying to locate some of the continent's most obscure places – the parts of Enclavia I had still to visit.

*   *   *

LIVIGNO

Coin-operated Valley

On the way to Samnaun, a tiny Swiss village lost in the Alps and only accessible from Austria (or so all existing sources asserted), I decided to make a detour to Livigno. This thirteen-kilometre-long Alpine valley in the Italian province of Sondrio, although not an enclave by definition, was a so-called "duty-free area" and as such was excluded from EU membership, like Campione. Also, Livigno, located high in the Retiche Alps between the valleys of Valtellina and Engadina, was officially part of the Danube Basin economic area, which was hundreds of miles away, and as such enjoyed the right of free mooring in the Black Sea ports – although the number of its maritime vessels was precisely zero. It would have been a shame to miss such an obvious European curiosity within the borders of Greater Enclavia, particularly at a time when Europe was in the throes of momentous monetary transformation.

With a long journey ahead of me, I stopped for an espresso at a tiny – phone-cabin-sized – street bar near Como train station. I had my coffee outside, on a small traffic island in the middle of a busy road, with cars roaring past me in both directions, their drivers honking at each other and gesticulating frantically – just for the sake of it, it seemed. They never braked at red-lights and would only let those pedestrians who totally ignored them cross the road. Those waiting patiently for a magnanimous driver to let them pass were bound to stay on the pavement until late in the evening, when the traffic would get less intense.

"Sally" was reclining comfortably (from her perspective) against my feet, her bulging thighs (sides) spelling out defiance and a total lack of desire to move on. I thought she was becoming too big (and far too heavy) for her wheels. It was as if she enjoyed posing as a leather-clad (although, in her case – or rather "suit-case" – the leather was artificial) dominatrix. She reminded me of many women in my life: easy-going and accommodating in the beginning, but eventually taking over.

"*Uno altro espresso, per favore*," I said to the barman, having succumbed to "Sally's" silent pleas. I was proud of my rudimentary Italian, which seemed to be improving by the day.

The "phone-cabin" barman proved to be the first un-mercenary Italian I had met during the trip: he actually undercharged me a little for my two double espressos and a bottle of *aqua minerale*! When I pointed out his mistake, he waved his hand and smiled: "*Bene!*"

Yes, Italians could be wonderfully generous and charmingly hospitable. I had another proof of that on the train to Tirano, where I was to be met by a Livigno Tourism Bureau driver. In fact, to get there from Como, I had to change trains several times. Before the first change in Monza, I asked the conductor when we were due there. The train had just stopped at some tiny Lombardy station. The conductor muttered "*Scusa!*", leapt off onto the platform and disappeared. A couple of minutes later, he returned holding a computer-printed timetable, which he gave to me. The moment he jumped back onboard, the train started. The poor man must have run to the station building in order to print out the timetable for me!

Countless little stations whooshed past behind the window. I thought that whistle-stop stations were true reflections of a nation's character. If Swiss, German and Dutch mini-stations were always neat, toy-like and semi-dead, Italian ones were invariably interesting and full of chaotic action: noisy passengers pushing things up and down the platform, small service engines chugging to and fro without an obvious purpose … And their names: *Bellano Tartavalle Terme* – it was like a short romantic poem by Petrarka.

The closer we came to Tirano, the sunnier it became. Terraced vineyards were on both sides of the track, and every other station had the word *terme* (spa) in its name. "Sally" was sleeping on the floor, blocking the aisle. I could almost hear her snoring. At Sondrio, I woke her up and dragged her along the platform to make our last connection. She resisted, rattling her little wheels against the asphalt like a steam engine – although, in all fairness, it was I who played the role of the engine, with her as a heavy cargo truck.

I whiled away several minutes between trains reading (aloud) another station sign: "*Vietato Attraversare i Binari, Servirsi de Sottopassagio.*" What a magnificent language that made a prosaic "Walking across the tracks is forbidden, use the underground passageway" sound so melodious and poetic!

Gianluca, a young minibus driver from Livigno's Azienda Promotione Turistica (Tourism Promotion Agency), was waiting for me in the square near Tirano station. We drove through the town, where Giacomo Negri had started his intercontinental journey more than one hundred and thirty years before, and soon hit a succession of tunnels, each several miles long. During short spells of daylight in between them, I could see snowy mountains, ski-slopes and chair lifts, which were to become permanent landscape features of my travels for many days to come.

From behind the wheel, Gianluca was telling me about Livigno, with its five thousand residents, one hundred and five hotels, nine hundred B&B apartments, fourteen petrol stations (duty-free petrol was one of Livigno's main trading items) and thirty-three chair lifts.

From what little I knew about the valley's history, Livigno had gone through numerous attempts to achieve sovereignty, starting in 1355, when it was effectively administered by two nominees of the Mayor of Bormio. In the early seventeenth century, Livigno enjoyed a short period of complete independence, when ruled by the Grigioni family, and a hundred years later it was given customs benefits by Napoleon (these were later confirmed by the Austro-Hungarian Empire in 1818, by Italy in 1910 and by the EEC in 1960), who effectively made it into what it was now – a duty-free area within Italy.

It was not long before my ears got clogged, as if after a hasty takeoff in a small plane. We were approaching Europe's highest populated area, which included the village of Trepalle – the continent's highest permanently inhabited settlement (administratively, part of Livigno), with Europe's highest parish church at two thousand, two hundred and fifty metres above the sea level. In just three days, I had moved from Europe's lowest point, the Netherlands, to its highest.

Livigno soon came into view – an amazingly long and flat valley, lined with ski-slopes and dotted with duty-free shops.

Before dropping me at my hotel, Gianluca gave me directions to the tourism office, run by a lady called – yes, you got it – Paola, and told me that all buses in Livigno were free for skiers.

"But I am not a skier, I am a smoker," I said, gasping from considerable oxygen deficiency, also known as "altitude sickness" or "altitude dizziness". Gianluca reassured me that buses were free for non-skiers too – a touch of high-altitude Alpine "communism" (read dizziness).

At the hotel, I dug out my "winter gear": a scarf, a knitted hat of artificial wool, gloves and a pair of wrinkled, as if constantly frowning, Marks & Spencer boots. I hadn't worn all these things for years – since skiing with Bill Bryson in the White Mountains of New Hampshire in January 1996.

The hotel's name was Adele, and like all of the other one hundred and four hotels in Livigno, it doubled as a ski lodge.

It was dark and freezing (-8°C) outside, but I nevertheless decided to venture out for a walk, hoping it would ease my splitting headache and my painful teary eyes – other common symptoms of "altitude dizziness".

Skiers in their fancy snowsuits were cheerfully falling out of free "communist" buses outside my hotel. Slipping over snowdrifts, I trudged up the street to the first duty-free shop, which sold, among other things, vodka and grappa for an astounding two Euros (£1.30) a litre. And although I had all but given up drinking spirits, I was unable to resist such an amazing bargain and bought a litre of grappa to keep me warm on my forthcoming Alpine travels. Across the road was a duty-free food shop, where I saw what could pass for the world's largest Mortadella sausage, the size of the leading wheel of a steamroller. Next to the deli was a *lavateria* – a launderette (not a lavatory). I wondered whether it was duty-free too.

More duty-free shops, separated by several metres of snow, were further up the street, their stock being roughly the same: perfumes, electronics, toiletries, clothes, rather expensive tobacco and extraordinarily cheap alcoholic drinks. Not a single customer (I didn't count myself as one) was to be found in any of them.

The loud bangs of church bells from a hidden *basilica* were floating over this snow-covered hub of consumerism. They sounded bizarre and out of place – like Chopin's funeral march played at a wedding. My poor oxygen-deficient head was tolling in unison with the bells.

Church bells above duty-free shops. Could there be a scene more Italian?

They say the surest way to aggravate altitude sickness and the resulting high blood pressure is to drink red wine, thus further increasing one's already high red-cell count. With pressurised blood pounding like a hammer inside my head and the red cells bouncing in front of my eyes, I was determined to stay away from wine – white or red – during the all-inclusive dinner at my Adele Hotel. But having looked at the wine list . . . Well, how can one resist a wine called "Vernaccia Di San Gimignano, 1944. Fattoria Abbazia Monte Oliveto", with a drawing of the medieval Mount Olive Abbey, founded in 1340, on the label? And all this poetry, history and art for just eight euros! Besides, the wine was white, not red, and also fruity, flavoury (especially when chased with fried cheese – a Livigno speciality) and seemingly helpful against my dizziness.

I was sitting in the corner of the small and cosy hotel restaurant watching loquacious Italian families gobbling up their *antipasti* and *primi piati*. From their puffed up, frost-bitten faces it was clear that all of them – including pregnant mums, grannies and toddlers – had spent the day skiing, which made me feel slightly guilty. It was time for another glass of *Fattoria Abbazia*. Cheers to the hardworking monks!

Snow was falling in large fluffy flakes behind my hotel window the next morning – quite a change from the previous one in Como. A gentle blizzard was keeping the flakes afloat and swirling in the air, as if they didn't feel like falling down – and when they finally did it was with reluctance, almost regret. Regretful snowfalls . . . How many times I woke up to them in Russia and Ukraine. *Snezhnoye sozhaleniye* – a "snowy regret" – two words with a beautiful onomatopoeic alliteration in Russian. The alliteration of snowy semi-silence . . .

CNN was reporting more bad news on the Euro falling against the US dollar, on growing unemployment in the Euro-zone countries. I flicked over to a special Livigno TV channel. "Livigno is a mini-world of its own among the mountains," a presenter's voice droned on in English.

My altitude sickness was getting better. It almost disappeared after two cups of espresso – an Italian version of the British "liquid breakfast", i.e. a pint of beer. I noted that even the tiny sugar sachets carried advertisements for duty-free shops.

Thus cured, I stepped out into Livigno – a bizarre duty-free "mini-world" of regretful snowfalls.

It was −11°C outside, only four degrees short of my ideal temperature of −15.

I went to see Paola at the tourism office, and she introduced me to my guide, Mladenka. A tall young Bosnian Serb with the looks of a supermodel, she had come to Livigno two years before. Bright, outgoing and fluent in four languages, she was a delight to be with, even if I made sure I kept at least a metre away from her when we walked the streets – to prevent her from towering above me like a railway signal above a pointsman's hut.

Mladenka seemed to know everyone in Livigno. At least she greeted almost everybody, and they greeted her. She introduced me to a lady from a perfume shop who was a member of the town council, and to another lady – from a clothes store – who was also the town's librarian. It looked as if everybody in Livigno doubled as either a duty-free shop owner or a duty-free shop assistant.

I wanted to buy a book on Livigno's history, but Mladenka told me there was not a single bookshop in the valley, just a couple of newsagents. Having checked both, I came to the conclusion that, on top of being duty-free, Livigno was also book-free. And English-language-newspaper-free, too.

The only readily available periodical was the free *Livigno* magazine, which was written partly in English. Here's an unedited extract from its front-page article:

> January has never granted us of such important dates. The coming of the Euro and its light coins able to derange history *[sic]*, uncovers a box full of dreams more than shower of one-hundred lira coins thrown into the Trevi Fountain. We will be able travel without the frustrating worry of exchanging currency which sometimes let us feel tardy and clumsy as the accountant Fantozzi.

This gobbledygook was followed by one of the most amazing sentences I have ever read in the English language (well, just about):

> Therefore, more than ever, our need to keep Livigno,s *[sic]* own identity which we are proud of: even if a train connection project is ready to bring us closer to Europe, opening us to novelties but not willing to abandon our traditions built throughout centuries of economic self-sufficiency when the passes were hermetically sealed by natural walls of snow and taking care of ourselves was a primary need while the rest of the world only knew of a mysterious place beyond the Foscagno pass.

119

My head started spinning, as if my altitude sickness had come pounding back, and Mladenka had to support me all the way to the tourism office, where I had a meeting with Giuseppe Longa – a teacher, amateur linguist (I hoped it was not he who had put together the "English" bits of "Livigno" magazine) and editor of *al Restel* (*The Rake)* – a monthly newsletter in the local dialect – Livignasc. He told me that, unlike other Sondrio dialects – Bormino, Tiranese, etc. – Livignasc incorporated lots of Romansch, Spanish and German words and therefore could not be understood in other parts of Italy. Signor Longa himself was now compiling the first Italian-Livignasc Dictionary.

I've always thought that minority European languages and dialects should be protected – like historic buildings[4] – and was therefore pleased to learn that, although all schools in Livigno were Italian, half of the valley's adults were fluent in Livignasc – a tribute to Giuseppe Longa and *The Rake*. The very name, "Livigno", as he told me, most probably derived from the Latin *lavina* meaning "avalanche of snow". Avalanches have always been a bane of Livigno's existence (the memories of one in 1951, when seven people were killed, were still very much alive in the valley). I told Signor Longo that in Russian *lavina* meant an avalanche too, and we both laughed out loud – like two little boys who had discovered their long-lost favourite toy at the bottom of granny's chest.

I have always loved languages. At the age of seven, I was cajoled (together with three other boys of the same age) into learning English. The name of the private teacher, hired by our persistent parents, was Grigoriy Alexandrovich Polonsky. He was a tall sturdy old man, with a loud voice and a droopy Cossack-style moustache. In his youth, he had studied at a pre-revolutionary grammar school, from which he graduated in 1917, the year of the Bolshevik *coup d'état*, having mastered – alongside all his classmates, no doubt – three living tongues and two dead ones (Latin and Ancient Greek).

---

4. *Here I am in total agreement with this book's chosen charity organisation –
the Foundation for Endangered Languages.*

Grigoriy Alexandrovich resided in the distant and obscure Kharkiv suburb of Kholodnaya Gora (Cold Mountain). I can still see his lanky snow-covered frame (it must have snowed constantly in Cold Mountain), energetically entering – almost falling into – our flat.

In his capacious battered brief-case our teacher carried – among other things – some faded postcards with coloured views of London. They came from a hard-to-obtain "Cities of the Capitalist Inferno" (or something of that sort) postcard set, shoddily printed by our local "Red Proletarian" publishing house. These postcards were given out to us – one at a time – as prizes for diligence in our studies of the English language. As "moral stimuli", so to speak.

For three "fives" (the highest mark in Russia and Ukraine) in a row we would be entitled to a bleak Piccadilly Circus postcard; for five to Buckingham Palace; for ten to something more politically significant, like, say, the grave of Karl Marx in Highgate Cemetery, featuring the cartoon-like bust, with disproportionably huge head and bulging eyes, staring at the world with a wild cretinous rage.

We were very proud of those postcards, gained in unfair battles with English irregular verbs. To please our parents, we even glued them into special albums.

I remember the badly drawn "British worker" hastily printed into my Piccadilly Circus picture – probably on the orders of a vigilant postcard censor – to add a proper political balance to the otherwise rather decadent "capitalist" view, with no tractors or red banners in sight. With a Soviet-style flat cap on his head, the "worker" stood on the stairs next to the Eros statue holding a poster that ran simply: "1st of Mey" (the spelling mistake here is not mine, for even at the tender age of seven I knew how to write the names of the months correctly).

This "Mey" poster added a feline touch to the picture. At least in our little boys' eyes it did (*Мяу* in Russian equals English "meow"). Even now, crossing Piccadilly Circus, I cannot help looking down to avoid the numerous cats that, as we had imagined, swarmed all over the square.

To earn enough "fives" for the "Piccadilly", let alone "Karl Marl", as we irreverently referred to the founder of Marxism, was not easy. And not just because of the fact that at the beginning of each lesson we had to recite from memory – in English! – "The Solemn Oath of the Young Pioneer"[5]: "I, a young pioneer of the Soviet Union, solemnly promise in the face of my comrades to love dearly my Soviet Motherland, to live, learn and fight [*sic*] as the great Lenin bequeathed to us, as the Communist party teaches us!" (not that Grigoriy Alexandrovich was so hooray-patriotic, but being a teacher, even if private, he had to play by the rules). No, the main difficulty lay in our Pestalozzi's rather unorthodox teaching methods. These days they would have probably been branded "forceful immersion into a foreign-language environment", or something like that.

The whole truth was that, due to the total absence of that very "foreign-language environment" in our industrial Ukrainian city, "closed" to all foreigners, apart from a few ever-tipsy Bulgarians, he had to invent it for us. That was why – as a way of introducing the verb "to pinch", for example – he would squeeze our cheeks with his stiff pre-revolutionary fingers and wouldn't let go until his victims wailed – in English – "Stop pinching!"

By modern politically correct standards, he could have easily been labelled a sadist – or even a paedophile – though in reality he was neither. On the contrary, he was an excellent teacher, and, thanks to his learn-as-you-play approach, alien-sounding foreign words were imprinted forever in our submissive brains. Yes, at times, on our cheeks, too.

One day, Grigoriy Alexandrovich left behind his glasses in our flat. A couple of days later, his wife called to cancel our next lesson (and all the following ones, too), because our playful teacher had died suddenly of a heart attack.

His glasses were still lying on our table, and I remember being amazed and somewhat puzzled by their sudden and rather scary good-for-nothing-ness.

---

5. *"Young Pioneers" – a state-run communist organisation for young children (between 9 and 14), membership in which was compulsory.*

At least he could now practise his two dead languages in peace, I thought.

The teacher passed away, but our trophies – the postcards – remained. I looked at them for hours, and, notwithstanding the awful quality of the printing, could not help admiring London's unique colour pattern: red buses and red pillar-boxes against the background of white Portland-stone houses.

That was probably how I became an Anglophile. Or rather – a Londonophile, if there's such a word.

When – many many years later – I came to London for the first time, my immediate impression was how much it resembled the fuzzy postcards of my childhood! Even the ridiculous "worker" was still stuck near Eros, only his poster ran not "1st of Mey", but "The End of the World is Nigh", which – as I already knew – was rubbish, because *my* real world was only just beginning.

I realised with sudden clarity that for all those years I had resided in an alien country and had only now found my true spiritual home.

With Giuseppe Longa, I played with some other Livignasc words: *tea* – house; *toila* – haystack; *troi* – mountain pass – trying to come up with similarly sounding words from ten other languages we knew between us. It was a fascinating word game.

With a sigh, my interlocutor informed me that there were only two part-time teachers of Livignasc left in the valley, including himself. "It is impractical to teach it at school, because of global-isation," he said. He told me how the EC had been blocking the efforts of the community to preserve its unique dialect by refusing to finance the publication of the first Livignasc-Italian dictionary, which he was compiling[6]. I thought I could understand why: in its strive for uniformity – monetary, legal, economic, cultural and so on – all attempts at individuality and/or versatility were (justly)

---

6. *I found exactly the same obstructionism while researching a column on the state of Scots Gaelic on the island of Skye. While Brussels was always willing to provide funds for a Gaelic song competition, a street festival or other window-dressing occasions, when it came to publication of the first comprehensive Gaelic-English Dictionary, all assistance was vehemently denied.*

regarded by the EU bureaucrats as direct threats to their own existence. No wonder Giuseppe Longa – a multi-talented writer and scholar – had to make his living by working as a hairdresser.

Signor Longa told me a couple of interesting facts about Livigno's history. According to him, the duty-free status was initially granted to the valley due to its poverty, as the only viable recipe for its survival. Even so, it did not bring any real benefits to the locals (apart from relatively cheap salt and flour) until 1951, when the first road that could be used in winter was built from Switzerland on the initiative of Italy's Minister of Finance – himself a native of Valtellina. I thought it was a very Italian story: there's no denying the fact that connections and mutual protection played and continue to play a pivotal role in Italian life and politics.

The first hotel in the valley was built in 1880, and a year later Livigno had its first tourist – an American, no doubt. It took another thirty-four years for the second hotel to be constructed.

With over a hundred hotels and dozens of duty-free shops, Livigno could safely be regarded as the hub of commercialism in the Retiche Alps. All Livigno shops were open from morning till late at night (with a two hour lunch break), seven days a week, three hundred and sixty-five days a year. Some time ago, one local shop owner, a devout Roman Catholic, wanted to have her store closed on Sundays, but the Livigno authorities did not allow her to do so. Duty-free obviously came before duty to God in Livigno, where the shops employed over three thousand people – more than half of all its residents – making them the community's main (and only) life line. Interestingly, the shops were not permitted to trade in Livigno's residential areas, which meant that all their employees and employers had to travel to work – on foot, by car or by free local buses.

Theoretically, a visitor (read shopper) could only take out of Livigno goods with total value of less than a hundred and seventy-five Euros. But, according to Signor Longa, customs controls on the Swiss border were lenient, if not to say non-existent. Livigno had become a sinecure for the no-longer-needed customs inspectors from the now defunct French-German border who were all sent there as an alternative to being sacked. "Our customs offices are very well staffed, yet there is nothing to worry about," Giuseppe Longa concluded with a cackle.

I was actually not at all worried: my only Livigno purchase was the bottle of extraordinarily cheap grappa – already one third empty, by the way.

After lunch, Mladenka drove me to the village of Trepalle – the highest permanently inhabited settlement in Europe, with Europe's highest church and a cluster of Europe's highest duty-free shops. The village was located at the very edge of the Livigno valley, but, although it was only a couple of hundred metres higher than the town, the difference was striking. It was much colder in Trepalle, and the washing on the balconies of its two-storied *teas* – traditional Valtellina houses, with stone basements and wooden tops – was stiff with frost. Unlike in the town, all houses in Trepalle doubled as shops selling spirits, perfumes and cigarettes, as if anyone could be bothered to climb that high only to get a carton of duty-free "Marlboros" or a bottle of mandarin-flavoured "Absolut".

We hid from the blizzard inside the "highly" famous church of St. Anna, which was unheated and felt like the inside of a freezer. But I didn't regret popping into this deep-frozen *basilica*, unremarkable in anything, apart from its height above sea level, for it was there that I spotted a detail which to me became the symbol of Livigno, and of the Italian character in general. Under the altar and along the walls there were rows of electric candles, which would light up only after a coin (of any country and denomination) was dropped into a special slot underneath! The slot was good enough for the Euros and Euro cents, too.

Pious commercialism (or commercialised piety?), manifesting itself in regulation crucifixes above cash registers and shop tills, had reached its absolute crescendo (or its maximum height above the sea level of decency, if you wish) inside Europe's highest church, with its cynical coin-activated candles – a sight that made America's shopping malls, factory outlets and incredibly tasteless gift shops (one in the Dallas museum, inside the house from which President Kennedy was shot dead in 1963, traded in porcelain salt and pepper grinders in the shape of JFK's head) look bleak in comparison.

From what I had seen of Livigno itself so far, I was able to conclude that the main principle of its existence was not that different from the mercenary church candles in Trepalle: it was by and large *a coin-operated valley*.

They had put a plate with my room number on it on my table in the restaurant. Having examined the tablecloth, complete with the stains of yesterday's monks' wine, I decided that it was just a simple ruse to allow them not to change the tablecloth.

Watching my fellow diners, I came to two profound conclusions: a) The secret of the Italian culture of dining – as opposed to the French cult of eating – lay in consuming plenty of wine and olive oil with every dish, and in having long breaks between courses filled with laughter and conversation; b) One obvious result of this culture was that Italians – both men and women – no matter how slim and graceful other parts of their bodies could be – had big floppy bums.

Having eaten my salad before the main course, I committed a crime by Italian culinary standards, for Italians always consume their salads last – at the end of the meal. An Italian-American mafioso in Nelson DeMille's *Gold Coast* once nearly shot a waiter who tried to remove his untouched salad while he was still "working" (as they say in the States) on his main course.

I also came up with a new recipe for beating altitude sickness: two shots of grappa, washed down with a bottle of good Italian red (or white) wine. Why not? On the Hebridean island of Tiree they treat all ailments – from cough to cancer – with whisky, and routinely apply whisky tampons to burns and wounds. In the absence of *Abbazia,* I had to opt for *Vernaccia di San Gimignano* – a white wine from Le Marche, my favourite part of Italy. It was lovely. The acclaimed Italian reds (in full accordance with the main rule of basic political economy: when demand outweighs supply, quality goes down the drain) often lack class and remain largely plebeian, whereas the little known young whites vie for excellency, like provincial school upstarts – and, more often than not, achieve it.

I had an urge to share these sublime conclusions with somebody, but because I didn't know any of the diners, who were unlikely to speak English anyway (my Livignasc was not adequate enough, despite several hours spent with Giuseppe Longa), I decided to address them to a stuffed stag's head hanging on the wall opposite my table and staring at me intently – as I thought, reproachfully – all through the meal, as if inviting me to a conversation.

"Sorry, mate, it was not I," I told him, referring to the deplorable absence of his body.

He didn't seem to believe me, and I didn't blame him. I told the head my after-dinner observations, but he did not respond, at which point I felt even lonelier than before: indeed, whereas everyone else in the restaurant was sitting with a friend or a partner, I had to face the stuffed head of a stag, with his conspicuously superfluous horns bringing about gruesome thoughts of infidelities and adulteries.

"Get stuffed!" – I told the head silently (which was unnecessary, for it had been already) and went back to my room to pack up "Sally", while watching a German TV channel which showed a group of fat men involved in a stone-lifting competition. I flicked over to another German channel broadcasting nothing but ads for phone sex, accompanied by orgasmic screams, then went back to the stone-lifters, who were now pushing truck tyres. I tried to imitate them by pushing "Sally" – by now fully packed – and was unable to move her one inch.

Distressed and shattered, as if I myself had done all the lifting and pushing on behalf of all those fat German men, I plopped down onto the bed and fell asleep straight away.

My short detour to high-altitude Livigno had proved, if anything, highly tiring.

*   *   *

3. Swastria (Switzerland and Austria)

SAMNAUN

Ski-less in the Alps

A pleasant surprise was waiting for me on my last morning in Livigno. Having looked at the thermometer outside my hotel window, I shouted "Yes-s-s!!" and jumped up in the air: it was −15°C – my ideal temperature, and the lowest I had been exposed to since leaving the Soviet Union. Back there minus fifteen would have been regarded as fairly mild. I was once on an assignment in Siberia, where it was minus thirty-three, but due to dry air and lack of wind it was bearable and not unpleasant.

The coldest temperature I have ever experienced was in Moscow on New Year's Eve 1980 – minus forty-two. It was hard to stay outside for more than five minutes: your eyes would start shedding uncontrollable salty tears that would freeze on your eyelids, blocking your vision. Scarves and *shapkas* (fur hats with ear-muffs) didn't help. The city was totally unprepared for such low

128

temperature: in many blocks of flats, heating, gas and electricity went off – all at the same time. People made bonfires on their high-rise balconies (the only place where one could actually see anything), trying to cook their festive meals. Metro stations were impossible to enter due to the huge clouds of thick vapour they were coated in. It was OK in our flat though: we had a bit of gas in the kitchen, where we all, dressed in hats and winter coats, huddled together for the New Year feast.

I ran out of the hotel. The frost was biting and invigorating, and I dashed back and forth through the snow – like a puppy taken out for a walk after a long day locked in a tiny flat. Several years in Australia, however, must have reduced my tolerance for cold: after ten minutes of frantic racing, my feet started to freeze and I had to return to Adele. A cup of steaming espresso made my face flush. I could almost feel the blood pulsate all over my body, charging it with warmth and energy. Frost is good for you. Especially when you hide from it inside a warm house.

Having said good-bye to the stag's head – my tolerant and taciturn dinner companion of the previous night – I climbed into Gianluca's car to start another long journey.

Italian border guards waved us through into Switzerland. Or, in the terms of my Greater Enclavia, into Swastria. Their Swiss counterparts at the *Dogana* ("customs office" in Romansch, which is spoken in that part of quatro-lingual "Doormania") stopped us only to say *buongiorno*. "They are normally lenient to cars with Livigno number plates," explained Gianluca. The reason was that everyone, even frontier-guards, would routinely travel to Livigno to stock up on cheap petrol and spirits, so they were just returning the favour, so to speak. Livigno cars were also spared the €1.50 toll for the nearest Swiss road tunnel. I was ready to bite my elbows[7]: had I known there would be no customs checks on the border, I would have bought another bottle of grappa!

---

7. *A peculiar Russian idiom describing the highest level of frustration.*

The moment we entered Switzerland, the landscape became picture-postcard-ish. At the end of every town and village there stood a regulation *A Revair* road sign in Romansch. "It is the first language here, they teach it at schools," said Gianluca.

We were driving through Engadina – Switzerland's national park. I spotted rows of fallen trees near the curb – a sight that didn't quite agree with Swiss neatness. According to Gianluca, those were traces of avalanches that had been stopped by controlled explosions.

Gianluca dropped me at Zermez – a little toy-like station which also doubled as a yellow post-bus stop. I had about an hour to kill. Having walked around the station square, where the only building of note was the Hotel La Staziun, I examined a gleaming *pulizia* car parked at its entrance. A bright yellow post-bus pulled over and disgorged a crowd of joyful skiers.

I went back inside the station, where I saw a curious multi-purpose vending machine. It was rather like a mini-corner shop dispensing a bit of everything: drinks, chocolates, crisps, sandwiches and even . . . condoms. With only Euros and Euro-cents in my pocket, I was unable to buy anything from that Swiss machine (not that I particularly wanted to). It was a welcome reminder that I was once again outside the Euro-zone.

A group of Romansch-speaking – or rather Romansch-giggling – schoolgirls in their early teens fluttered in and proceeded straight towards the vending machine. I didn't like their naughty giggles and, while acknowledging the positive effects of early sex education, still hoped it was not the *ceylor preservatifs* that they were after . . . To my considerable relief, they all opted for chocolate bars.

Waiting for my train on the sterile platform, I suffered a panic attack, having accidentally dropped my fag onto its crystal-clean surface. I picked it up promptly, pretending nothing extraordinary had happened. To my relief, no one seemed to have noticed my heinous, if unintended, crime against the Swiss way of life: the skiers were busy cleaning their snowboards.

Soon I boarded my *ratische bahn* train to Scuol. It was lunchtime. Having settled myself next to the window, I unpacked my lunch bag, containing bread, cheese and a couple of boiled eggs, nicked from the Adele Hotel breakfast buffet. I cracked one egg against the edge of a squeaky clean table – and a disaster followed. The window, the floor and half of the spotless carriage were suddenly covered with the egg's slimy contents. It was fresh – not boiled! What a silly thing to offer raw eggs for breakfast!

I was half-expecting the train to come to a halt to let in a special *Pulizia* Cleanliness Squad to frogmarch me to the nearest prison. Well, at least, my cell was bound to be dirt-free, and, possibly, they would even bring my meals from a local restaurant in a van inscribed "Gourmet Foods", like they did to the lucky inmates of Liechtenstein's only jail in Vaduz.

Thank God for Kleenex tissues – one of humankind's best inventions. I had actually managed to wipe the egg off the window and the floor before anyone noticed. The realisation of how close I came to becoming a Swiss jailbird was enough to curtail my appetite. I threw the remaining – fresh – egg into a plastic-lined litter bin, where it exploded in a peaceful, controlled manner.

"Sally" was sprawled over two seats like a fat Italian *mamma* – a silent witness to my punishment for being greedy. She must have thoroughly enjoyed the sight. I went to the toilet and experienced a fiendish pleasure weeing (legally!) onto the sterile Swiss track through the hole at the bottom of the cubicle.

The train was playing hide-and-seek with the Alps by diving into countless tunnels and peeping out again with a high-pitched little-boy-like whistle, as if yelling mischievously: "Here I am! Try and catch me!"

Because of the snowy conditions, the stretch of railway from Guarda to Scuol was closed and, as they say in Britain, "replacement buses" had to be used. A couple of yellow post-autos were waiting near the station with their engines running. We arrived at Scuol on the dot, as if we had never left the train.

Another train ride to Etan, and another post-bus – this time for me alone – to Landeck. This post-bus had come from Austria (Swiss "post-autos" also operate in the Alpine areas of Austria and Germany close to the Swiss border), and I was able to pay for my ticket in Euros. The driver pressed the button – and my change jumped out. The recorded announcements on this bus were in all four official languages of Switzerland.

The history of the post-bus – a great Swiss institution on wheels – goes back to 1849, when the Swiss postal service was first made a monopoly of the young Confederation. The role of the yellow buses was then played by horse-drawn carriages – also yellow. It was not long before they started carrying passengers too, although Swiss Post opened the first scheduled service between Berne and Detligen only in 1906. This line is still in operation.

In winter, some carriages had to be replaced with sleighs. With time, the longest and busiest routes were gradually taken over by railways, though most Alpine destinations were still served by mail coaches. After World War I, Swiss Post bought a fleet of decommissioned military trucks, which were converted into the first mechanical post-buses – predecessors of modern post-autos.

In all these years, there was hardly a serious accident involving a post-bus – quite an achievement, if we remember that they operate mostly in mountainous areas. I also suspect there has never been more than a one minute deviation from the timetable. Like many years ago, yellow carriages with two hundred and fifty-horsepower engines still carry passengers and mail. As in the old times, the drivers blow their melodious three-note (C sharp, E and A, spelling out an A major chord) post-horns, still playing the same wistfully nostalgic tune from the andante of the overture to Rossini's *William Tell*. It is not widely known, however, that these horns also allow post-buses to "talk" to post offices and to each other from a distance, for different combinations of the notes announce: "departure of post", "arrival of post", "arrival of special post", "bus swerving out" and so on – so much more romantic (and probably more reliable) than radio or mobile phones. This musical language started in the mid-nineteenth century, when the coach drivers blew their horns on approaching a destination to forewarn the station about the number of horses that needed to be fed.

An Austrian frontier guard boarded our post-bus near a town with the unappealing, as if spat out, name of Pfunds. He threw a quick look at my Australian passport, but stopped short of touching it, as if it were infected with some obscure antipodean disease. "*Gut!*" he muttered through clenched teeth and went on. I was back in the Euro-land, having travelled through three countries within a couple of hours.

I have always liked Austria: its quirky old towns, its (relatively) friendly people, with their melodious, almost mellifluous, German and a peculiar self-deprecating humour. "We are clever people. We turned Hitler into a German and Beethoven into an Austrian," they say in Vienna.

I have noticed that in Britain, for some obscure reason, Austrians are often regarded with scorn. One of the meanest comments I have read in the British press in all my fifteen years in the UK comes from the September 2002 issue of the Scottish edition of the *Daily Express*: "To their credit, most Germans have worked hard to disown the Nazi past – unlike the Austrians who shrug their shoulders, presumably to stop their arms snapping into a reflex *Sieg Heil*, and mutter into their strudels every time the war is mentioned."

The Austrian Alpine villages behind the squeaky-clean windows of our post-bus were less picturesque and more run-down than the Swiss ones. Yet they were also more colourful in everything, apart from the names of their hotels, which were all called Edelweiss, Belvedere or Lowen. And the mountains no longer looked man-made and picture-postcard-ish.

The new passengers on the bus were chatting loudly in what sounded like a Tyrolean dialect of German, possibly Ladin. They were laughing a lot. It was hard to believe that the bus – totally silent minutes ago – was still the same: in Switzerland one doesn't often hear people laugh in public. Can it be that a vehicle – be it a train, a bus, or even a private car – acquires some of the personality (identity?) of the country it passes through?

I was also enjoying my first (albeit temporary) separation from "Sally", who was riding in the boot in the company of skis and ski-boards. I hoped they would bully her a little for being so fat and capricious.

The bus arrived at Landeck railway station at precisely 14:21 – as per the timetable. After Switzerland, the station looked pleasantly dirty(ish).

I was met by an obese and apoplectic driver who didn't speak a word of English. For some reason he held a hand-written poster saying "Birgit" in his hand. I said: "Vitali?" and he nodded. Well, I had been called all sorts of names (Vassili, Vitari, Vitara, Vitau, even Vivaldi), but never Birgit. Never mind. All the way to Ischgl – my base for exploring Samnaun – he puffed and wheezed behind the wheel and I was seriously worried that he would have a stroke while driving.

Ischgl was a popular Austrian skiing resort. Walking to the tourist office, I saw organised crowds of German skiers marching from cable cars to their hotels and pounding the ground with their ski boots – as if goose-stepping on the snow.

My contact at the tourism office turned out to be a lady called Birgit, which explained my little misunderstanding with the driver. Birgit was apologetic: her husband was taking her for a weekend in Vienna to see an opera (it was Friday). "I am so sorry I cannot be with you tomorrow," she said. I assured her that I was a big boy and could survive on my own. "Yes, but I am worried for you," she kept repeating. "You can see some strange people here in the evening . . ." I told her I had a red belt in Tae-kwon-do, but this did not alleviate her motherly anxiety.

I then announced that I wanted to go across the mountains to Samnaun next morning. "Do you ski?" she asked me. "Yes, but not at the moment. Firstly, I don't have the gear. Secondly, tomorrow is my only full day in the area, and I have no time for skiing." "But . . . but," she muttered, her anxiety levels going through the roof. "But it is not possible without skis, unless you take a bus which will take you five and a half hours." "No more buses for me!" I said resolutely. I knew it was possible (well, theoretically at least) to short cut to Samnaun by crossing the Alps in a cable car or a chair lift, even without skis.

She gave up. "But I must draw you a plan," she said. I thought she meant the plan of Ischgl, but she took out a map of the surrounding mountains and drew some curved red lines on it. Then she wrote on a piece of paper:

1. Silveretta Bahn – Idalp
2. Flimjochbahn (border) – down
3. Flihsattelbahn – Alp Trida
4. Alp Trida – Sattelbahn
5. Pendelbahn – Samnaun

This was supposed to be my itinerary for tomorrow. It was mind-boggling, but I decided not to show my concern, which might have led to Birgit having a panic attack and cancelling her trip to Vienna.

"No problem," I said cheerfully and, having picked up my *Tag Schmuggler* (Smuggler's Day Ticket), a voucher entitling a non-skier to use the area's chair lifts and cable cars, I went out into the snow.

It was dusk. The mountains surrounding Ischgl looked dark and uninviting. Close to the top of one of the peaks I could discern ant-like dots of skiers descending back into Austria across the imaginary Swiss border, behind which the village of Samnaun was nestling somewhere on the other side of the mountain. I wondered whether the skiers were stopped by frontier guards and asked to show their passports while coming down the slope – and made a mental note to take mine with me tomorrow just in case.

Near Silverbahn station, a large group of German skiers was crowded outside a beer kiosk. They were swinging and singing a German song in an amazingly synchronised chorus. In their hands, they were clutching plastic cups of beer. Their skis and poles stood next to them in the snow like temporarily discarded halberds while they got seriously drunk after a day of skiing. The kiosk was appropriately called Après Ski.

The narrow, snow-ridden streets of Ischgl were full of people. In the crowd, I could hear occasional British voices: "Hey, girls! Come with us! F*** you!" (this came from a group of tipsy British teenagers). A self-confessed Anglophile, I had been dying to hear English speech, but now I wished I hadn't. I suddenly realised that ninety percent of the crowd were already very drunk (it was not yet 6pm!) which made me understand the nature of Birgit's concern about "strange people in the evening". German and British holidaymakers had a lot in common when drunk, the only difference being that the Germans, while equally boorish, seemed to be much better organised.

A huge queue, the like of which I hadn't seen since Russia, was snaking in the snow around the town's only supermarket. It reminded me of the seven-mile-long line to Moscow's first McDonald's on the day of its opening in January 1990. Well, to be honest, the Ischgl queue was a little bit shorter.

Squeezed by dripping skis and boots protruding from all sides, I bought myself some cheese and salami after a mere thirty minutes of queuing at a tiny, yet outrageously expensive *backerei* (deli) before retiring to my Garni Hotel. I had had enough of Ischgl – this Alpine mini-Blackpool – and was looking forward to a quiet, solitary evening before tomorrow's adventure.

My hotel "suite" consisted of two separate premises: a fairly unremarkable windowless bedroom and a so-called s*tube* – a spacious room with large ivy-lined bay windows all along the front wall. Apart from a comfy rocking chair and several pots with flowers, the *stube* was empty. Rooms like this were often to be found in German and Austrian rural households. I had also seen them in Romania, where they were called *casa mare* – a room with sea view. Their sole purpose was quiet contemplation and relaxation at the end of a working day. The *stube*'s peculiar layout corresponded to an observation of Bernard van Beurden, a Dutch writer: "The Austrian has a two-roomed house. One room is bright and friendly, a well-furnished room, where he receives his guests. The other room is dark, with the blinds down, locked, inaccessible, completely out of bounds to strangers." According to Prof. Erwin Ringel, an Austrian scholar, this reflected a dichotomy of the Austrian mind – friendly and conformist on the surface, yet angry and jealous underneath – with both anger and jealousy directed primarily at the Germans, who had, allegedly, hijacked their culture and were now basking in wealth. Having observed the behaviour of German skiers in Ischgl, I could understand, if not the jealousy, then definitely the anger.

Unfortunately, instead of a sea view, my *stube* was facing Ischgl's main street, with a bright neon Casino sign across the road. I drew the curtains and, having taken a bath, lowered myself into the rocking chair only to realise that relaxation and/or contemplation were going to be hard to achieve. The drunken din behind the curtained bay windows was growing by the minute. From time to time, piercing human shrieks could be heard. Watching the endless procession of unsteady human shadows, I wished spring would come soon and the screaming skiers would melt away with the snow.

Closer to midnight, the noise died down somewhat. I opened the curtains and, soothed by a sharp-ish Austrian Riesling, chased with stinky Tyrolean cheese, I sat in the dark, watching. It felt like being in front of a TV screen: no one could see me from the street, but I could see them. The *Stube* was a good vantage point for a writer, allowing him to observe without being noticed.

Outside, in the nearly deserted street, an empty bottle was tossed about by the wind. Whenever it hit the curb, it clinked submissively – like wind chimes disturbed by a passing drunk.

*   *   *

"*Umniy v goru ne poidiot – umniy goru oboidiot*" is a wise Russian proverb translating simply as "He who is clever won't climb the mountain, but will walk around it." I had a chance to fully appreciate its wisdom during my foolhardy attempt at crossing the Alps to get to Samnaun.

There is a famous painting called *Suvorov Crossing the Alps* by Surikov – a late-nineteenth-century Russian artist. It depicts a scene from Russia's successful military campaign to expel the French from Italy (Russia was then part of the anti-French coalition) led by a renowned military commander, Count Alexander Vassilyevich Suvorov. During the 1799 Swiss expedition, Suvorov's troops had to go across the Alps. The painting shows Suvorov's soldiers, sliding down a snow-covered mountain on their bottoms, laughing. For some reason, I couldn't help thinking of it when walking to Silveretta Bahn the following morning.

Even and orderly formations of German skiers – skis on their shoulders and hangovers on their faces – were marching purposefully in the same direction. They looked like New Age Crusaders out to conquer some infidel mountain peaks. As they were boarding a cable car – in a rush, yet without fuss – I suddenly realised that I was the only person around without skis. With the "Smuggler's Day Ticket" on a rope around my neck – like my accreditation for an adventure – I squeezed myself inside the cabin, crowded like a Moscow rush-hour tram.

As the cable car was climbing higher and higher up, I couldn't help registering how hostile and forbidding the Alps looked close up. I thought of the daring smugglers (real ones, not "accredited" like myself), who used to criss-cross these treacherous slopes on primitive skis, with bags of cheap Swiss sugar (or flour) on their backs. Our cabin, albeit full to bursting point, was a much safer way to cross the mountains – if you forgot the American military jet that, having gone off course, had accidentally flown through and broken a cable car cord in the Italian Alps a couple of years before. Through the plexiglass roof of the cabin, I looked up at the low, clouded sky: there were no stranded planes in sight, thank goodness, and even if there had been, I wouldn't have been able to spot them.

With relief, I jumped out of the cabin at Idalp and immediately fell up to my knees through the snow. As I was trying to extricate my feet from its tight ice-cold grip, skiers were whooshing past me indifferently: the snow was "consolidated" enough to support the skis, but not my cranky M&S boots. Above my head, cable car ropes criss-crossed on different levels, like roads at a spaghetti junction.

Eventually, I made it to the Flimjochbahn station, about a hundred yards away. It was a chair lift, and the cabins were much smaller than Silveretta's: each had only two seats. Apart from a plastic roof, they were open to the elements, with passengers' legs hanging precariously above the abyss. Pressing my shoulder bag to my chest (among other things, it contained my passport – just in case), I travelled further up in the company of a sexless creature wearing a helmet and a thick ski suit and pressing a snowboard to his (her? its?) chest. It was also wearing skis, as was everybody else in the cabins travelling in the opposite direction. They stared at my dangling boots with a mixture of pity and disdain, as if I had no feet.

When we arrived at the next station, my chair lift companion took off its helmet and turned out to be a young German woman.

I was now on the very top of the mountain, where a heavy blizzard was raging. It suddenly became bitterly cold. My next chair lift station was about three hundred yards away. I crawled towards it on my belly to stop myself from falling through the snow. Having reached it in a mere forty minutes, I learnt that they were about to close the chair lift down because of the blizzard. I was the only person trying to get in.

I knocked on the window of a small booth, where a chair lift operator was sitting. He peeped out and said just one word: "*Geschlossen!*" ("Closed!")

"But I have to get to Samnaun, and I have no skis!" I screamed. "What am I going to do, if you close the chair lift?!"

My frozen voice drowned in the hooliganistic whistles of the wind.

The operator must have pitied me, for after about five minutes, during which I kept cursing myself for being so stupid as to have ventured across the Alps without skis, he briskly walked out of his booth and pushed me into an open cabin with a plastic screen in front. I was shivering all the way down to Altrida – either with bone-piercing cold or with fear that they would stop the chair lift any moment and I would be left dangling in the air above the precipice until the blizzard died down, or, possibly, until spring arrived – like a frozen turkey left to thaw on the balcony of a sky scraper.

Sinisterly, I seemed to be the only passenger going down or up. At times, my cabin would screech to a near-complete halt ("This is it! The end of the line!"), but after some shilly-shallying, it would reluctantly resume its slow downward progress.

I was frozen stiff by the time I reached Altrida. Of course, the moment I stepped out of the chair lift, I fell through the snow again and was nearly run over by a passing skier. In the distance, about two hundred yards away, I saw a large log cabin, with the word "Restaurant" on top. I needed some warming up, or rather defrosting, before I could proceed to Samnaun (there were still two more chair lifts to go). Using my freshly acquired crawling skills and propelled by a hallucinatory vision of a steaming espresso cup, I reached the log-cabin in record time – less than half an hour.

They did have espresso inside! It cost me €3.70 – the most I had ever paid for a coffee. But I did not mind. Holding the cup with stiff frozen fingers, I drank the hot watery liquid in small sips, savouring the warmth of every swallow. Soon my fingers could bend again. The rest of my body was thawing off too, and I suddenly realised that my defrosting feet were wet through: my boots must have been leaking.

"It is not easy without skis," the young man who had sold me the coffee commented gravely, after a quick sorrowful look at my boots. He continued in bad English: "I did not see somebody do it here . . ."

He was obviously telling the truth, for even the daring smugglers of yesteryear crossed the Alps on skis. I was probably the first fool to undertake a ski-less crossing after Suvorov's soldiers in 1799. I promised to myself that I would go back to Ischgl by bus, even if it took me a week.

"Were they serious about shutting down the chair lift in my face?" I asked the youngster.

"Sometimes they close the lift, and you have to ask ski police to take you down," he said.

I had heard of secret police, of the thought police from Orwell's *Nineteen Eighty-Four*, but never of ski police. How would they take me down, I wondered? By helicopter?

I went to the bathroom and put my red hands under the stream of hot water. Yes, they had hot water, electronic soap dispensers and paper flowers on the walls in this high-altitude Alpine bathroom. "Can it be that I am already in Switzerland?" I thought. And, indeed, I was! Another confirmation of the fact that nowhere else is a national character manifested so clearly as in bathrooms.

On the very last leg to Samnaun I travelled in the relative comfort of a warm Pendelbahn cable car, with soft music playing from invisible loudspeakers. I looked at my fellow passengers – all skiers – with a bit of triumph: I bet none of them had made it there from Ischgl on foot and belly.

Having dipped into my pocket, I discovered they had given me change in Swiss francs in the log cabin of the Alpine restaurant (no wonder, it being in Switzerland). There was no choice but to spend them in the Swiss semi-enclave of Samnaun, which I was – now unstoppably – approaching.

I fell out of the cable car at the foot of a mountain. My fellow mountaineers were all met by a minibus. One of them told me that Samnaun was several miles away from the cable car station, and I felt too frozen and too exhausted to walk that far across the snow. I thought of using my freshly acquired skills and crawling to Samnaun on my tummy, or even taking a cable car back to the mountain top, when an accidental minibus, with *Samnaundorf* written on its sides, pulled over next to me. "Samnaun?" an amiable young driver inquired merrily. I nodded and climbed in. It was an hourly shuttle-bus to one of Samnaun's hotels, picking up its guests arriving by cable car. Since there were none, I had a free ride to the village.

Samnaun was tiny: just a cluster of restaurants and duty-free shops plus the minuscule church of St. Jakobus, looking so neat and new that it could pass for a duty-free item too. It was my second duty-free settlement in as many days. Samnaun looked like a smaller copy of Livigno: the same jolly crowds of skiers, the same familiar brands in shops, even the same tacky postcards of naked men standing in the snow, their penises wrapped in scarves – sold in the only newsagent, which stocked no books, but just a couple of Swiss newspapers (and the postcards of course).

There was one obvious difference, though: giant Swiss Army knives, displayed in every other shop window and leaving a visitor with no doubt that he was in Switzerland. A number of those enormous knives were installed outside the shops in the snow. Like troubled octopi, they stretched their constantly-moving tentacles (blades) towards me threateningly. I already had a multi-function Swiss Army knife, bought in Lucerne in 1991, which I tended to regard not only as the best ever Swiss invention (miles ahead of the cuckoo clock), but also as one of my most treasured possessions and, maybe, even one of my best friends. For all those years the knife had been my faithful travel companion. It had opened innumerable wine bottles. It had cut through countless chunks of cheese and sausage. At home, it had helped me carry out numerous domestic chores, thus redeeming me in the critical eyes of my wives and girlfriends, who otherwise thought that my hands "grew from a wrong place", as they say in Russia. (They were right, of course: I was – and still am – the world's most hopeless DIY person.)

Having narrowly escaped the aggressive blades, I took shelter in a small tourism office next to the post-bus station, not knowing what a blow was awaiting me there.

The office was empty, except for a young female tourism official, who was about to close it down and go home. She was clearly annoyed by my intrusion (or, possibly, she simply looked permanently annoyed, as many Swiss do). She was even further irritated when I asked her about Samnaun's history – information I had been unable to get from any Internet (or other) sources. Yet, being Swiss, she had a high sense of duty. With a deep sigh, she told me that the duty-free rank, bestowed on the village in 1892, was an object of contention for the other four villages of the area, which were desperate for the same status, but had never been granted it. Like jealous Soviet housewives, unable to cope with their neighbour's well-being and hence writing letters of slanderous complaints to the local communist party committee, the residents of the four "deprived" villages were bombarding the Swiss parliament with demands of either giving the same status to them or withdrawing it from Samnaun, using the logic of a spoilt brat: if I cannot have the sweetie, then no one can!

"The Swiss government, however, stays firm. And although Samnaun is no longer considered a semi-enclave, it keeps refusing to revoke our duty free . . ."

"Wait a moment!" I interrupted her quite rudely. "What do you mean 'no longer considered a semi-enclave'? Considered by whom?"

"The thing is that a way has been discovered to reach Samnaun by road from Switzerland without entering Austria. This is a bad country road, but, if you follow it, you can actually arrive here without leaving Switzerland. However, it is only open in summer, so theoretically in winter time Samnaun remains an enclave . . ."

"Do you mean to say that I have crawled across the Alps on my belly all for nothing?" I yelled.

The young woman seemed unaffected by my emotional outburst. Like the Swiss government, she "stayed firm".

"Well, it is winter now," she said somewhat apologetically.

As if trying to alleviate her non-existent "guilt", she stayed on at the office for another ten minutes to draft and print out the itinerary for my return to Ischgl by three different post-buses.

Waiting for her to finish, I picked up a free "Samnaun" tourism pamphlet (in German) from a stack on her desk. A small bird's quill was glued to its cover.

"Its message," explained the lady, "is that after skiing holidays in Samnaun one's body is supposed to feel as light as a feather."

"With so many duty-free shops, this could rather apply to one's wallet," I grumbled, being shocked and angered by the sudden "disenclavement" of Samnaun, in which I almost lost interest. I felt like leaving it immediately, but had to wait for a couple of hours for the post-bus to Martina – the only one to leave the village on that February afternoon.

I had lunch at the nondescript and squeaky-clean Chasa Hotel restaurant, next to the Snow-How (!) ski-hire shop. Unable to understand the intricacies of the Romansch menu, I asked the waitress what sort of soup (a word that sounds roughly the same in most European languages) was offered as a daily "special".

"This soup is with . . . er . . . how is it in English . . . you know . . . Bambi!" she mumbled.

The plate of venison soup had a fried egg floating in it like a water lily.

As there was nothing much else to do in this tiny and fairly unremarkable (apart from its ex-enclave status that is) duty-free village, after lunch I wandered aimlessly into a large duty-free shop next to Chasa Hotel where I spotted large bags of sugar in the corner under shelves of perfumes.

"Are these for sale?" I asked a shop assistant with a dose of sarcasm in my voice.

"Yes, of course!" was the reply.

To my growing surprise, I noticed more sugar bags in another shop and in yet another one. It took me a while to remember that sugar, alongside flour, used to be the main item of early twentieth century Alpine smuggling.

Could it still be the case? I addressed this question to an English-speaking shop manager, who explained that the price of sugar in Switzerland was indeed almost half of that in Austria.

"*Plus ça change*," I said to myself, mincing from one foot to the other at the post-bus stop. That little detail made me feel that my hardship-ridden sojourn to Samnaun had not been entirely worthless.

I nearly ended up being left behind in Samnaun by a post-bus driver who refused to accept Euros as my fare. And I had no Swiss francs left. In the end, I persuaded him to accept a ten Euro note, and his ticket machine spat out some francs as change. A victim of the common European currency, I now had to carry the maverick Swiss francs until the Busingen leg of my journey, when I was going to travel across Switzerland again.

I plopped myself onto the bus seat. The departure time was 13:11. At 13:09, the driver started the engine. At 13:10, he shut the door. Exactly one minute later, the bus started moving.

Having had to dispose of the Swiss francs, dispensed to me at the top-of-the-mountain restaurant, I did purchase one duty-free item in Samnaun, but I didn't think it would cause me any trouble at the Austrian border in Martina. Having promised myself not to buy anything in overpriced Ischgl, I had acquired and was now carrying a long bazooka-shaped Swiss baguette, which had to be bent in the middle to fit into my shoulder bag. As I was wondering whether to declare my freshly baked duty-free loaf, a bored Austrian customs officer, sporting a green uniform and a red cap – an outfit that made him look like an oversize woodpecker – waved our bus through. My next connecting post-bus was due to arrive at 15:01. To my surprise, it pulled over two minutes early – at 14:59. I rushed towards it only to discover that it was *not* my Landeck-bound bus, but a different one. As its tail lights disappeared behind the road turn at 15:00, I could see MY bus approach.

Shockingly, it was three minutes late to depart! I thought this would make for a good front-page headline for tomorrow's Swiss (and, possibly, Austrian) national newspapers – "SWISS LIFESTYLE UNDER THREAT AFTER POST-AUTO GETS DELAYED AT BORDER", or something of that sort.

In actual fact, the delay was caused by the driver talking on his mobile phone. The conversation, I was sure, was work-related. Most likely, he was getting a warning of an approaching avalanche from his controller, who advised him of an alternative route.

We drove through sunset, past snow-covered mountain peaks, engulfed in bright white flames. I was starting to get somewhat fed up with mountains. Looking up at the unwelcoming summits, I thought it was good NOT to be up there any longer. Remembering the wise Russian proverb, I was now doing the clever thing – circumventing the mountain, rather than climbing it.

*   *   *

The last stretch of my five-and-a-half-hour return journey was marred by a group of Ischgl-bound drunken German skiers, who were so noisy and obstreperous that the driver had to pull over and order them off the bus. They obeyed immediately and stumbled out. Skiing for them was probably like ice-fishing in Russia – an excuse for getting drunk in the snow.

Back in my hotel room, I discovered with awe that I had lost my cigarette-rolling kit (I call it my portable cigarette factory) – a compact leather pouch containing a German cigarette-rolling machine, tobacco, papers and filters. It must have happened at Landeck station, where I rolled a couple of cigarettes while waiting for the bus. I had to wait until the next morning to try and retrieve it.

This kit of mine used to cause a furore during my travels across America. There was no better conversation starter than to produce my little machine and roll a fag or two in public. Whole restaurants would come to a stop. The patrons would abandon their meals, flock around me and applaud every time a cigarette jumped out of the machine. A chef would materialise from the kitchen wiping his greasy hands on his apron. Every other onlooker wanted to own this "nice European toy" and pleaded with me to send one from London. "Are you a smoker?" I would ask. "No, but I just love it . . ." A couple of times, my kit even got me free drinks at bars, offered by (non-smoking!) barmen who wanted to have the machine, too. What a shame it would be to lose it!

In panic, I ran outside and, in breach of my resolution not to buy anything in Ischgl, purchased a packet of overpriced Marlboros from a cigarette vending machine. I hadn't smoked factory-made cigarettes for several years, and they tasted awful.

My only consolation was that if the kit was indeed left behind at Landeck station, I stood a pretty good chance of having it returned to me the next day, for, as far as I knew, Austrians stood pretty high up the unofficial ladder of honesty – probably occupying the second step from the top after Germans. Several years ago, a group of British sociologists conducted an experiment whereby wallets with small amounts of cash were scattered around randomly selected cities and towns – twenty wallets in each. Apart from coins and banknotes, the wallets contained a piece of paper, with the address of the "owner" clearly written on it. As far as I can remember, Glasgow came first in this honesty test, with twelve wallets out of twenty duly returned to the experiment's "field offices". London – unsurprisingly – was last, with only eight. I thought that had such an experiment been conducted in Moscow, all twenty-one wallets would have gone missing – including one stolen from a pocket of an organiser while he or she was scattering the wallets around.

Back in my *stube* that evening, I experienced what could best be described as bliss after the blizzard. Having taken a leisurely hot bath, I sat in the rocking chair, wearing thermal socks (I should have put them on in the morning), munching my duty-free Samnaun baguette and watching the murky, unsteady silhouettes of passers-by behind the curtains. It was like a recreation of the poem by Yevtushenko about a misty park in March, populated with "neither women nor men, but only the shadows of women and men".

Time ceased to exist. The chair next to me was empty, and I was imagining my various friends and loved ones – dead and alive – taking turns sitting in it.

A heavy snowfall fitted all the windows of the *stube* with thick, yet translucent, white curtains the following morning. Through the veil of snow, I could see bulldozers, with blinking hazard lights on their roofs, trying to clean the road – a futile task given the density of the snow. I was wondering how I was going to travel to Jungholz – my next destination – later in the afternoon. According to the local TV channel, the temperature on the mountaintop was –13°C; the speed of wind -43 m/h, and none of the chair lifts or cable cars were operating. I was lucky to have undertaken the crossing the day before.

Before leaving Ischgl, I was to receive a guest – Herr Rudolf Vogt, a local historian, hotelier, ski-instructor and mountain guide, specialising in "smugglers' tours" from Ischgl to Samnaun (on skis, of course). I was interested in Alpine smugglers of the past (particularly so after my previous day's adventure), who could be regarded as the precursors of free European trade, possibly even of the Euro itself.

The moment Herr Vogt – a sprightly middle-aged man with a red, frostbitten face – shook the snow off his ski-boots and reclined in a rocking chair inside the *stube*, I asked him about the sugar bags in the duty-free shops of Samnaun.

"Until the 1950s, sugar was fairly hard to get in Austria," he said. "Also, in Samnaun it was twice as cheap – and still is! Near Kapl, there's a hamlet, locally known as "saccharine village", where all the houses were built with the money earned by sugar smuggling. Displaying packets of sugar outside duty-free shops these days is a tribute to this age-old tradition."

Herr Vogt's story was fascinating. It was hard to believe that smugglers from Ischgl – these "hard Tyrolean guys" and excellent skiers– had been able to cover the distance to and from Samnaun in just four hours. They always travelled in small groups under cover of darkness and had designated hiding places along the route where they could conceal themselves while a border patrol was skiing past. If spotted, they would take to their heels (or rather skis) and, being far better skiers than the border guards, would normally get away with all their goodies. Almost all local farmers were involved in some part-time smuggling to keep ends met.

Between the wars – the period that was known as the heyday of professional smuggling – contrabandists mostly specialised in cigarettes, which they carried inside wine barrels (!). They bought tobacco in Samnaun and sold it in Austria. Once a barrel fell off the cart and broke open in Landeck station. The inventive smuggler, whose name was Josef Kurtz, instead of panicking, offered cigarettes to the spellbound locals and told them to keep quiet. Then he unhurriedly patched up the barrel and rolled it on along the platform, as if nothing had happened (at this point, I couldn't help a rather far-fetched association with my cigarette-rolling machine, also at Landeck station – or so I hoped).

"My father was a part-time smuggler, too," Herr Vogt confessed, not without a touch of pride. "Being a poor farmer, he smuggled a bit of coffee, butter and cheese in his spare time. What else could he do? Smuggling was pretty much the way of life for this impoverished community."

He went on to acknowledge that his great uncle was also a smuggler, yet not a petty one, like his father, but a celebrity. He was in cahoots with the border guards and always used one simple trick when apprehended: he quickly hid his bag of loot under the snow, took out an axe (he always carried one) and pretended to be cutting wood.

Smuggling definitely ran strong in Herr Vogt's family.

I asked him (with fiendish hope) whether there were any smugglers left in the area.

"Smuggling as a business came to a stop in the 1950s, with the advent of tourism that gave the community a new means of subsistence," he replied with what I thought was a hastily-repressed sigh of nostalgia. To me, one valid reason to regret the decline of smuggling was that its courageous perpetrators sounded much more colourful (and much quieter) than the drunken German skiers who had come in their stead.

We talked a bit about Samnaun, which Herr Vogt knew well. He told me that, being part of Switzerland, the semi-enclaved (until they had found and officially mapped the damn road) valley had not been occupied during World War II. German troops were deployed along its perimeter, but never ventured across the border. For the *Vehrmacht* deserters Samnaun was a godsend, for the locals were always happy to help them reach "mainland" Switzerland. The villagers' considerable skiing (read smuggling) skills came in handy (or rather "footy").

For me, this story somewhat redeemed the over-commercialised image of modern duty-free Samnaun, which, according to Herr Vogt, was coming to an end.

The reality was that, by law, Samnaun's duty-free status (which among other things meant an almost guaranteed affluence) had to be confirmed every ten years by a referendum in the whole of the Graubunden Canton of Switzerland, to which the village territorially belonged. Echoing the words of the irritated young lady from Samnaun's tourism office, my guest assured me that, due to the constant lobbying by other (jealous) villages in the area, desperate to get the same status, the next referendum was almost certain to terminate it for Samnaun.

I felt sorry for Samnaun, which now faced a double blow: the loss of its pene-enclave status plus the end of duty-free trade (these two were obviously interconnected and – at least in the eyes of the officialdom – one very much depended upon the other). But I was also sure that, being Swiss and with thick smugglers' blood in their veins, Samnauners would find another way of surviving and would keep on annoying the neighbours by their everlasting prosperity.

*   *   *

4. Austmany (Austria and Germany)

JUNGHOLZ

A One-Haus Village

It is with relief that I am starting this new chapter on yet another part of Enclavia – Austmany, an imaginary "province" incorporating two Austrian semi-enclaves inside Germany – the village of Jungholz and Kleinwalsertal Valley. Why? One reason is that I won't have to spell Ischgl any longer! Well, just once more perhaps (see the following sentence).

I had no regrets leaving Ischgl.

My driver to Jungholz was an Austrian called Arnie. A strong-minded and no-nonsense character, he reminded me of his famous namesake and compatriot.

"Samnaun?" he chuckled, on hearing about my mountaineering adventure. "I don't like the people there: they are slow, arrogant and too serious." To me, it sounded as if Arnie was describing himself, for he was definitely in possession, if not of all three above-mentioned qualities, then definitely of the last two – and in abundance. "I don't like Swiss," he carried on. "They think they are the best."

When not driving his taxi, Arnie worked as a ski instructor. If formerly most Tyrolean men had been part-time smugglers, these days they all doubled as ski instructors. Arnie's "students", as he called them, were mostly Germans, whom he did not like either, although occasionally he had some "new Russians", whom he liked even less. "They are all Mafia. Very rich," he declared from behind the wheel. I had to admit that this last characterisation was not that far from reality.

A reformed smoker, Arnie had an annoying habit of picking up lollies from the glove compartment and sucking them noisily as he drove, without offering any to me (not that I particularly wanted them).

Eureka! My "Porta" cigarette roller was waiting for me at the newspaper kiosk at Landeck station (we had to make a little detour to liberate it). Who said it was the Germans that were the most honest people in the world? I now knew it was the Austrians! I was so grateful to the man at the kiosk that, without thinking, I bought a copy of the previous day's *Independent*, which cost me a small fortune (€3.25), just to do something nice for him. From the look on his face, I could see he was impressed.

We drove towards the German border through corridors of snow-covered pines. Arnie pointed out Germany's highest mountain peak – Zugspitz (we were still in Austria, by the way) and next to it one of the highest Austrian summits: an Alpine Anschluss of sorts. And in between the peaks, a lonely high-altitude McDonalds was nestling in the snow. Just like its twin brother in the Melbourne suburb of Templestowe (or anywhere else in the world), it had an open air playground outside – an amazing uniformity of design. The presence of this unlikely fast food joint in the heart of the Tyrolean Alps made the mountains look Americanised and strangely "domesticated".

We were getting further and further away from the high mountains: both Jungholz and Kleinwalsertal were located in fairly low-altitude valleys. I suddenly thought I was going to miss the glistening Alpine peaks, which were slowly receding from us and soon disappeared from view.

A couple of hours into the journey, Arnie started fidgeting nervously in his seat and throwing furtive looks at road signs.

"I am going to have coffee at the next restaurant," he declared, and added unnecessarily and somewhat Terminator-like: "I drink coffee!"

We stopped at a small roadside inn, with an old-fashioned wooden cupboard built into the bar. A small group of men, sporting *lederhosen*, braces and snow boots, were perched on high stools around it.

The white-aproned waitress brought us coffees and two miniature biscuits in wrappers featuring Euro conversion tables on one side and Euro banknotes on the other. Mine had a hundred-Euro note printed on it, Arnie's a fifty-Euro one. From the sour look on his face, I deduced that he would have rather have had this Euro-propaganda order reversed. To restore justice, I offered him a cigarette, which he grabbed eagerly, despite being a "reformed smoker". He lit it up and inhaled deeply, turning into a reformed non-smoker in front of my eyes. I realised that, on top of all his other unenviable character traits, Arnie was rather tight and greedy.

The blizzard caught up with us near Vils, *eine kleine stadt mit grossen geschifte*. Soon, a modest *Deutschland* road sign flashed past behind the car window. We had temporarily left Tyrol and entered Bavaria.

We had also entered the EU's largest, most populous and economically advanced country, separated from Austria by two semi-rotten stumps of former border posts. The houses immediately grew bigger, their roofs steep and red-tiled, and the roads grew cleaner. I ticked off such unmistakable German sights as blue-and-white Bavarian flags near petrol stations; Salamander supermarkets; posters of forthcoming German elections featuring a certain "Dr. Marcus Schiek"; and pink Deutsche Telecom cabins.

In Fronten, the first German town on our way, I spotted a huge life-size mannequin of a white-hatted chef, sitting on the steps of a restaurant. This is what Germany is all about – size, cleanliness, comfort: even the mannequins are supposed to be sitting!

The number of cars on the road had grown considerably – as had their average speed. This was another German trait that I had always admired: dynamism.

From time to time we overtook buses, packed with ragged-looking German skiers returning home after the boozy skiing weekend. It was getting dark.

"Jungholz – 3km" ran the sign near the village called Gschwend – a name that made Ischgl seem easy to spell in comparison. A couple of minutes later, we crossed the (Austrian) border of the Jungholz semi-enclave and were thus officially back in the Austrian province of Tyrol. Unlike Samnaun, with its (blasted) newly-discovered Swiss-bound road, Jungholz was fully surrounded by Germany and was only connected to Austria at one point – the one thousand, six hundred and forty-metre-high Sorgschrofen mountain peak. As far as I knew, there were neither mountain paths nor hiking trails across Sorgschrofen. There were no chair lifts either. It was only well-trained mountain climbers who could actually reach it from Austria (I didn't think I would be able to crawl across the peak on my stomach) – a fact that made Jungholz an exemplary and undisputed pene-enclave.

The village itself was so tiny that we missed it at first, and drove past it. A man walking his dog gave us directions to my hotel, Vital Sporthaus (this was what it was called, I swear! And the area surrounding Jungholz was officially known as "Vitales Land"!). The hotel's name simultaneously evoked two feelings in me: 1. Guilt for having given up "sport" and exercise; 2. Fear that it would resemble the Sporthauss Bruurs hotel in Baarle. I hasten to say that the latter apprehension proved wrong.

Countless chandeliers adorned the hotel's lobby, decorated in *belle époque* style. It was spacious, yet warm, heated up by enormous fireplaces. A smiling blonde receptionist offered Arnie a cup of coffee. His eyes lit up: he could not believe his luck. Having guzzled the free coffee in one quick gulp (as if afraid that the unexpected freebie would be taken away from him any moment), he asked me for another cigarette and left without thanking the receptionist or saying good-bye.

With only two nights in Jungholz, I had little time to lose. Having taken the antiquated one-door lift to my room, I dropped my bags and returned to the lobby to try and find out more about the village. I was lucky. The blonde hotel receptionist (in actual fact, she was a "shift manager"), whose name was Charlotte, proved to be an invaluable source of information.

Initially, I took her for an Aussie, for she spoke perfect English with an unmistakable Australian accent and characteristically uncertain – somewhat feline – intonations. She was actually one hundred percent German, and her accent was the result of six months of travelling down under. Charlotte was an exceptionally capable linguist, also fluent in half-a-dozen European languages ("Not bad for a sheila, d'you reckon, mate?" she laughed when I praised her unaccented "Strine"). She also represented the first ever "Australophile" (not to be confused with australopithecine) I had ever come across. Her admiration for Oz had no limits, and I didn't feel like arguing with her about Australia's multiple complexes and limitations, which had made me leave it permanently over ten years before. In fact, I was quite pleased to see a person so fascinated with one of my two adopted countries. In my heart of hearts, I have lots of warm feelings for Australia for having harboured me at a time of troubles.

I ended up in Australia largely by accident after defecting from the USSR in January 1990. At that time the Soviet Union was still there, and my natural desire was to take my family and myself as far away from the "Evil Empire" and the KGB as possible. I hadn't heard about the "tyranny of distance" then. Despite all the material wellbeing (including a totally superfluous indoor swimming pool in my Melbourne bungalow), looking back, I can see very clearly that emigrating down under was a mistake. Possibly, the biggest mistake I had ever made. The truth is that, apart from when standing in the "Other Passports" queue at a Heathrow or Gatwick immigration counter, I had never felt particularly Australian. Nor have I been often (mis)taken for one, if you don't count the occasional comments in Eastern Europe provoked by the sight of my coveted, dog-eared Australian passport: "Oh, Australia is my dream!" (a young gooey-eyed hotel receptionist in Gdansk, Poland), "Sitting pretty, buddy!" (another hotel receptionist in Kiev, Ukraine) and: "How do you live with all these creepy-crawlies?" (an immigration officer in Riga, Latvia).

Jungholz was certainly an unlikely place to bump into a German "sheila", yet here she was sitting opposite me in the Vital Hotel lobby and telling me about this peculiar Austrian village, lost in the Bavarian Alps.

With just over three hundred residents spread over an area of seven square kilometres, the village was located on a flat "sundeck" plateau, which accounted for the relatively warm and sunny climate all year round. It began as a small German farmstead, sold to a Tyrolean (Austrian) owner in 1342. When the first borders between Austria and Germany were drafted in 1463, the village was given to Tyrol, at which point the ongoing duality of the place began. The Germans (Bavarians) kept trying to reclaim Jungholz (peacefully) until 1773, when the frontiers were finally agreed upon. After the Napoleonic wars, the whole of Austrian Tyrol was incorporated into Bavaria, apart from Jungholz, which was forgotten and omitted from all annexation protocols. Similar to the principality of Monaco, Jungholz owed its status to a historical boo-boo.

Unable to correct the mistake, the Bavarian authorities chose to make Jungholz a tax-free haven, which it remains, if only to a certain extent: all German food in the village is tax-free, but alcohol isn't.

During World War I, the men of Jungholz fought in the Austrian army, yet during World War II they had to enlist in the Vehrmacht, for the village had been temporarily re-attached to Germany to become part of its Sorgschrofen district in 1938–45.

In the 1950s, the village received two different phone codes – German and Austrian. Nowadays, one could dial Jungholz from Austria using the 056 Austrian area code, whereas calls from the neighbouring German villages and towns required dialling the 083

German one. Every phone number in Jungholz could be accessed by either country's local area code, which, for some obscure reason, did not mean that the villagers could dial both countries at local rates: whereas calling Austria from Jungholz was a local call (this started in 1957, when a phone cable was stretched across the mountain – until then the village could only connect to its mother country via Germany), calls to Germany were charged at international rates. Before the Euro, the village's few public telephones simultaneously accepted Austrian phone cards and/or German coins.

Postal services were regulated in a slightly less illogical way: from both Austria and Germany one could send a letter at national rates, using either of the village's two post codes – "D-87491 Jungholz (Oberallgau)" from Germany, and "A-6691 Jungholz (Tyrol)" from Austria, yet letters from all other countries were supposed to use only the German code.

This Austrian village, whose residents voted in Austrian elections, received its water and electricity from Germany and was privy to the superb German National Health System. The villagers were the world's only non-Germans entitled to use the German Health Insurance Scheme. It was baffling to learn that Jungholz was part of the German Trade Area, yet somehow outside the German Economic Area, and its Austrian residents were allowed to shop tax-free in Germany, yet not in Austria (outside Jungholz). To get employment in the village, foreigners, including Germans like Charlotte, were supposed to obtain Austrian work-permits in the nearest Austrian town of Reuter which housed, among other things, a tiny police station, responsible for maintaining law and order in Jungholz. It took weapons-carrying Austrian *gendarmes* about thirty minutes to reach the village via Germany – a procedure regulated by a special bilateral agreement. The same agreement stipulated that, in cases of emergency, German *polizei* were allowed to operate in Jungholz, too.

The village's only primary school offered its pupils an Austrian curriculum, taught in *Allemansch* – "High German" – by two German teachers. Most Jungholz children continued their education in German secondary schools, which were nearer and, unlike the area's Austrian schools, provided school buses.

Apart from skiing and tourism, the village's main industry and employer was banking. Jungholz was home to three big branches of Austria's main banks, operating with two SWIFT codes – Austrian and German. This meant that money could be transferred to and from Germany with no fees and taxes – like domestic transactions. On the other hand, they were regulated by extremely strict Austrian banking laws, barring German auditors from accessing the records – an ideal scenario for money-laundering.

"The banks employ some locals, but mostly Germans, who live here, pay local taxes and have lunches at our hotel," said Charlotte.

It was increasingly bizarre to listen to her knowledgeable account of Jungholz's controversies, delivered not in "High German" but in "Low Australian" – unaccented "Strine".

"We are the living model of unified Europe, yet they don't want to know about us either in Vienna or in Berlin," she sighed, echoing the familiar mantra I had heard in all the enclaves I had visited so far.

The Vital Sporthaus Hotel had the biggest restaurant I had ever eaten in. It took me ten minutes to return to my table after visiting the bathroom. The only English-speaking patron, I had problems reading the German (possibly even the "High German") menu, and Christian, an outgoing barman with a pony-tailed goatee beard, kindly volunteered to translate it for me.

"It is something coming from pig's backside," he mumbled, pointing with one hand at an obscure Gothic-script entry starting with "*Schwein* . . ." and touching his own "backside" with the other. I had noticed that most German speakers (both in Germany and in Austria) tended to misuse the word "backside", thinking it described anything that was behind them. A hotel receptionist in Leipzig, whom I once asked for directions to the railway station, politely advised me to go through her backside (she meant the hotel's back door, of course) and then turn left. Walking there, I had noted with satisfaction that her ample backside stretched for a good couple of miles.

Whatever it was that had come "from pig's backside", I decided to stay away from it and opted for some German beef, swimming in sticky horseradish sauce, half of which ended up on my sweater – to the amusement of an elderly German couple at a neighbouring table. They kept smirking at me and shaking their heads in disapproval. Their own table was a shining example of neatness, with no traces of food on it. I wouldn't have been surprised to learn that they came to the restaurant not to eat, but primarily to tut-tut at uncouth foreigners' lack of manners.

For all I knew, they could have been Austrian, too: I had read in a paper several days before that in Vienna they were seriously considering obliging the city's police horses to wear nappies – a move opposed by animal rights activists, who said that nappies would make the horses sore between their legs.

"To hell with you!" I said silently to the smirking German/Austrian couple, wrapping a napkin around my neck.

It was MY hotel, after all! To prove the point (mostly to myself), I ordered a glass of "Vitality" house wine. Sipping "Vitality" at the Vital Sporthaus Hotel in Vitales Land was bound to make Vitali Vitaliev brim with *vita* (life). I wish . . .

"You can sit at my bar and make your notes," Christian, the barman, suggested as I was ordering coffee. Remembering his obsession with "backsides", I chose to stay at my table, where Charlotte – the implausible German fair dinkum Aussie, who had finished her evening shift – joined me. We talked a bit about "Tassie" (Tasmania), which she liked almost as much as I did; about "sheilas", "Abos", "tinnies" and "tucker". A Capricorn, like me, she was probably pre-destined for some cultural dichotomy. Soon I had to excuse myself and retire to my room: the blasted horseradish sauce was causing me stomach cramps.

Next morning, I trudged up the hill to the village's *gemeinderhaus* (municipal building) – through heavy snowfall, sleet and melting slush. As I was approaching the oblong two-storey building, a diminutive Vietnamese lady emerged from a car and made a dash for it. The first living being I saw in Jungholz outside Vital Hotel, she was cradling a baby in her hands. Both were heavily wrapped in scarves and thick sweaters. I soon found out that *gemeinderhaus* was, among other things, home to the village nursery.

Apart from the nursery, this capacious multi-purpose building housed the mayor's office, the primary school, the kindergarten, the fire brigade, the library, the post office and the tourism bureau, to which I was heading. All Jungholz officialdom seemed to have been gathered together under one roof. Theoretically speaking, the whole life cycle of a Jungholz resident was represented in *gemeinderhaus* – starting with the nursery and kindergarten and going up to the tourism bureau for the village retirees wanting to see the world. Only the final link in this in-house chain of life was missing – an undertaker. Although, for all I knew, there could have been a small funeral parlour hidden somewhere in the basement.

Jungholz's *gemeinderhaus* reminded me of Whittier in Alaska – by far the most peculiar town I had ever visited.

This "city" (as it insisted) on the shores of Prince William Sound was the world's only one-house municipality. As part of an attempt to minimise the clearing away of snow, of which Whittier had plenty in winter, the decision was taken to house all three hundred and thirty-four of the town's residents in the fourteen-storied Begich Tower – until recently, Alaska's tallest building. Well, to be precise, only three hundred and thirty-three people resided in the skyscraper: one maverick chose to escape the high-rise hustle and bustle by settling down in an abandoned bus, terminally parked in the harbour.

The Tower, built by the US military during World War II, had all necessary conveniences: shops, restaurants, a laundromat, a post office, a museum (down the hall from the post-office), a beauty salon, and even a church. There used to be a small jail there too, but it had closed down for lack of offenders. The "city government", headed by Carrie Williams, the outgoing and chain-smoking "City Manager", occupied one floor. The Tower also accommodated two rival newspapers – the mild-mannered *Whittier Sentinel* and the censorious *Turnagain Times*, but had only one public "restroom".

Of course, when inside the Jungholz *Haus* (let's call it that), I first wandered into a kindergarten, then the fire station, before ending up at the tourism bureau, also doubling as the village library, which in turn doubled as the bureau's conference room. The only other room in the office was the bureau itself. It was there that the bureau's head – a blonde, bespectacled and insultingly young man called Christian Liechtenberg, greeted me.

"Last time I spoke English was two years ago," he smiled, extending his hand. I liked him immediately.

I asked Christian about Vitales Land, and he explained that the term was used to describe an area incorporating parts of Allgau province of Germany and of Austrian Tyrol, including Jungholz. So Vitales Land had a mixed identity – not to the extent of Vitali Vitaliev, yet still fairly uncertain. I should have felt more or less at home in Vitales Land, but, for some reason, I didn't.

Christian was busy. He asked me to hang around and make myself at home. With the heavy snowfall outside, I didn't feel like venturing out of the *Haus* – and I could do most of my research without leaving it.

I crossed the corridor to the tiny village post-office, proudly calling itself "Postampt", only to discover that the man behind the counter didn't speak a word of English and was therefore unsuitable for an interview. The Mayor's office and the fire brigade HQ were locked; the school was in the middle of a lesson. I tried one unmarked door, only to find myself inside an electric cables closet, which I hastily exited.

Wanting to have a look at the library, I retraced my steps to the tourism bureau. The library consisted of six shelves of books in the bureau's side room. Out of a couple of hundred volumes, only one was in English. Its title struck me as somewhat mysterious – *The Bird of Self-Knowledge: Folk Art and Current Artists' Positions*. No wonder: the book had been printed in Innsbruck. To deepen the mystery, it was sealed in cellophane, so that it could not be opened and browsed through. With a sigh, I put the volume back on the shelf. I was not destined to find out what the "current artists' positions" were like.

Having nothing else to do, I stared out of the window. A modest obelisk, diplomatically inscribed *"Deutsche Soldaten"* (it was probably erected after World War II, when the men of Jungholz were drafted into the *Vehrmacht*), was half-covered with snow. The obelisk was surrounded by several abstract wooden sculptures. I knew that Jungholz hosted an international woodcarving competition every summer.

Christian was still busy. I took several German books off the shelves and was amazed to see that many of them had English titles: *Tiger Eyes, Good-bye, Archie* – and so on. The books themselves were in German, except for the titles!

I remembered wandering into a large German bookshop in the centre of Stuttgart a couple of years before and thinking at first it was an English bookshop, for half of the section names – "Best Sellers", "Thrillers", "Science Fiction", "Cook Books" etc. – were in English. They only sold books written and printed in German (although many had English titles, especially in the "Cook Books" section), and I wondered whether the language of Goethe had no words for "Cook Books" and "Best Sellers".

Travelling in Europe, particularly inside the EU, one gets used to the ubiquitous "Snack Bar", "Car Park," "Fast Food", etc. signs – be it in Italy, Spain, Germany or France, where I once saw a "Sandwicherie" bistro. Listening to a situational lesson of German on *Deutsche Welle* radio station, in which a German birthday party was re-enacted, I was stunned to discover that "Happy Birthday!" in German was actually . . . "Happy Birthday!"

In the bulging newspaper folder I was carrying with me, there was an advertising supplement from a regional German rag, flashing with "Hot!", "Best Buy", "Special Offer", "Hi-Fi Receiver", "Digital Camcorder", "Toaster", "Notebooks" and dozens of other "plug" words and phrases in English (or rather, American English). In actual fact, the few German words they had in that German supplement to the German newspaper were all in small print and looked like poor relatives and (literally) pale shadows of all those eye-catching five-inch-tall red-and-black "Best Buys".

What's going on? Have the nations of Western Europe – with the possible exception of the Faroe Islands, where the use of foreign borrowings and foreign names is strictly regulated by special language-protecting legislation – all but given up on their indigenous mother tongues? The answer can be found in one particular European capital – Brussels.

The reality is that, alongside the Euro-currency, Euro-President, Euro-Court, Euro-Army and Euro-Police Force, the European super-state needs a common super-tongue, and the Euro-bureaucrats probably decided that English, with its flexibility and – to my mind – relative simplicity, would suit this purpose better than German, French or Flemish.

Unlike the introduction of the Euro, this clandestine policy has never been proclaimed publicly, but Brussels' obstinate refusal to support minority European languages (e.g. Livignasc, Scots Gaelic, etc.) and its tireless pushing of English, which – despite the much-publicised "equality" of all member countries' national tongues – has effectively become the main (and often the only) language of all major EU gatherings, speak for themselves. Different languages mean different cultures, read nationalistic feelings and aspirations. One common tongue means homogenisation and centralised control from Brussels.

This isn't just my opinion. Some time ago Maria Campogrande, the Italian Representative in the EC, wrote to Romano Prodi, then the Commission President, to protest against what she described as the "stifling and constant evangelism of English". In the same year, when the EC decreed that France must allow the sale of products with labels in English, thus overruling the existing French legislation, the so-called *Loi Tourbon* that forbade it, Dominique Noguez, a French author, wrote in *Le Monde*: "What will be imposed on us next? Will it be clothes – a unisex, uncoloured uniform, labelled in English? Will the French have to use English for teaching in all their schools?" His rhetorical questions might have sounded grossly hyperbolical, had it not been for the fact that, according to two recent French surveys, parents in the EU countries are increasingly choosing similar names for their offspring. The Euro-bureaucrats' dream is coming true . . .

Don't get me wrong: for as long as I can remember, I have been a proponent, an enthusiast and an avid learner of the English language, which makes it even more painful for me to see how this great tongue is being used by the EU autocracy in their strive for European domination. "Learn a new language – get a new soul," they say in the Czech Republic. By imposing one common language on different European nations, the EC is undermining the very spirit of Europe.

Christian finally finished whatever he was busy with and said he was ready to help me communicate with the people inside the *Haus*.

From my conversation with the postmaster in a tiny cubicle of the village Postampt across the corridor, I grasped that, although the double postcoded post office was truly "Austmanian" – half-German, half-Austrian (with no visible border cutting through it), it was only selling Austrian stamps: being technically on Austrian territory, it was not allowed to have a German seal. BE[8], the stamps, priced – naturally – in Austrian schillings, could also be paid for in deutschemarks and pfennigs, just as all government transactions in Jungholz had to be done in schillings first, and then converted into marks. For this particular village therefore the Euro was a blessing.

The postmaster went on to say that a letter to Germany could be sent from Jungholz as a local missive, which was obviously cheaper. The same did not necessarily stand for a parcel, which sometimes cost less if sent to Germany via Austria.

By the time we had finished talking, the bell sounded from the primary school premises at the end of the corridor. We opened the door to the "staff room" and met the whole of the school's teaching force of two (one part-time, one full-time).

"Frena Corinna," – the young lady introduced herself in the Austrian fashion: putting her last name first. That was strange, for

---

8. *Before the Euro: an abbreviation, coined – or shall I say "Euro-cented"? – by me.*

she was actually German. The only explanation was that we were in Austria, after all.

The male half of the staff, also German, avoided this controversy by introducing himself simply as Gerhard (I was left to guess whether it was his first name or last: both are common in Germany).

The teachers told me that their school had fifteen pupils ranging from first to fourth class. They all studied in one and the same large room.

"It is like a family – the older kids help the smaller ones," explained Gerhard, who taught Maths, German, Sports, Natural Sciences, Music and Art – what a polymath! Frena's, sorry Corinna's, subjects were English, plus Sports and Maths for years one and two.

"Here in Germany [sic], we teach the so-called "integrated English" in accordance with a special German curriculum, whereas all other subjects are taught to the Austrian one," Gerhard was saying.

I coughed to remind him politely that we were actually in Austria, not Germany. As a teacher, he was supposed to know at least which country his school was in (I didn't voice this thought of course).

"This is an amazing community," continued his female colleague (I feel safer referring to her like this). "The kids are easy to teach, and the parents are very supportive which is unusual for an Austrian village."

It was not very nice of her to say so – being a German, I thought.

I asked whether the children saw themselves as German or Austrian.

"Their dialect makes them sound more German than Austrian," replied Gerhard (I wondered whether this was a bit of wishful thinking on his part), and he added, as if to redeem himself: "Otherwise, they are just normal kids: they fight and they can be naughty, too."

This was not exactly the answer I wanted to hear, so I asked the teachers for permission to conduct a little survey of their pupils.

We all entered the studying room, buzzing with all the habitual noises "normal" school kids make during break time. The racket immediately died down. Thirteen pairs of curious, intelligent and mischievous eyes (the other two pupils were off sick) stared at me expectantly.

I asked those who thought they were Austrian to raise their hands. Ten hands went up willingly (the children seemed to be enjoying this unexpected "nationality game"). I then invited the kids who considered themselves German to do the same. Two more lifted their hands. One bespectacled girl, her young face showing signs of internal struggle, did not take part in the voting. When questioned by Gerhard, she mumbled something in German.

"She says she is unsure," he translated.

The most interesting result of that mini-experiment of mine was that the vast majority of the kids thought they were definitely Austrian. With forty-nine percent of Jungholz's population being Austrian and fifty-one percent German, I – as a "rootless cosmopolitan" (*pace* Comrade Stalin) – had expected many more of them to be "unsure" – like the honest bespectacled girl.

"*In Bayern Gehen Die Uhren Andeis*" – "In Bavaria, everything goes backwards" was inscribed across the face of a big "souvenir" clock inside the Hotel Alpenhof restaurant, where I had lunch with Christian, Gerhard and Corinna (aka Frena). The clock's face looked normal from a distance, yet, on closer examination, I discovered that, instead of digits from 1 to 12, it only had one – "4", repeated twelve times. 4pm was when most German offices would close down for the day, after an early start of 7–7:30am. Also, both hands of that peculiar clock moved anti-clockwise (as if it mattered) to substantiate the proverb, which initially (as you might have guessed already) was translated to me by my German hosts as "In Bavaria, everything goes to the backside".

The most curious thing, however, was that we were NOT in Bavaria, but in Austrian Tyrol. One proof of that was steaming on our plates in the form of "Tyrolean potato soup", served by another – living – proof of the same point: a buxom blonde waitress in a Tyrolean dress. Yet everyone at our table (including Christian, but excluding myself) was German.

"There are places in Europe where the EU has been practised for many years but Euro-bureaucrats refuse to acknowledge it," Christian, a recent graduate of the faculty of business and tourism of the University of Ravensbruck, was saying, echoing the words of Charlotte, the German "sheila" from my hotel, and of so many other residents of Enclavia. "Here in Jungholz, people had to learn to live peacefully with their neighbours. One thing to remember was to carry your passport at all times. We still do it, although the border doesn't exist any more. Out of habit, ha ha . . ."

"True, it is easy to remove border posts, but getting rid of mental barriers is much harder," Gerhard added philosophically. "We now have common European currency, but no common European mentality. A cross-border way of thinking, which we practise in Jungholz, is probably the first step towards it."

I could not agree with him more.

After lunch, we all returned to the *Haus*: Frena (alias Corinna) and Gerhard went back to their pupils, while Christian and I headed upstairs to the Mayor's office.

"Here we have no red tape," Christian commented facetiously as we negotiated two flights of steps. "Most outgoing correspondence simply has to be taken across the corridor or upstairs, and you can get a reply on the spot. An ideal community."

He had a dry, self-deprecating and, if I may say so, rather un-German sense of irony.

Bernhard Eggel (or vice versa), the Mayor of Jungholz and a member of the Tyrol *Landtag*, was a middle-aged Hemingway look-alike, with short grey-ish hair and designer stubble on his face. He was dressed in a traditional embroidered Tyrolean (or was it Bavarian?) shirt. Two other casually dressed men sat in his office looking impatient. The Mayor explained that they were to go to a wedding, and he only had ten minutes to talk to me.

A native of Jungholz and an electrician by profession, the Mayor had been elected by the village residents. His post was part-time, and the only remuneration he received for it was a small compensation package to reimburse him for the time that could otherwise be spent repairing wires and fixing fuses.

"The Mayor's office here is like a service point for the community. It provides ID cards, issues building permissions and so on," the Mayor told me, looking at his watch. The two men in the corner did the same – simultaneously

It turned out that the Mayor also doubled (or rather "trebled") as the village's only resident police officer, entitled to carry out citizen arrests and to detain offenders (inside the *Haus*, no doubt) until "proper" policemen (*gendarmes*) arrived from Austria.

He assured me that, despite the fact that only forty-nine percent of Jungholz residents were Austrian and that economically the village was all but German, it was a clearly Austrian community. "We have to fight two formidable bureaucracies – the EU and the Austrian one, plus some off-shoots of the German, although in Vienna they prefer to ignore our existence to avoid complications."

He then added, as I had expected, that in Jungholz they had "had the EU long before Maastricht".

Above his desk, next to a crucifix, I saw a large photo of Herr Eggel himself with a well-groomed, aristocratic-looking old man.

"This is me with Otto von Hapsburg here in Jungholz," said the Mayor. "Until recently, there was a law in Austria, according to which members of the Austrian royal family were not allowed on Austrian territory. Yet, due to the absence of border controls in Jungholz, Baron [I was right about the old guy's classy looks] Otto von Hapsburg was able to come here some time ago. It was a highly symbolic visit, for Jungholz was the only bit of Austria the Hapsburgs were able to set their feet upon."

At this point, the two waiting men all but grabbed the Mayor under his armpits and frogmarched him out of the office. I wished all three of them a good time.

On his way out, the Mayor handed me his business card – a masterpiece of practicality. In the amount of information it carried, it could only be compared to the *Haus* itself. Apart from the Mayor's own smiling photo, it featured: two (German and Austrian) postal addresses, two (German and Austrian) phone and fax numbers (as well as one mobile), the emblem of Jungholz, the banner of the OVP – the political party the Mayor belonged to –

and the current year's calendar on the back, all in full colour. I wouldn't have been surprised to find multiplication tables and a minuscule village map somewhere in the corner.

It was probably a peculiarly "Enclavian" habit – trying to fit as many things as possible into a limited space. As opposed to Americans, Australians and even Asians (including Russians), all of whom resided on vast and largely under-populated continents, Europeans inhabited a relatively small and overcrowded space – a fact that accounted for their instinctive strive for *compactness* in everyday life. I put it down in my notebook as another likely sign of "European-ness".

In the downstairs corridor the school kids, dressed in tracksuits, were merrily carrying stacks of tourist brochures from the van, parked outside the *Haus*, to the tourism office.

"It is their physical education lesson," explained Christian, who was overseeing the unloading from inside the building. "They exercise and help the community – at the same time. When they finish, we take them all for a free ice cream at Alpenhof restaurant."

"How ingenious and pragmatic," thought I.

The kids were clearly enjoying their brochure-carrying lesson. "*Schneller, Stefan, Schneller!*" they were shouting. Free ice cream, it seemed, was a powerful stimulant to inspired labour. To say nothing of good physical exercise . . .

The working day inside the all-in-one *Haus* was coming to an end. Christian said he would like to have dinner with me at my hotel that evening and would bring his girlfriend too. He had to drive home to a neighbouring German village, where they had just bought a house.

It was already dusk when I left the *Haus*, and the snow was still falling relentlessly. Not a single soul was trudging the streets, and most of the windows were dark. Have they all gone to Germany, I wondered, before overhearing the muffled whining sounds of an accordion from one of the seemingly lifeless cottages. The monotonous um-pah-pah melody was like a painless toothache. It was probably the villagers' favourite pastime outside moneymaking hours: to lock themselves up inside their houses and to play the accordion in the dark.

At the edge of the village, three "high-rise" offices (three to four stories each) of three different banks stood next to each other, like incongruous village guards. Unlike the residential cottages, all their windows were brightly lit up. For the guys inside, moneymaking (money-laundering?) hours were obviously going on. I lingered in front of the modernistic Reisebank building and took a photo. Immediately, a black-suited clerk appeared in a second floor window. He was eyeing me – a solitary snow-covered figure with a camera and a shoulder bag – with suspicion. I didn't blame him: I have always looked suspicious to bankers.

One thing I was finding hard to cope with during this journey was the sheer miserliness of some Germanic (German, Austrian, Swiss) hotels. My (German) Vital Sporthaus hotel in (Austrian) Jungholz had four stars, yet only one flimsy, pocket-handkerchief-size towel in my bathroom, which they didn't bother to change. The one match-box-sized (and seemingly irreplaceable) soap-bar was so thin that it was almost transparent on the night of my arrival. Twenty-four hours later, it could easily have been taken for a tiny piece of slippery mica: I had to put on my reading glasses to locate it on the rack. A plastic container above the bath that should have contained shampoo-cum-bath gel emitted a semi-audible melancholic whistle – and nothing else – when I squeezed it while taking my pre-dinner shower. The Germans could well be the world's most honest people, but they were also the world's most parsimonious.

I found yet another proof of the above waiting for me on my restaurant table in the shape of the half-empty bottle of mineral water which I hadn't finished the previous evening. One might argue that it was not parsimony but mere practicality: why pour away half a bottle of nice German water when I was likely to order it again the next day? Yet I couldn't help the feeling that I was being treated like a poor relation in the house of richer cousins – tolerated, yet not particularly welcome.

Christian was running late. Unlike practicality, punctuality as a stereotypical German character trait seemed largely a thing of the past: even the German trains that used to run on the dot only several years before were now routinely ten to fifteen minutes late.

"*Guten Abend!*" – the grinning German couple who had sat at the neighbouring table the night before entered the restaurant with a sad-looking and anaemic daughter in tow. Having quickly swallowed their dinner, they dragged the daughter back to their room. It was only 8pm, and she clearly wanted to stay on, to have another drink or seven, maybe even to flirt with somebody (possibly, even with me), but they were adamant. She gave in eventually and followed them upstairs, her head down. Poor thing . . .

In the restaurant toilet, a respectable German gentleman (I had seen him coming in) was moaning and shouting: "Oh la! Oh la!" in his cubicle. I wondered what he was up (or down) to in there and whether he was on his own.

Christian finally arrived with his girlfriend, who looked annoyed. They had probably had a row on the way – hence the delay. We talked about all sorts of things (I mean Christian and I chatted, while his girlfriend stayed silent and sulked throughout the dinner – as if she had a mouthful of water, as we used to say in Russia). Unlike earlier in the day, none of us was totally relaxed, due to a substantial generation gap (or could it be the sulking girlfriend?) – as if we had to yell at each other to bridge it, but were unable to communicate properly nevertheless. Christian told me about his recent skiing holidays – with his grandparents. Skiing with one's grandparents – what could be a clearer sign of youth?

The barman with a pony-tailed beard wished me "a good flight". I was wondering where one could possibly fly to from Jungholz as the squeaky lift reluctantly took me upstairs to my room, where I was about to test my only chance of Jungholz flying – in my dreams.

Not willing to bump into the grinning German couple yet again, I forsook the hotel breakfast on my last morning in Jungholz and opted for a cup of coffee at Connie's Coffeehouse (*pace*

Anglicisation), which I had spotted the day before near the village centre. The Coffeehouse doubled as Jungholz's only general store, selling pretty much everything – from wine to ski gear. So it was probably the other way around: a store, doubling as a café. Just like in Ischgl, where every local hotel owner was also a ski instructor (and – formerly – a smuggler) and every hotel was also a ski lodge, everything doubled in Jungholz, too: shop as cafe, mayor as electrician and policeman, municipal building as school and nursery, tourism office as library, business cards as calendars, and so on. And the surrounding mountains doubled too. As more and more mountains.

My last morning in Jungholz was to be spent outside the *Haus*, looking at the village's main "industry" – the banks. Christian had told me at dinner the night before that, due to the presence of three big banks in one small village, Jungholz boasted the world's highest rate of deposited money per person and hence the world's highest concentration of capital. In plain words, it was officially the world's wealthiest spot – a fact that did not quite agree with the miserly supply of toiletries at my hotel.

Free "please pick one up" electronic Euro-converters (I did pick up three as souvenirs for my London friends: what the hell, it was the world's wealthiest place, after all!) were neatly stacked on a table at the plush reception hall of Reiffeisenbank – marble, wooden sculptures, winter gardens, original old masters, indoor fountains, etc. – and totally empty, where I had an appointment with a young executive called Wolfgang. He told me that the attraction of Jungholz for investors lay in the fact that it had all the benefits of an offshore haven and many more.

"Here we have three one hundred percent Austrian banks operating within the German financial system – the best of both worlds, so to speak. All three banks have permanent seats at the Frankfurt Stock Exchange, and our clients are mostly German."

The real allure for investors and money-launderers was that Austrian banking secrecy regulations, laid down in the country's constitution, were among the world's strictest, second only to those in Switzerland. Wolfgang showed me an English copy of his bank's

"Private Banking" portfolio – a document that I found darkly fascinating.

It began on a somewhat philosophical note: "There are moments in life when you can't compromise on confidentiality. [Like, say, when having an affair?] For instance, when it comes to your money. Our Goldfinger Numbered Account makes absolute confidentiality a reality."

I rather liked the straightforwardness of the account name – "Goldfinger", bringing about associations with James Bond, gangsters, international fraudsters, etc. Confidentiality made reality, indeed. Or vice versa: reality made complete confidentiality.

"The name and address of the account holder(s) are not entered in the computer system and thus do not appear on the account statements or invoices. Only selected management-level employees and those vested with special power of attorney have access to this data."

As I read on, the mystery kept deepening:

"We hold the copyright on the Goldfinger Numbered Account – the only one of its kind in the world. When you open your account, your electronic fingerprint [this was where "Goldfinger" came from!], stored in your account, gives you that extra margin of security."

The most amazing – and rather spooky – feature of the account was that the transactions did not have to stop even with the account holder's sudden demise (e.g. murder by a rival gang or Mafia clan, etc):

"Raiffeisenbank in Jungholz has no obligation to report the death of a foreign account holder to the probate courts. You can make your own individual arrangements right away by naming additional individuals authorised to sign. That way you can grant authorisation now for someone to sign even after your death."

The late Captain Bob, alias Robert Maxwell, would have loved this financial immortality. As for myself, the whole "Goldfinger" scenario was as relevant as a pair of skis for a camel. "Poverty makes writers' eyes sharper," said one American author. I think it was the look-alike of the Mayor of Jungholz – Ernest Hemingway.

"Why can't I see any clients?" I asked Wolfgang, when we returned to the fountain-ridden reception lounge.

"They seldom come here, as most of our transactions are done either by phone or on the Internet," he smiled and added: "Some of our clients come from Eastern Europe."

By saying that, he was obviously trying to please me. Possibly, even to reassure me that I could still make it big, if I wanted to, like some of my former compatriots. To be honest, I was not interested. I knew precisely what their East European "clients" did for a living, and that sort of "Goldfinger" lifestyle was certainly not my cup of tea. At least, I had a much better chance of dying of natural causes.

Being poor in the world's wealthiest place did not feel awkward. In fact, figuratively speaking, I was wealthier that most – having discovered Jungholz.

Packing up "Sally" in my hotel room half an hour later, I remembered that I had forgotten to ask Wolfgang how they were able to verify electronic fingerprints by phone or by the Internet.

Not that it really mattered . . .

*   *   *

KLEINWALSERTAL

A "Yummy" Little Valley

It happens sometimes that two people "click" the moment they meet, and half an hour later they feel as if they have known each other for years. Ten minutes after Rolf Koeberle, the head of Kleinwalsertal's tourist office, picked me up at the Vital Hotel in Jungholz, it was obvious we had plenty in common.

To begin with, he reminded me of my old friend Charlie Garside, the former editor of the *European* and now a successful Lake District hotelier, not so much in appearance as in mannerisms. Taciturn and somewhat withdrawn, Rolf had Charlie's warm, dark brown eyes, with a touch of melancholy in them. Like Charles (and myself) he was a heavy smoker. We were of the same age, had similar views on a number of issues and also shared a certain mildly self-destructive streak. On top of all these, Rolf had done a spell at a school of English in Folkestone when he was a teenager. He had lived in Dover Street, round the corner from my own abode, where, incidentally, I am writing these lines.

It was the shortest "transfer" I had made in Enclavia so far. Or maybe it simply felt like that because we so enjoyed each other's company.

"At my office, we answer to both Austrian and German tourism authorities. Our stand at international travel markets is at times part of Austrian, at times of German, exhibits," Rolf was saying from behind the wheel, through clouds of tobacco smoke. It was a good introduction to Kleinwalsertal, which – like Jungholz – was an Austrian pene-enclave in Germany. Unlike Jungholz, however, it was connected to Germany not at one, but at three points – all high up in the mountains and accessible only to well-trained mountaineers, and only in summer. The oblong and narrow, almost Chile-shaped, small valley (forty-five kilometres squares) had not one, but three villages: Riezlern, Hirschegg and Mittelberg.

Smoking like two human chimneys, we drove through a patch of Germany and soon crossed back into Austria, immediately recognisable by the "B" – for "Bregenz" – car number plates on the road. Multiple chair lift wires criss-crossed in the sky above our heads like the railway tracks at Clapham Junction. Skiing was one of Kleinwalsertal's main lifelines.

My hotel was in Riezlern – the valley's main village, or "capital", as Rolf put it. Called Walserstuba, it was owned by the Riezler family. Although geographically in Austria, the hotel nevertheless had a website with the address www.walserstuba.de (where "de" stood for "Deutschland" – Germany). After many days in enclaves and semi-enclaves, I wasn't particularly surprised by this relatively small incongruity.

Rolf kindly agreed to spend the rest of the day with me.

We started our exploration of the valley with a quick visit to the police station – or, as they say in Austria, *gendermerie* – next to my hotel. Of all Kleinwalsertal's eleven *gendermes*, only one was inside. Dressed in their uniform (a stylish grey pullover, with white shirt and tie underneath), he sat under the portrait of the Austrian Chancellor and typed away on his computer.

According to the *genderme* on duty, the most common crime in the valley was . . . stolen skis. The most common offender? The local tourism office – ha, ha! (he scowled at Rolf).

"What happens if you detain a German subject?"

"We call a German police helicopter to take him to Germany, and we are not even allowed to escort him there."

The young *genderme* was rather intrigued by my interest in police matters. "Are you a *polizei*?" he enquired, not realising that the very German word "*polizei*" was a term of abuse in Russia, where it implied (and still does) a war-time collaborator with the Nazis – read a traitor.

"I want to introduce you to the valley's most famous person," said Rolf as he was driving me away from the police station. He meant Luggi Leitner – an Olympic skiing champion at Innsbruck (1964), a multiple World champion, and now a local hotelier. (I remembered following Leitner's spectacular Innsbruck performance as a ten-year-old in Kharkiv – on our antediluvian KVN TV set, with a magnifying glass in front of the screen to make it look larger.)

Paradoxically, although a native of Kleinwalsertal and an Austrian, Luggi Leitner had won the Olympic gold (and all his other titles) as part of the German national team and was, among other things, the former skiing champion of Germany – not once, not twice, but sixteen times! The explanation was simple: the tiny Austrian valley lacked the appropriate world-class training facilities, and Germany, which had plenty, was just around the corner- a fact that was sufficient for the famous Austrian skier to take up German citizenship. Nevertheless, the residents of Kleinwalsertal were proud of the locally bred Olympic champion and regarded him as one of their own.

Rolf decided to drop in on Luggi Leitner at his hotel unannounced. It was not a good idea.

The former sporting legend was drunk.

With trembling hands and several days of stubble, he was drinking and chain-smoking in the empty bar of his small hotel, brimming with trophies of his past glory. With disbelief, I looked at the photo of a smiling young man in a ski suit, with a number 3 on his chest, on one of the walls. His resemblance to the present-day Luggi Leitner – a stooping and unclean old man, with an alcohol-sodden face – was limited to the same protruding cheek-bones and the similarly shaped, albeit now grossly enlarged, nose. The youthful twinkle in his eyes had faded completely and had been replaced by the blank and watery stare of an alcoholic.

He offered us a drink, which we refused – to his considerable dismay – and opted for a coffee. With the last glimmer of hope in his voice, he implored us to add grappa to our coffees (*"Zer Gut!"*). When we refused that too, he all but lost interest in us.

I tried to question him about his past, but the only thing I managed to squeeze out of him was a semi-audible mumble to the effect that "the gear is much better these days".

Another unshaven character stumbled into the bar and started a drunken squabble with Luggi. We excused ourselves and moved to an empty dining room, overhung with displays of photos, cups, diplomas and other trophies of the famous skier. Medals were blinking ruefully under the glass.

Never before had I seen a better illustration to the Roman dictum *sic transit gloria mundi*. It must have been that very *gloria mundi* that made it so hard for Luggi to face up to the dire reality of running a small hotel in the enclosed and fairly claustrophobic Valley. Having experienced similar isolation first in the Soviet Union and then in Australia, I thought I knew precisely how he felt.

Back in the car, Rolf surprised me by saying that both Luggi Leitner and himself (as well as fifty percent of the Valley's population) were neither Austrian nor German but Walser. The name Kleinwalsertal spoke for itself. "Walser people are habitually shy and introverted," explained my shy and introverted host.

I had first learned about the Walser people in Liechtenstein while researching one of my previous books. They came there from Switzerland in the thirteenth century and settled around the

177

mountain village of Triesenberg. I was amazed by how they had managed to preserve their own distinctive language, costumes, customs and dances (including the good old waltz). I also remembered a story of an old Walser woman, who single-handedly chased a unit of Swiss soldiers back across the border, when they had mistakenly crossed into Liechtenstein and tried to camp there.

The Walser people (or the Walsers), one of Europe's most ancient ethnic minorities and descendants of pre-historic nomads, came to what was now Kleinwalsertal from Bernese Oberland (Switzerland). By the end of the thirteenth century, they had spread over other Alpine valleys, where they set up numerous organic farms – the first of their kind in Europe. Soon, the Walsers established their own independent mini-sate, with its centre in Tannberg. Their sovereignty, however, was brought to an end in 1451 by the invasion of Sigmund, Count of Tyrol, which made Kleinwalsertal part of Austria. Organic farmers and cattle-breeders, the Walsers had to move higher up the mountains (they were used to high-altitude farming), but many continued to reside in the Valley, now resplendent with their peculiar brick-and-wood dwellings.

We drove back to Riezlern, the Valley's self-proclaimed "capital", to meet Werner Strohmaier – the Mayor of Kleinwalsertal. "Is he a Walser too?" I asked Rolf. "I am not sure about that," he replied, and added: "One thing I am positive about is that he is a former butcher."

From time to time, our car overtook colourful "Walserbuses" – the Valley's only form of public transport. Just like in Livigno, the buses were free – another touch of Alpine "communism".

A live rock band was playing on the snow in the square outside the Mayor's office. They played badly, but a handful of skiers, flocking around them, listened with fascination. From inside the building, however, the music, muffled by the walls, sounded bearable and even soothing.

Unlike his counterpart in Jungholz, who managed to combine carrying out his mayoral duties with those of an electrician, Werner Strohmaier, the Mayor of Kleinwalsertal, had had to (temporarily) stop selling meat and poultry. Dressed in an immaculate three-piece suit, he looked smart and not at all butcher-ish. It was only his ruddy face and the bulging muscles under his sleeves that gave away his main – physically demanding – occupation.

"We have very good contacts with our German neighbours, without whom we would have become a social enclave," he told me, and he explained that the Austrian Valley had been economically German since 1891.

"It was only after the formation of the EU that we started receiving Austrian goods," he carried on. "Prior to that, only German products were on sale. We were even unable to buy our famous Austrian rum in the Valley. These days we keep getting gas and electricity from Germany, but supply our own water."

He then surprised me by praising the EU:

"You wait, it won't be long before Britain and Denmark start screaming with envy at not joining the Euro Zone in the first place."

The reason for such pro-EU ardour was simple: it turned out that Herr Strohmaier was himself a high-ranking Euro-bureaucrat – a member of the EU General Directorate for Euregios. It was the first time I had heard about Euregios – the randomly drafted ninety-two border areas of Europe. Each of them had been turned by Brussels into a separate administrative (or rather bureaucratic) entity, with its own governing body and its own hefty budget. Naturally, they were all answerable to and controlled by the above mentioned General Directorate. I asked the Mayor what the exact purpose of Euregios was.

"Unified Europe can only be achieved through powerful regions and communities," he declared in what sounded like yet another Brussels-coined cliché, which to me reeked of Stalin's frequent lip-service to the "strong Soviet Republics" – but he failed to provide an answer to my question. From my own impressions, I knew that "strong regions" (or strong minority groups) were in reality anathema to Brussels, which wanted to control everything itself. As long as Brussels itself was "strong", nothing else mattered.

I told him I was planning to visit Brussels in the near future and asked for the name of a person in the EU headquarters, who could enlighten me about Euregios.

He mentioned a certain "Mr. Duprès", but was unable to provide me with either his contact number or an address. I promised myself to try and pin him down one day.

Before saying goodbye to the Mayor, I asked him what political party he represented. Herr Strohmaier's already ruddy face grew purple – as if I had inadvertently enquired about the state of his sex life. Fidgeting awkwardly in his chair, he muttered something about media stereotyping before blurting out that he belonged to the FPO – Jorg Heider's ultra right-wing Austrian National party. I assured him that it was better to be open about one's beliefs – no matter what they were – as long as they were genuine.

But the Mayor *was* clearly ashamed. As though he was afraid I could somehow spot a blood-stained butcher's apron concealed underneath his smart Armani suit.

"Have a nice time in my country!" he said (with an emphasis on "my"). I shivered, for without realising it, the Mayor had repeated word-for-word Count Dracula's favourite form of greeting and farewell.

The skiers outside were dancing in the snow to a bad rendition of *O-bla-di O-bla-da* – a melody of my youth.

A plump blonde receptionist was singing a Walser song into the telephone at my Walserstuba hotel. The small in-house restaurant was full, and would-be patrons were queuing up at the door. I was shown to an unclean table, with a messed-up ashtray and spots of ice cream on the cloth. "Just sit down, or else other people will come and sit down," Jodok Riezler, the hotel owner doubling as head waiter, told me peremptorily. I needed a table (preferably a clean one) for myself, for I had a meeting with Wolfgang Hilbrand – a local teacher and historian.

My dinner companion was running late, and, having nothing better to do, I studied the restaurant's book-sized menu. It was a truly extraordinary document (at least, the English language part of it was). Like any other book, it started with an Introduction:

> You can taste it – cultivating nature! We just use fresh products – so you can't find any industrially prepared food in our house.

The used products of local farmers will be prepared in harmony with nature. Result: on the one hand we have nice meadows, on the other hand we get a lot of different culinary specialities. Here's a list of our "Free Walser Farmers" [names] – our direct agricultural partners. They are cultivating the meadows and Alps of our valley with largest engagement and you can taste everything. We receive our game just from local 'Wild Walser Hunters' [names]. So we can guarantee the best quality and highest freshness of our products. Enjoy your meals and have nice days here in our valley! Your family Riezler.

Having read this lively "preface" with "largest engagement", I proceeded to the menu itself:

Fresh salades of our buffet. Eat your own composition Roasted slices of mini-pumpkins with potatoes in their jackets and sour cream
Fresh selfmade pancake in rags
Bauernschmals with selfmade cheese sausage
Roast neck with selfmade red cabbage
Escalope with sauted mushrooms and dumplings in a napkin
Mixed rice and sauce of cognak.

And so on. I felt tempted to order every single "selfmade" dish on the menu.

So engrossed was I in this charming culinary volume that I didn't notice my dinner companion had come in and sat down opposite me.

Wolfgang Hilbrand had the soft kindly face of an intellectual. He spoke with authority and passion. I first asked him to expand on Kleinwalsertal's dichotomy, which had begun in 1453 when the Valley became Austrian (since then, it had changed hands a number of times and was finally returned to Austria in 1945 after the 1938 annexation by Germany).

Like most of the enclaves and semi-enclaves that I had visited before, Kleinwalsertal had two different international phone codes, yet six (!) different postcodes – two for each of its three village post offices. Before the Euro, taxes in the Valley – slightly lower than in the rest of Austria – were calculated in Austrian shillings, yet payable in German marks. The same was true about Austrian postage stamps. The Valley's free buses were actually run by a German company, and the residents were allowed to choose between either Austrian or German health insurance schemes.

As part of the German economic area, Kleinwalsertal was patrolled by armed German customs officers, imposing quotas on certain Austrian goods to be "imported" into the Austrian Valley (prior to 1891, Austrian cows, wine, cheese, lard and spirits were allowed to be brought into the Valley duty-free). In the eighteenth century there existed a peculiar regulation, according to which any carriage driven by a resident of Kleinwalsertal was supposed to make way for a German vehicle when coming face-to-face with it on the only (and, naturally, one-lane) road connecting the Valley with the nearest German town of Oberstdorf. Even now, an Austrian subject detained by Kleinwalsertal police (*gendermerie*) theoretically had the right to ask for asylum in Germany, when (and if) driven to "mainland" Austria along the same road. That was why the Valley's *gendermes*, as I knew already, preferred to transport detainees by helicopter.

After World War II, the residents of Kleinwalsertal were reluctant to grant the Germans building permissions in the Valley, but soon the situation began to reverse. The power of German investment and superior technology was irresistible (one example was that phone lines from Kleinwalsertal to Germany were always perfect, whereas the ones to Austria were invariably faulty). In short, Germany was increasingly dominating the Valley economically and "in many other Big Brother ways", as Herr Hilbrand chose to put it.

As a form of mild anti-Big Brother protest, I asked the waitress for a non-German (and a non-Austrian, for that matter) red wine. From the sour look on her face, it was obvious she was cheesed off. There's no better way to upset a German (or an Austrian) waitress.

Over a "selfmade" main course of something in a napkin (or was it in rags?), we talked about enclaves and semi-enclaves. Of all my interlocutors in Enclavia, Herr Hilbrand proved to be the most outspoken on the subject.

"Enclaves are like mini-states in their own right, the only real difference being that their very existence is staunchly denied by Euro-bureaucrats," he said, echoing my own thoughts. "For the functionaries in Brussels, acknowledging our existence is tantamount to confessing their own irrelevance. They sit there in Brussels, Strasbourg and Luxembourg producing circulars and meaningless instructions on cross-border co-operation, which has been happening in the enclaves for ages without their intervention. The legitimate question is: who needs them?" (He meant both the bureaucrats and the instructions, I assumed).

Distinctively anti-Brussels, Herr Hilbrand, however, put part of the blame for the obscurity of the enclaves on the enclaves' residents themselves.

"The enclave mentality as such is largely to blame for the lack of awareness . . . Hush-hush . . . Let's keep it quiet as long as we live well . . . Otherwise, they will find out about us and will try to take away our prosperity . . . It is like a smaller version of the notorious British 'island psychology'."

"Believe it or not, but ninety percent of the Valley's own population are unaware of Kleinwalsertal's enclave status," he carried on after a pause. "They think they are Germans, and Chancellor Schroeder is their head of state . . . I regret such an attitude – just like I deplore the persisting German feeling of guilt which has made them capitulate in the face of American cultural imperialism."

At this point, I remembered a brochure in German, with the English title "Tourist Information", that I had seen in Rolf's office earlier. "This shows you how internationalist we are," Rolf had told me then with a cackle.

He was very pro-European, Herr Wolfgang Hilbrand. And, at the same time, ardently anti-EU.

"Brussels has spent four hundred and fifty million dollars on the Euro propaganda. It has become politically incorrect to voice one's doubts over the Euro, which automatically brands you 'anti-European' and a near-Nazi," he said bitterly.

We touched upon the subject of "European-ness" and what it involved.

"Living in an enclave or a semi-enclave makes one feel more European than anywhere else. The ancestors of modern enclave dwellers were the first true Europeans and the first proper citizens of united Europe," said Herr Hilbrand, to my enthusiastic agreement.

He told me that his first awareness of his own "European-ness" went back to his early teens, when he attended a boarding school in "mainland" Austria.

"They called me *Wirtschaftswunder* – "economic wonder" – a derogatory nickname for a German, although I was actually their fellow Austrian."

My dinner with Wolfgang Hilbrand cheered me up a great deal. It is not often that I meet a like-minded person with an equally messed-up – truly "European"? – identity. I was also reassured about the purpose of my whole enclave-hopping exercise: living in an enclave may indeed feel enormously "European", yet – whether I wanted it or not – even visiting them briefly made me feel profoundly "European", too. And no less profoundly anti-EU. Not a "Euro-sceptic", as all those trying to criticise Brussels are so easily branded these days, but an "EU-sceptic", for Europe and the EU have very little (if anything) in common.

I returned to my room in high spirits. Even a morose ad for an "Effective All-Round Cleaner – Simply the Best!", overheard on one of the German TV channels, failed to spoil my mood.

The next morning I saw my first sunshine in over a week. "Isn't the weather yummy?" Rolf asked me first thing after picking me up.

I had taught him the word "yummy" the day before, while commenting on the Italian grappa I had bought in Livigno (the two Euro bottle was still with me, nearly empty by now). I had probably failed to convey all the subtleties of the word's usage, for Rolf, having liked the sound of it, started inserting it into every English sentence he uttered. "Was your last night's meeting yummy?" "Was your evening yummy?" he kept questioning me, clearly savouring the word and rolling it in his mouth, as if it were indeed a yummy "long-playing" lollipop.

Rolf was keen to show me the valley's most famous cheese shop (we shared a passion for good cheeses – another common "European" trait of ours, on top of smoking and drinking) in the outskirts of Mittelberg, run by his Walser friend Georg Feurstein. In line with the age-old Walser tradition of organic farming, Georg's *Berskase* cheeses were made of "Alpine milk", produced by cows grazing on high-altitude meadows, resplendent with "yummy" mountain flowers and herbs.

The shop itself was but a small Walser cabin, with a cheese cellar and a cow-shed at the back.

Having put on white gowns and rubber boots, we went down to the cellar, where dozens of huge round cheeses were duly maturing on wooden shelves, with what I thought were almost inaudible sighs (or, maybe, it was the sound of our wellies shuffling against the cemented floor?).

Georg explained that for the first two months in the life of a cheese, it had to be sprayed with water and covered with salt twice a day. As the cheese grew older, the same ritual had to be repeated weekly. In summer, he would take his cows up the mountains, where cheese-making went on in specially designed Alpine cheese-huts.

We tasted the freshly-made *Berskase* and both came to the conclusion that it was "yummy".

After the cheese-shop, we visited the offices of *Der Walser* – a local weekly, written in High German interspersed with occasional Walser words. In its format and lay-out, the paper reminded me of *Penguin News*, the Falkland Islands' weekly newsletter, produced in Port Stanley and selling more copies overseas than on the Islands themselves. Likewise, *Der Walser* sent a substantial part of its one thousand seven hundred circulation to the Walser "expatriates" in different countries, including Australia and New Zealand.

"What was your last week's lead story?" I asked the editor.

"It was about a big bonfire to celebrate the end of winter," he replied.

Outside the newsletter offices, we lit up and looked around at the mountains, surrounding the valley on all sides. Suddenly, we both felt somewhat claustrophobic.

"Kleinwalsertal is yummy, but you have to leave it from time to time not to go mad," said Rolf, puffing at his Golden Virginia rollie. It was mutually agreed that we would go for lunch in Germany.

We stopped feeling claustrophobic the moment we left the Valley and crossed into *Bundesrepublik Deutschland*. It was nice to be back in a big and spacious country, whose very mentality defied claustrophobia: I knew, for example, that a German law forbade offices without windows.

On the way to Oberstdorf, the nearest German town, we stopped to have a look at what was, allegedly, the world's highest ski jump.

The facility itself was closed (Rolf told me it only came to life a couple of times a year during major competitions), and the snow around it was melting. Yet the ski-jump's car park was nearly full. Small groups of people strolled in the forest around it. From time to time, they stopped and stared up at the dead ski jump, as if it were some kind of a giant monument. A minibus, inscribed *Kleinwalsertal Gendermerie*, pulled over near us and disgorged six police officers – more than half of the Valley's whole police force of eleven. Rolf suggested that they were heading to Germany for lunch, too, and, like us, had stopped to gape at the closed ski jump on their way. I thought that, with over half of the Valley's *gendermes* in Germany, Kleinwalsertal was an easy target for lunchtime offenders. On second thoughts, however, I decided that all potential Kleinwalsertal felons were probably here too: gaping at the empty ski jump on the way to a nice German dinner.

I could understand the peculiar fascination the residents of the "sheltered" valley felt for this impressive sportive structure, built for the purpose of propelling skiers into the air – the closest sensation to flying a human being could experience, except for being on board a plane.

Yet most of the cars in the ski jump car park carried German number plates. What was it that brought the Germans here, I wondered. Could it be the curious German fascination with man-made objects (dams, pylons, pill-boxes, etc.) in the midst of wild nature, so brilliantly described by Jerome K. Jerome in *Three Men on the Bummel*?:

"Your German is not averse . . . to wild scenery, provided it be not too wild. But if he considers it too savage, he sets to work to tame it . . . In Germany nature has got to behave itself, and not set a bad example to the children. A German poet, noticing waters coming down as Southey describes, somewhat inexactly . . . would be too shocked to stop and write alliterative verse about them. He would hurry away, and at once report them to the police . . . And the local German council would provide those waters with zinc pipes and wooden troughs, and a corkscrew staircase, and show them how to come down sensibly, in the German manner. It is a tidy land, Germany."

And Oberstdorf was a "tidy" town, too. A local English-language tourism brochure, with the somewhat dubious title *Gay Goings-on, Tranquil Nooks and Crannies*, which would ideally suit London's Hampstead Heath, described it as "a top village", where "the wild, romantic character is coupled ingeniously with cultural highlights of international ranking" (probably meaning the ski jump). "Live and let die – where could there be a better place to do just that, if not here?" it concluded rhetorically.

With its sterile cobbled streets, lined with shops and *kirchen*, Oberstdorf did look semi-dead on that dull winter afternoon. We left the car in a shopping centre car park, and Rolf showed me his last one-deutschemark coin, which he kept to hire a trolley at the Oberstdorf superstore where he did his weekly shopping. The deutschemark was due to go out of circulation the day after next (it was the twenty-seventh of February), yet Rolf had reasons to believe it might take slightly longer to re-adjust all the shopping trolleys' coin-slots.

We had a heavy Bavarian dinner, washed down with lots of *Allgauer* – a light local beer, brewed in Kempen. After Kleinwalsertal, everything seemed disproportionately big in the pub: an enormous dining hall with high vaulted ceilings, tall and capacious *steins* (beer glasses) and huge portions of food.

I ordered "Pig's feet with sauerkraut" for my main course. Judging by the size of the feet, the pig must have been a boar.

A poshly dressed German couple, with dull sauerkraut faces, were sitting next to us. They didn't exchange a single word during the meal, proving an old observation of a fellow British hack that Germans were, for the most part, comfortable but not happy.

The restaurant manager, in a white apron, asked me where I was from. "From London," I said. "You must be a Cockney then!" he asserted cheerfully, mystified by my accent. It was the first time I had ever been taken for a Cockney. He made my day.

Loud (much too loud) um-pah-pah music was playing in the pub. I had noticed the annoying German tradition of eating to the accompaniment of deafening music many times before. Looking at the taciturn sauerkraut couple at the neighbouring table, I suddenly realised that loud music was a convenient alternative to conversation.

"Is this local music?" I asked Rolf. "No, it is German," he replied mysteriously. I knew we WERE in Germany, but, burdened with too many confusing enclave experiences, decided not to press the point any further.

Back in Kleinwalsertal, Rolf pointed out a number of table-dancing outlets – newcomers to the valley. "They are staffed exclusively by Russian girls," he asserted. Starting with the two antiques wheeler-dealers on the train from Brussels to Amsterdam, all the Russians I had come across during this journey seemed to be involved in some shadowy activities, of which table dancing was probably the most exposed (in more than one sense) and straightforward one.

After the wide expanses of Germany, it was somehow depressing to be back in "sheltered" Kleinwalsertal. Having dropped me at my hotel, Rolf said he would go home for a quick "snap" – the word he used for a "nap", as they had probably taught him at the English-language school in Folkestone. Having exhausted all the valley's attractions (except, perhaps, for table-dancing outlets), I decided that I could do with a quick "snap" myself.

Walserstuba's restaurant was full again that evening. I was studying the original "selfmade" menu, when the manager came up to my table and asked whether I would mind some company. I didn't. A slim young man, with an inspired round face, was seated at my table. He produced a packet of "blue" Samson tobacco (my brand!) and started making "rollies" with his bare hands – something that I always found impossible. My neighbour had no problem rolling up cigarettes with his long supple fingers – as if specially designed for that unwholesome occupation. Those were the fingers of a musician. And a musician he was.

Christoph was German. A composer and a violinist with the Osnabruck Symphony Orchestra, he was on a nostalgic journey to revisit the holiday spots of his childhood, taking advantage of a five-day window between concerts. Like Christian Lichtenberg, he used to ski in Kleinwalsertal with his grandparents – something that I had never had a chance to do, for my grandparents (as well as my parents) all died much too early.

He said he had his violin with him and practised it every morning in his hotel room, using a special "silencer" so as not to disturb the other guests. I thought that "Violin with a Silencer" would pass for a good title of a John Le Carré-type spy thriller.

"While skiing, I have to take care of my fingers," he said lifting up his bird-like hands, as if to make sure that all his precious musical fingers were still there. "If I fall, I instinctively protect my fingers first, and only then my head."

He told me about a small accident he had had the day before: a chair lift had swung into his shoulder and twisted his arm. Luckily, the fingers had remained intact.

At that point, we had to stop talking. Ulrike, the hotel owner's wife, dressed in a traditional Walser costume, with a no-less-traditional *kronele* (little crown) on her head, began singing Walser songs – and all the patrons went silent. She had a strong clear voice, and each song was rewarded with a generous round of applause. I noticed that – unlike other patrons – Christoph applauded by tapping his right palm on his left wrist, as if – with an imaginary bow in his hand – he was greeting an orchestra conductor.

189

"Serious musicians should never wear costumes," Christoph commented, when, having finished her last number, Ulrike returned to her post at the hotel's reception desk. "I noticed that when our orchestra is asked to perform in period costumes, the audience inevitably concentrates on our attire, not on the music."

I asked him who his favourite composer was.

"When I play Mozart, I always feel I should give up trying to compose myself, for Mozart had said it all. To me, playing a classical piece of music is more creative than reading a book. When you perform, you add a bit of yourself to the piece, particularly if it is the violin you are playing. When you play the violin, your whole body takes part – not just your hands. This is why I think that kids should start learning music with the violin, not the piano, which does a lot of work for you."

Having seen a number of brilliant pianists who had also "played with their whole bodies", I could have argued with Christoph over that last point.

I remembered an old music teacher from Isaac Babel's *Odessa Stories* telling his young Jewish disciple that mediocre violin-playing was unbearable, and good-quality playing hardly tolerable, hence the only way to play the violin was to do it *brilliantly*. I myself was put off learning music for good (at the tender age of seven) by my first piano teacher, who would slap me on my finger-tips with a wooden ruler the moment I pressed a wrong key. Even now, when I hear piano playing, my fingers occasionally respond with dull gnawing pain.

Christoph then told me about the German concept of *heimut*, meaning "homeland" or "motherland", only "with much more emotion". He said that for him *heimut* was Osnabruck.

I was pleased he didn't question me about my *heimut*, for I would have been at a loss as to what to say.

Instead, he introduced me to another German word and concept: *heimatverein* – compatriots, but, again, "with much more emotion". "It is like a club – a very German phenomenon," he said.

I had witnessed real *heimatverein* once – on a train from Moscow to Grozny, the capital of Chechnya, long before the recent Russian invasions. As the train was approaching Chechen "soil", all the Chechen men in the restaurant car burst into wild folk dancing. Never before or after had I witnessed such genuine exhilaration at the would-be reunion with one's long-suffering motherland. *Heimut* would have probably been the most appropriate word to describe what it meant for the Chechens. And although it is hard to find two more different nations – in every possible way – than Germans and Chechens, they were both united by the feeling of *heimut*. They were both part of the same *heimatverein* of Europe.

How about my own *heimatverein*? If I have one, it is probably called "London". London – as a state of mind, as a chameleon city, effortlessly adjusting to my changing moods: grieving and rejoicing with me – like no other place in the world; constantly opening up new horizons, offering hope and snatching it away the moment you succumb to its treacherous charms.

Karl Baedeker once called Paris "the temptress of a city". If so, London is probably the bitch of a city. An expensive and devious, yet totally irresistible, whore. A dangerous liaison for a writer . . .

"Having become a Westerner, better, a Londoner . . ." – this is a snippet from a *Financial Times* review of one of my books. I like this ostentatious and somewhat cocky praise and tend to regard it as the highest I have ever received.

The reviewer, whose name I cannot recall, was right, for "Londoner" is not just a term of residence, but rather an honorary title (like a knighthood, perhaps?), bestowed on those, who – whether they realise it or not – have won the main prize in the lottery of life; a title that is awarded for good and – like a "final and unchangeable" Soviet-style court verdict – cannot be altered or annulled.

Lots and lots of murky Thames waters have flown under the bridges since my first ever visit to London in October 1988, when – for the first time in my life – I experienced a very strong feeling of belonging. Eventually, I did settle in London and started studying it diligently – as I had studied the basics of English many years before. I was learning London by heart (a wonderfully precise idiom) – like a poem that has a beginning, but no end.

I soon discovered that Londonology – like every other science – had its own dons and professors: Charles Dickens, Walter Besant, H.V. Morton, Peter Ackroyd and "London perambulator" James Bone.

Eventually, I found in London all the elements of my missing spiritual motherland: the house where I was born (as a "Westerner, better – a Londoner") – with a red dragon on its roof and a foaming cherry tree in the front garden; my first ("Western") love; a first school (even if not mine, but my son's); devoted friends; a dream job; and wealth; and poverty; and joy; and depression . . .

I have discovered my favourite London spots:

A little cafe in a vaulted basement, with tiny windows under the ceiling through which one can only see the heads of passers-by floating above the street. Among them, I often discern the faces of long-deceased friends and loved ones.

A lush Spanish garden – complete with chestnut trees, rustling willows, acacias, shady alleys, ducks and even flamingos – on the roof (!) of a department store in Kensington. To get to it, one has to ascend to the sixth floor in an ordinary office lift. The garden looks exactly like the one I used to conjure up in my travel-hungry mind while an enforced "armchair buccaneer", encaged for over thirty-five years in the world's largest prison cell – the Soviet Union.

An abandoned and nearly always deserted little park in the very centre of London adjoining Lincoln's Inn Court, whose members, incidentally, have for centuries enjoyed the rare privilege of not having to stand up when a toast to the Queen or King is pronounced.

A much bigger park, a real forest – Highgate Wood, full of birds, bats and squirrels, the latter so neat, orderly and civilised that I wouldn't be surprised to learn that they pay taxes to the forest authorities.

A tiny Sunday market in Dulwich, where – for next to nothing – one can buy time-beaten antiquarian guidebooks, which I have been collecting for many years.

The Tyburn Convent next to Marble Arch, which one can visit only between 3 and 4pm – the only hour of the day when the twenty-one Franciscan nuns living in it are allowed to talk. "What's wrong with me? I cannot stop blabbering today ..." an old hunchbacked Sister kept muttering as she showed me around the Convent's chapel.

And Ely Place, of course, whose very name implies uncertainty and dislocation.

After visiting Ely Place, I love walking through the deserted and misty streets of the City (fuzzy, like in those postcards of my childhood!), which on weekends comes to resemble the house of a close friend from which all excessive furniture has been removed. And in the stillness of a Sunday morning, only occasionally broken by a police siren, one can almost hear from afar the muffled sound of Roman legionnaires' worn-out sandals shuffling against the cobbles.

I love crisp October mornings, when strolling through London is like walking inside a huge chilled wine glass, and fallen leaves rest on the windscreens of parked cars, like yellow parking tickets issued by the strict traffic warden of autumn.

I love London's velvety summer nights, when nightingales scream their little lungs out in Berkeley Square, and a podgy full moon mooches about in the brandy-coloured sky, like a pot-bellied drunk trudging home from the pub.

I love its stormy nights, too, for when it stops raining the young hook-like crescent breaks through the clouds and hangs precariously above Parliament Hill. I always feel tempted to hang my soaked umbrella onto it, before remembering that I have left it behind at Heathrow airport the other day ...

"What's wrong with me? I cannot stop blabbering today ..." Indeed.

I never get tired of talking about my adopted home town – London.

In my travel writing, I have always liked to personify places. I once compared Venice to an ageing, yet still graceful lady, suffering from insomnia and shuffling around the house in her loose and worn-out slippers in the night. And living down under, I visualised Australia as a freckled and angular, albeit sporty, teenager. There's little doubt that towns, cities, villages and countries – just like people –have identities of their own.

So what (or who) is London?

There is no consensus as to the great city's nature, character or even "gender". When London is depicted as human in British literary sources, it is almost always as a woman ("she"). However, London's significant parts are often represented by male figures – as in "Old Father Thames".

Interestingly, in Russian, the word "London" is masculine ("on" = "he"), and a female Russian friend told me repeatedly that for her London was definitely a *muzhchina* ("a man") – an attitude shared, surprisingly, by the renowned English travel writer H.V. Morton, who regarded London as "the most masculine city in the world".

Peter Ackroyd in his *London: The Biography* sees London as "a human body": "The byways of the city resemble thin veins and its parks are like lungs. In the mist and rain of an urban autumn, the shining stones and cobbles of the older thoroughfares look as if they are bleeding." Likewise, H.V. Morton was convinced that London had a "heart". On the other hand, the late Ian Nairn, one of the most brilliant architectural commentators of modern times, once noted authoritatively that "London as a single personality simply does not exist."

Personality or not, London has always been able to evoke purely human emotions. T.E. Lawrence had missed it (him? her?) so much, when in Arabia, that, on his return, he was ready "to eat the pavement of the Strand". And according to the confession of Charles Lamb in 1801, "The wonder of these [London] sights impels me into night walks about the crowded streets, and I often shed tears in the motley Strand from fullness of joy at so much life . . ."

I strongly believe in Sydney Smith's pronouncement that any life led out of London is a mistake – bigger or smaller, but still a mistake . . .

We finished our dinner with two fairly mediocre espressos. Just like average violin-playing, they were hardly bearable, read undrinkable. But I drank mine anyway. And so did Christoph.

It snowed heavily next morning – as it routinely did on almost every morning during my wanderings in Enclavia.

Ulrike gave me a spoon to use on the train to Schaffhausen. I put it inside "Sally", next to the fork donated by a blonde salesgirl in a Baarle supermarket.

In Russia, a spoon was a regulation house-warming present symbolising a happy and plentiful household. In my case, it was a symbol of my continuing journey. As for the fork ... God only knows what it was supposed to symbolise (the thorny path of a travel writer, perhaps?).

Whatever their meanings, a spoon from Walserstuba and a fork from Baarle were so far my journey's main (and only) trophies.

Rolf – more taciturn than usual – gave me a lift to Oberstdorf station. As we were saying goodbye, I felt sadness in my generally sanguine host. I was feeling sad, too: with all the similarities we shared, we had come to like each other.

Or, maybe, Rolf was simply reluctant to go back to his small and claustrophobic valley, surrounded by the mountains?

I shall probably never know the answer.

5. Swimany (Switzerland and Germany)

BUSINGEN

A Small Corner of Germany that is Forever Switzerland

"Do you want a German espresso or an Italian one?"

A barman at Oberstdorf station buffet was trying to be helpful, not realising that he had coined an oxymoron. "German espresso" was a pure contradiction in terms – on a par with "four-angled triangle", French sushi, Hungarian samosa, or Italian sauerkraut.

I opted for an Italian espresso, of course, but ended up with something that looked and tasted like weak Russian black tea. He had probably made me a "German espresso" by mistake.

I boarded a gleaming red *DB* train to Immenstadt and took a seat next to an unmanned "Snack Point" (they couldn't find a proper German equivalent of course), which, among other gadgets, contained a hissing coffee machine making decent "German" cappuccino.

Travelling by German trains is always a delight. Five minutes into the journey, a uniformed conductor brought me a stack of printed timetables, with platform numbers, departure times and tips as to the quickest way to change trains.

Unlike their British counterparts, German railways had certainly changed a lot in the last 100 years or so. In 1900, according to Jerome K. Jerome, to board a train in Germany one had to buy four different tickets, including a platform ticket, a *schnellzug* ticket if you wanted to travel with the speed of more than a couple of miles per hour, and a *platz* ticket if you wanted to sit (or even to stand) during the journey. These days, one InterRail Pass, acquired in Britain, was enough to take me through the whole of Europe (except, for some reason, Britain and Russia), as long as I kept writing every destination down on a special page attached to it.

At Sonthofen, a small German boy boarded the carriage with his mum. He carried a huge toy rifle – twice his size – and could have easily been mistaken for the living embodiment of the stereotypical jingoistic German, had his toy not been a life-size plastic copy of an Israeli Uzi submachine gun.

Waiting for a connecting train at Immenstadt, I decided to stock up on my reading matter. The station's newspaper kiosk displayed several dozen British and American thrillers (by Frederick Forsyth, John Grisham, etc.) – in German, yet with their original English titles on the covers. There were also several comics – all in English – and a facsimile edition of *Baedeker Deutschland* Guide-Book celebrating one hundred and seventy-five years of Baedeker. Had I known German, I would have definitely bought the latter, but because I didn't, I had to be satisfied with reading a sign above the station buffet: "*Original Italienische Pizza*". Consisting of just three words, it somehow managed to combine at least two, possibly even three, different languages: English and/or German ("original" – same spelling in both), definitely German (*Italienische*) and definitely Italian (*Pizza*) which made it one of the most striking linguistic mongrels I had ever come across. Yet, curiously, I was not put off by this sign – not half as much as I was by all those German "Snack Points". To me, it was charmingly idiosyncratic and messed up in a truly cosmopolitan European way. A three-word linguistic Baarle, so to speak.

On the platform, I spotted a drunken German youth, guzzling cheap German champagne (another European oxymoron!) from the bottle and chanting: "Happy birthday to me!" Herr Karl Baedeker would have got a shock, if he had known that even drunks chanted in English in the twenty-first century Germany – which, I was sure, was not the case one hundred and seventy-five years ago.

Then – something incredible happened. The lanky pimpled youth dropped a bottle cork onto the ground. Bullish and obstreperous as he was, he took an effort to bend down, pick the cork up and – unsteadily – carry it to the nearest rubbish bin (and although I couldn't see it, I was somehow certain that he had placed the cork in a special "corks" compartment of that bin – if there was such a thing). Can you imagine this happening in any other country but Germany?

This episode gave a new meaning to Lenin's famous description of German socialists (he hated Germans, socialists and almost everyone else) as the people who would buy platform tickets prior to storming a railway station – a quotation that could be applied to other Germans in equal measure.

The train left the province of Allgau and rattled along the shore of Lake Konstanz, from where Charlotte – the Australophile German "sheila" from Jungholz – originated. It is good to be able to tie an area to a person you know.

The lake was lined with vineyards producing what my wine-critic friend once called "immoral German wines". Whatever the morality of their final product, the vineyards looked beautiful.

I got off at Lindau to wait for my last connection to Schaffhausen. My personal timetable said I had an hour to kill, so I went for an early lunch at the station buffet – empty, except for a couple of rough-looking men with scratched faces, sitting quietly at the bar.

Eating sausages with boiled potatoes – the German answer to bangers'n'mash – I watched a green *polizei* car, with an American-style Sheriff Star on its door, circling around a deserted cobbled square behind the buffet window. It was all peace and quiet, if you didn't count the loud German pop songs blasting from the buffet's radio (loud music, as I had established already, was as essential a component of a German meal as a tin of mustard on the table). The songs were in German, yet with English refrains, one of which was:

> I lost my way,
> I can't believe in yesterday . . .
> Yeah . . . Yeah . . .

I thought these lines could be applied to the shrivelling status of the German language in modern Germany which seemed to have largely lost its way, too.

The only book in English (I mean fully in English – not just the title) at the station kiosk was *Faceless Killers* – a thriller by a certain Henning Mankell, translated from Swedish. Having run out of things to read, I reluctantly bought it. It turned out to be one of the biggest discoveries I made during my journey.

From the very first pages, I was mesmerised by Mankell's lucid and economic style and the intricacy of the plot. It was a thriller alright (and a pretty unputdownable one at that), but it was also literature. The book's main character – police inspector Kurt Wallander from the small Swedish town of Ystad (an unlikely location for a thriller) struck me as one of the most memorable heroes in modern European literature. A lonely workaholic (his wife had left him for another man), Wallander had lots of self-destructive (European?) habits: overeating, addiction to coffee, working crazy hours, not looking after himself, and so on. Constantly unsure of himself, he had disastrous relationships not just with women, but with his own father and daughter, too. The only people he was able to communicate with properly were his police colleagues – all of whom had similar-sounding names: Rydberg, Svedberg, Martinsson. Brusque and snappy on the surface, yet warm and sentimental underneath, Wallander had a brilliant analytic brain, helping him to solve even the most heinous crimes. He also had a high sense of morality, brooding a lot about the growing moral degradation (from his point of view) of Swedish society.

In short, Kurt Wallander (aka Henning Mankell) became my favourite travel companion for days to come. Mankell's easily flowing narrative never failed to have a soothing effect on me – as if I was indeed exposed to the severe, yet calming, beauty of the Swedish rural landscape, where most of the action was set. The qualities that made Wallander an archetypal European were not limited to his well-pronounced self-destructive streak and/or his love of strong coffee. They also included his innate resistance to bureaucracy and his broadmindedness in the face of other cultures and beliefs, which he always tried to understand – even if at times he failed.

"Come on, let's twist again . . ." a Walkman-wearing German girl sitting next to me was humming all the way to Schaffhausen. A man opposite was browsing through the Classifieds supplement of *Freiburger Zeitung*, advertising all sorts of "Veggie Deals", "Best Buys", "Special Offers" and other "faceless killers" of the embittered German culture as the train left Germany and rolled into Switzerland. It arrived in Schaffhausen five minutes behind schedule.

I put Mankell's book – my last Euro purchase – into my shoulder bag and pulled "Sally" along the platform to the nearest Currency Exchange Office to convert my remaining Euros into Swiss francs.

The only reason for coming to Schaffhausen, a fairly unremarkable Swiss canton centre on the banks of the Rhine, was that Busingen – Germany's only exclave – was effectively one of the town's suburbs. Like Campione, it had neither a hotel nor even a B&B. From my previous visits to Schaffhausen, I knew that most of its residents were totally unaware of having a little pocket of Germany on their doorstep.

A local tourism brochure described Schaffhausen as a "dreamy" town, although, to my mind, "sleepy" would have been a more appropriate adjective for the place. They still sold cattle in the central square on Sundays, and the town would routinely go dead after 6pm every night. With the Swiss referendum on whether to join the UN only a couple of days away, one could expect some excitement in the town's streets, but no: the well-preserved traffic-free Old Town, with its medieval fortifications, guildhalls and burgher houses, remained pretty much people-free too.

It was too late to go to Busingen: Germany (as well as Switzerland) all but closed down at 4pm. Having dropped "Sally" at Hotel Kronenhof in Kirchplatz, I decided to revisit my favourite spot in Schaffhausen – the railway station. Well, to be perfectly honest, not the station as such, but a cosy Paris-style café on Platform One.

This French-style café on the platform of a Swiss railway station was called Aperto – a nice European mix. The name suited an establishment that, indeed, seemed to be open at all times.

I sat on the café's open-plan veranda among some red-nosed Swiss old age pensioners. Nursing a drink, I looked at the passing trains, at the passengers moving to and fro – whereas I myself remained *stationary* for a change.

Stationary at a station . . . After many days on the move, it was a welcome twist, even if just for an hour or so. I felt as if the whole of Europe was passing by me – its progress both chaotic and unstoppable.

On the way back to my hotel, I popped into a supermarket to buy a couple of things for dinner.

When I approached the till, the female teller suddenly bent down, peeped into my shopping basket (uninvited!) and triumphantly ferreted out a semi-rotten tomato. Having demonstrated it to the people queuing behind me, she put up a *Geschlossen* sign above her till and went away. A couple of minutes later, she returned with a fresh tomato, which she solemnly handed over to me. All this was done without a murmur from other queuers. Charging a customer for a rotten tomato was probably a punishable offence in Switzerland.

The weighty and battered Swiss franc coins weighing down my pockets, felt solid and reliable after the gleaming, yet nearly weightless (and nearly worthless) Euros.

Checking my e-mails on the coin-operated hotel computer, I discovered that the miserly Swiss PC had a peculiar speech defect: it was printing "y", instead of "z" and "z" instead of "y". It was only when I got an e-mail reply from a London friend that I realised that I had actually wished him to have a "lovelz holidaz", as if my writing had suddenly acquired a Hungarian accent. The lisping computer meanwhile kept gobbling up coins like crazy (or rather like "crayz"), and I suddenly thought that whoever it was who called Swiss hotels "suicidal" had a point.

On BBC World that evening (the TV set in my room was – surprisingly – not coin-operated), they had the first feedback from Germany, where the Euro had just pushed out the last remaining deutschemarks. The latest survey showed that half of the Germans would have preferred keeping their old currency. As it was, consumer confidence was falling. People complained of creeping price rises and uncertainty as to how much goods actually cost. The Euro itself kept plunging against the US dollar, but "the grey men of Brussels" remained seemingly unperturbed.

I was looking forward to my next day's foray into Germany – or rather into the tiny forgotten bit of that great country lost in the outskirts of Schaffhausen.

Unlike other enclaves and semi-enclaves of Europe, Busingen – a one-street German village (population nine hundred, area 7.62 kilometres square), fully surrounded by Switzerland – was not to be found on any maps, not even on the most detailed ones, simply because in reality it was but a suburb of Schaffhausen, where Busingers would routinely do their shopping. By far the most obscure of the four remaining full-scale enclaves of Western Europe (the other three are Campione d'Italia, Baarle and Llivia), Busingen was nevertheless extremely interesting. I would call it Enclavia's second most idiosyncratic settlement after Baarle.

On a quiet (if not to say boring) Swiss morning – having dodged several permanently red pedestrian crossing lights (with no pedestrians in sight) and a crazy fat man riding a minuscule toy-size bicycle – I arrived at the Schaffhausen pier to catch a boat to Busingen. I had about forty minutes to spare and sat down for a coffee in a café next to the jetty, where I was immediately joined (or rather pounced on) by a red-faced old man – drunk out of his mind at this morning hour (it was about 10am). He was yelling something passionately in the odd Schaffhausen dialect of Swiss German, which included some French words, such as *merci* for *danke* and *bonsoir* for *guten abend*.

Fed up with the intruder, I wished him "*Bonsoir!*" and boarded the boat – only to find dozens of his look-alikes (male and female) on board. They were all Swiss, old, drunk, red-faced and noisy. Sitting on the upper deck, they kept downing their glasses of wine as if there was no tomorrow. What was it that made Swiss old-age pensioners get plastered first thing in the morning? Could it be some perverse form of revenge for their over-regulated lives, spent on money-making and endless waiting at red traffic lights? By breaking the rules they had themselves helped to establish, were they trying to bring some long-awaited "green light" of freedom into their existence?

Anyway ... the boat was chugging up the Rhine – against the current. I knew there were no German border markings separating Swiss Schaffhausen from German Busingen, either on land or on water, and kept my eyes open for any signs of the elusive border. There were none – unless one was prepared to regard a flock of white swans, sliding noiselessly in front of the boat, as well-camouflaged frontier guards.

Soon I spotted a lonely angler, fishing from the bank in breach of German law, which forbade angling from banks and piers anywhere on the Rhine. So we were still in Switzerland. Several minutes later, I saw another man, urinating blissfully into the water, and realised that we must have crossed into Germany.

I was right: we soon moored at a nameless pier which was in Busingen. I was the only person to get off the boat. An elegant middle-aged woman with a silk scarf around her neck was waiting for me. It was Ursula Barner, Busingen's Deputy Mayor, with whom I had spoken more than once over the phone.

Ursula was a delightful lady, who combined her social duties as Deputy Mayor with those of a teacher at Busingen's only primary school, where she taught, in her own words, "sports and knitting". She stood on the pier next to her car, its number plate starting with "BUS". Busingen was Germany's only village with its own "personalised" car number plates! It was also the only bit of Germany which was not part of the EU: like Campione d'Italia, the economically Swiss German village was excluded from the EU membership by a special protocol.

I shook hands with Frau Barner and looked around: the natural setting of Busingen was nothing short of stunning. The picture-postcard village stretched for over a mile along the right bank of the Rhine, lined with weeping willows and sunflower fields. The only village structure, visible from the pier, was the steep Gothic spire of St. Michael's Church on the hill towering above the trees. In her charming English, Ursula remarked that the Church had "a special room for the dead people before they go to grave".

Modern Busingen originally developed from a German settlement, founded around 500 AD, but its official designation – "Bosinga" – did not appear until 1090.

Until it became a dependency of the Austrian Hapsburgs in 1465, Busingen was ruled by the Counts of Nellenburg. In 1535, the Austrian King Ferdinand I granted the local Im Thurn family feudal tenure over the village – a grand royal thank you gesture for their services to the Crown. Since then, the Swiss canton of Schaffhausen had repeatedly tried to annex Busingen, but never quite succeeded. In April 1694, the council of Schaffhausen kidnapped and arrested the bailiff of Busingen, Eberhardt Im Thurn, and sentenced him to life imprisonment for alleged blasphemy – an incident that went down in history as the "first Busingen affair". Under the pressure of the Hapsburg emperor Leopold I, Im Thurn was released five years later, but Busingers had a long memory and when Schaffhausen undertook yet another attempt to incorporate the village into the Swiss Confederation in 1723, they adamantly came out against it. It was their revenge for the mistreatment of their leading citizen.

During the Napoleonic era, French, Austrian and Russian troops fought battles to control Busingen, which frequently changed hands. French troops were quartered in the village for a while, and the Russian Tsar Alexander plundered it in search of provisions. In the aftermath of the Pressburg Peace Treaty of 1805, Busingen became part of Wurttemberg and five years later it was incorporated into the Great Duchy of Baden, which, in its turn, was absorbed into the German Reich in 1871.

Since the end of World War I, the enclave-dwellers had been campaigning for incorporation into Switzerland – a movement that had been repeatedly suppressed by the Weimar Republic police and ignored by Hitler's government.

During World War II, Busingen was briefly occupied by the Red Army. The Soviets built a pontoon bridge across the Rhine and – in line with their ancestors – subjected the village to several days of merciless looting. In other words, they built and burnt their bridges almost simultaneously.

An interesting episode occurred shortly after the end of World War II, when the French occupation authorities discovered Busingen and wanted to take possession of it – for, although surrounded by neutral Switzerland, it legally belonged to their zone of occupation in Germany. But the Swiss, fearing a violation of their much-valued neutrality, barred access to Busingen by the French – or any other foreign troops. After the prolonged negotiations that followed, an agreement was reached whereby a squad of French soldiers was allowed to cross Swiss territory to occupy the village.

The German-appointed post-war Mayor of Busingen – a certain Herr Hugo, an engineer from Hanover – unexpectedly sided with the villagers in their pro-Swiss position. He even changed all the German village signs into Swiss ones. After two months, the maverick Mayor was recalled by the German authorities, yet he refused to leave Busingen, and lived there as an independent citizen until his death in 1959.

In the following years, Busingen residents, inspired by the 1964 example of nearby Verenahof (see next chapter), continued to agitate for annexation by Switzerland. And although the authorities of Schaffhausen openly sided with them, the ever-cautious Swiss Federal parliament staunchly refused to consider the village's disenclavement. Eventually, the villagers had to give up the idea and to limit themselves to displaying Swiss flags in the windows of their houses, which even now far outnumbered German ones.

In July 1967, an international treaty between the Federal Republic of Germany and the Swiss Confederation placed Busingen in the Swiss Customs area. From that time on, the Busingers were treated by Customs as Swiss citizens and had to pay customs duties if they exceeded the limit of goods "imported" (!) from their native Germany. This effectively meant that, whereas Busingen remained German politically and geographically, Swiss laws applied to the village's economy (farming and agriculture) and public health, including food and drug control, although its residents still had to pay German income taxes. It also meant that Switzerland, not Germany, was responsible for Busingen's economic support in the (now unlikely) case of war.

Being economically Swiss, Busingen was supposed to conduct all monetary transactions in Swiss francs, before and after the Euro. Officially, German marks and later Euros were only accepted at the post office, yet in reality most Busingen retailers would accept them, too.

The 1967 treaty also established an intergovernmental consultative body – the so-called Busingen Assembly – to help in solving the enclave's multiple problems. The Assembly had so far proved impotent and only able to regulate some minor taxation matters.

We drove along Busingen's main (and only) street, known locally as "The Broadway". In the small village square, next to the modernistic *gemeindehaus*, I spotted two differently-coloured public phone cabins next to each other: grey Swisscom's and pink Deutsche Telecom's. Ursula explained that all private telephones in the village had German numbers, which effectively meant that to call the nearest cinema or a supermarket (all less than a mile away in Schaffhausen), one had to dial the Swiss international code. The alternative was to come to the village square and to use the pink Swisscom cabin. "The only other phone with a direct Swiss connection and its own Swiss number is in the Mayor's office," she said.

Behind the phone cabins, I could discern the village post office, with two postcodes, written in large black letters above the door: D-78266 Busingen (German) and CH-8238 Busingen (Swiss). "It is very simple: when you send a letter to Busingen from Switzerland you use the Swiss code, when from Germany the German one, when from the rest of the world – either of them," Ursula explained, and added: "For me, this is all normal, but for visitors – it must be a nightmare."

Having compared the situation with that of Baarle, Campione and Jungholz, I didn't find it at all nightmarish. On the contrary, it looked relatively simple and wonderfully practical.

We soon left the village and drove through some potato and sunflower fields towards the Swiss border. Unmarked on the Schaffhausen side, it was designated on the opposite – Eastern – side of the village by one hundred and twenty-three (as Ursula informed me with truly German precision) old moss-covered border stones, installed in 1839. On some of the boulders, faded letters were still readable: "GB" for *Grossherzogtum Baden* (Grand Duchy of Baden) on the Germany-facing side, and "CS" for *Canton Schaffhausen* on the side that faced Switzerland.

Straddling the invisible border line a couple of hundred yards ahead of us was the Waldheim Restaurant. "Enjoy the Silence!" ran a banner above the entrance to its spacious beer garden, dissected by the frontier. It was rather a dubious slogan for a restaurant, which, according to Ursula, did remained silent – and empty – most of the time due to its exorbitant prices: an average main course would set you back the equivalent of twenty pounds.

In Waldheim's empty – and, yes, silent! – beer garden, over-looking the Rhine, Ursula playfully posed for a cross-border photo, with one leg in Switzerland and the other in Germany. The border was marked by a curved green line painted on the ground. If the line was telling the truth, all restaurant tables were in Switzerland, whereas the kitchen and the bar were in Germany. I wondered whether the waiters had to stick to Customs quotas while carrying food and booze from the kitchen and the bar (in Germany) to the patrons (in Switzerland). The question was purely hypothetical – just like the customers themselves. I thought that the Waldheim would have done much better had it invited its prospective patrons to enjoy not "the silence", but the restaurant's unique location – having reduced its prices first, no doubt.

Ursula reminisced about how the German Ambassador to Switzerland had come to the restaurant to sign an official protocol in the year 2000. Due to the fact that, under international legislation, an Ambassador's authority can only be exercised in the country to which he had been dispatched by his government, the German Envoy had to be careful to stay on the Swiss side of the restaurant while signing the document, with no part of his body overlapping into Germany. It was good to know that the Waldheim had once had a customer after all, even if a while ago.

"You have to drive very carefully in Switzerland, because the fines are big," Ursula said from behind the wheel of her car. We were crossing a small patch of Switzerland separating Busingen from the German border. In Busingen itself German traffic rules applied. They were imposed by two policemen from Gallingen, the nearest German village, whose rare visits to the virtually crime-free enclave – part of the German policing area – mostly coincided with home games of the Busingen football team which competed, incidentally, in the Swiss amateur soccer league.

We stopped at the border, next to two neat portakabins – one somewhat larger than the other – both decorated with a *Zoll* (Customs) sign. The bigger hut housed the German Customs office, staffed that morning by *Zollhauptsekretar* Volfgang Gunter – a dark-haired man in jeans and a leather jacket, with a gun dangling from his belt. The smaller cubicle was the Swiss Customs point, manned by *Chef de Post Veldwebel* Schwizer Niklauc, sporting a neat dark-grey uniform complete with a red beret and red lapels, but with no gun.

Standing outside their respective cubicles and watching the passing cars, the two Customs officers were direct opposites of each other. The German one was tall, brown-eyed and broad-shouldered, whereas his Swiss counterpart was short, blue-eyed and fair-haired. The German inspector was grinning, while the Swiss one looked serious and unsmiling. Their makeshift "offices" were also as different as (German) chalk and (Swiss) cheese. The German portakabin was larger. One was allowed to smoke there. An electronic typewriter stood on the desk. The Swiss cubicle was smaller, neater and strictly non-smoking, but had a PC, which – as I was assured by its occupier – the German "colleague" was not allowed to use. One common feature was that both offices closed down at 4pm every afternoon and stayed unmanned and firmly locked on Saturdays, Sundays and public holidays – which, in my view, made this whole double-checkpoint exercise totally absurd.

"What are you watching out for?" I asked the vigilant inspectors.

"We are looking for drugs and forbidden goods," Volfgang Gunter replied with a wry smile.

"We also impose quotas and check passports," his Swiss colleague added gravely.

"Why aren't you stopping any cars then?" I inquired.

"It's the experience that prompts us which car to stop." The German officer seemed to be struggling not to laugh out loud.

He then flagged down a passing post-bus – just for the sake of it (or rather for my sake, I guess) – and conducted a peremptory two-minute-long "inspection" of its passengers' faces, which immediately acquired a peculiar – seemingly indifferent, yet somewhat tense – expression.

While he was doing so, a red VW pulled over at the Swiss Customs post. A man carrying a large parcel climbed out and went to the Swiss cubicle, where *Veldwebel* Nicklauc scrutinised it carefully and took some banknotes from the man.

"Is that man a devious smuggler, caught red-handed?" I asked Volfgang Gunter, who had let the post-bus proceed in peace.

This time he couldn't contain his laughter: "*Nein*! Ha ha! He simply brought a pizza to my Swiss colleague!"

"How about the money that changed hands?"

"It was probably the change – ha, ha, ha!"

He then showed me a full-colour German pamphlet, with the title "News and Tips" (in English, of course) on the cover. The booklet clearly specified the quotas on the amount of German goods the Swiss (and the Busingers) were allowed to carry into Switzerland (and into German Busingen): no more than half a kilo of meat, a hundred and twenty-five grams of butter, a kilo of sausages and so on.

From what I had seen already, it was clear that "smuggling" an extra kilo of coveted German sausages into Switzerland (or Busingen) was not too much of a problem, particularly on weekends, public holidays and in the evenings. The inspectors' obvious lack of enthusiasm for exposing potential contrabandists could also be explained by the fact that all customs barriers between Germany and Switzerland were due to be removed soon.

"This is not exactly the South–North Korea border situation here," I remarked to the German inspector before we drove off.

A powerful burst of laughter sounded in response.

We continued our drive along the erratic Swiss-German border and passed by several other superfluous customs posts – all duly manned by uniformed Swiss and casually-dressed German inspectors. Swiss or German, formally dressed or not – they all looked bored out of their minds.

Busingen's only restaurant – La Gondola – was closed "for holidays", and we went for lunch to the only village pub. A German Tattslotto poster on its doors advertised the forthcoming Saturday's draw, promising "Millions of deutschemarks to be won" (the words "deutschemarks" were painted over and "Euros" written on top of them). The German lotto, with its huge payouts, was Busingen's biggest attraction in the eyes of the residents of the neighbouring Swiss cantons, who would arrive there in droves on Fridays to buy the tickets, banned from sale in Switzerland.

Most patrons in the pub were reading *Schaffhauser Nachrichter* – a Schaffhausen daily. German newspapers, for some reason, had failed to arrive that morning, and one man at the bar was engrossed in yesterday's issue of *Bild*, a vivacious German tabloid. Its front page story exposed the corrupt German Defence Minister Rudolf Scharping, who had allegedly taken fifty trips from Berlin to his girlfriend in Frankfurt by a specially commandeered military jet. In his defence, the embattled defence minister was saying that he had only taken thirty flights – not fifty. He was later sacked by Chancellor Schroeder, who himself came under fire for allegedly dying his hair – a claim he vigorously denied.

We lunched on German soup with liver dumplings, followed by crunchy Swiss *Rosti* – truly "Enclavian" fare. Halfway through the meal, we were joined at our table by Busingen's old pier master, whose brother had been living in Britain since 1944, when he ended up there as a prisoner of war.

A couple of flies were buzzing under the ceiling, and all through the meal I kept wondering whether they were Swiss or German.

Ursula was in a hurry: the pupils at Busingen's primary school were waiting for her to teach them some more "sport and knitting".

Wandering through the village on my own, I popped into a general store and bought (for Swiss francs!) two bottles of local "Businger" wine – one white and one red. The labels had the names and addresses (!) of the wine-makers, Andreas and Helen von Ow, printed on them. Instead of normal corks, they were crowned with metallic screw-on caps – not unusual for cheap German wines. (As I discovered later, they also had a bland – if not to say "immoral" – "German" taste.)

Continuing my exploration of the village, I was surprised to learn that tiny Busingen was home to an international higher-education establishment – the European Nazarene College. Run by the Nazarene Mission, with headquarters in Kansas City, Missouri, it had forty-five residential students from many European countries who majored in Biblical Languages, Church History, Philosophy, Theological Studies and so on. The College also offered a Master of Arts degree program in Mission Studies.

But why in Busingen? I addressed this question to Dr. Corlis MacGee, the College's Rector – a black-clad American lady. She was unable to give me the answer, only saying that Switzerland was a convenient country for the students.

"But this is not Switzerland," I remarked. "This is Germany." From the look on her face, it was obvious she didn't believe me. She probably thought I was either mad, or was just pulling her leg. Having excused herself, she left her little office, where we were talking, and gave me her business card. The College's address on the card was indeed "Busingen, Switzerland"! The same address was printed on all the College's promotional brochures, piled on her desk.

I thought that the students, too, were probably dead sure they lived and studied in Switzerland, whereas in fact they were in Germany – a striking case of massive delusion, better known as ignorance. Unfortunately, I could not confirm or deny my suspicion, for all the students and staff, except for the Rector that is, were away on holiday.

"*Neveroyatno*!" (Unbelievable!) I exclaimed in Russian – out of pure frustration (these days I only speak Russian when under stress, and occasionally in my dreams – as my girlfriend assures me), for how could one blame the residents of Schaffhausen for not knowing they had a German exclave on their doorstep, when some dwellers of the exclave itself had no idea of its existence?

My outburst attracted the attention of a young char-lady, sweeping the empty corridor. She then addressed me in unaccented (if somewhat unsophisticated) "countryside" Russian.

We sat down on a windowsill for a quick chat.

Lisa was a Russian German from Kazakhstan – a descendant of several million Volga Germans – exiled to the virgin lands of Central Asia by Stalin in the wake of World War II, simply for being ethnically German.[9] Brought up in a remote Kazakh village, she spoke a rough and not very literate Russian. After the Soviet Union's collapse, all Russian Germans were allowed to emigrate to Germany (or to be repatriated, as the German government preferred to put it). Unlike other migrants, they were treated as ethnically

---

9. *A similar fate befell many other USSR ethnic minorities: Chechens, Crimean Tartars, Kabardins, etc were all treated by Stalin as sympathisers and potential collaborators with Nazi Germany.*

German (which they were) and were immediately granted German citizenship and full rights.

Shortly after coming to live in Germany, Lisa had met her husband-to-be, with whom she now had three little children. A couple of years before, he had been to study in Nazarene College, and Lisa had followed him. Amazingly, she had no idea that Busingen was in Germany either. "It doesn't feel like Germany here," she muttered – her crude Russian sounds rolling out of her mouth like heavy, irregularly shaped pebbles. "People are quiet and withdrawn – typically Swiss."

I asked her how she was coping with looking after three kids, and she assured me it was not a problem, for "in Switzerland, nurseries are compulsory and free".

I thought I'd better give up trying to persuade her she was not in Switzerland. To be honest, I had started doubting it myself.

For reassurance, I went to see Gunnar Lang, the Mayor of Busingen, in his modest office inside *gemeindehaus*, which also housed the village's library, art gallery, marriage bureau and what-not – almost like the similar *Haus* in Jungholz (unlike in Jungholz, however, it did not house the post office, situated across the square, or a library-cum-tourism office, for Busingen had neither). He was sitting at his desk, speaking into one of his two telephones – I couldn't say whether it was the German or the Swiss one.

"Are we really in Germany?" I asked him.

"We certainly are," he replied, with a nice gentle smile. "We are in Germany, although it is easier for me to deal with the Swiss Canton authorities in Schaffhausen than with our own German government in Berlin, which keeps stubbornly ignoring our problems, and at times our very existence."

A quiet, soft-spoken man, Gunnar Lang was a professional accountant, an expert in international taxation. Busingen, where they had to pay German income tax and Swiss sales tax, would have been an ideal place for him to practise his trade. Yet, as a full-time appointee of German authorities, he had to limit himself to his mayoral duties.

"We have lots of legal abnormalities here," he went on. "For example, I hold a German passport which allows me to be the Mayor of this German village. Had I been a Swiss passport holder, I wouldn't have been able to do so, for Switzerland is not a member of the EU. On the other hand, if I had any other EU nationality – Italian, Swedish, Greek – I would have had the right to be appointed *Burgmeister* (Mayor), although Busingen is officially not part of the EU, yet it is a part of Germany, which is!"

I tried to imagine a Greek Mayor of Busingen.

"I had repeatedly explained to various German ambassadors in Bern what Busingen was about," the Mayor went on. "For the most part, they chose not to be bothered. You see, ambassadorship in Switzerland is thought to be the biggest sinecure of the German diplomatic service, and normally the post is taken by an elderly Foreign Ministry apparatchik, nearing retirement, as a reward for many years of good service. The last thing these people want is to get themselves into any sort of trouble."

This situation was not dissimilar to that of Soviet – and later Russian – official envoys dispatched to Canberra, the world's biggest diplomatic sinecure from their (Soviet) point of view.

"Did you notice the village's marriage hall next to my office?" the Mayor pointed to a polished wooden door in the corner. "Not too many young people are getting married here these days. Not too many of them are left in the village, to be honest, and I don't blame them: who would want to live all his life in a place with double taxation? They all try to relocate to Switzerland, with its much lower taxes and better job opportunities. There are two ways of doing this: getting a Swiss work permit, which is extremely hard, for one has to reside in Switzerland for a number of years (paradoxically, despite being economically Swiss, Busingers are treated by Swiss authorities like any other foreigners). The easier way is to get married to a Swiss subject and to get residence in Switzerland automatically. Our marriage room stays empty, while our youngsters are tying the knots in Switzerland. In short, Busingen is facing extinction in the not-so-distant future."

I asked the Mayor how (and whether) this classic catch-22 situation – a nightmare scenario for "unified", yet still thoroughly "dis-united", Europe – could be stopped.

"We are hoping that a new Swiss-EU Treaty will allow EU subjects to live and to work in Switzerland which will make it easier for Busingers, who are Germans and hence the EU subjects, although living outside the EU, to find jobs in Switzerland without leaving their village . . . But whether this happens or not, it is high time for the German and Swiss governments to sit down and resolve the issue of Busingen once and for all. To begin with, they can abolish the double taxation. Otherwise, with the intended scrapping of customs duties between Switzerland and Germany, Busingen will be in danger of becoming just another *Swiss* suburb of Schaffhausen. The village will cease to exist, and I shall be the last person to leave the sinking ship . . ."

Herr Lang was effectively talking about the possible disenclavement of Busingen – a complicated intergovernmental process, last undergone by Verenahof, a small patch of German farmland in the Schaffhausen area, given back to Switzerland in 1964. Gunnar Lang himself was a guest at the disenclavement ceremony then. But Busingen, with its nine hundred German subjects, peculiar history and sizeable area, was a different matter. In the existing geopolitical climate, it was highly unlikely that the German (or any other modern European) government would give up any bit of its territory, even if the majority of its residents so wished.

"There must be other ways of stopping the exodus from Busingen," I suggested to the Mayor. I told him about the Enclaves Assembly they were trying to create in Baarle. I suggested they might capitalise on their unique status as Germany's only exclave to raise awareness about themselves and to attract tourists. For starters, they could release several English-language brochures telling the world about Busingen and ask the German Tourism Office to distribute them around Europe and the world, for Germany at least owed them that much. They would have to open more shops and several B&Bs to accommodate the visitors, thus creating jobs for the villagers. In short, a big PR campaign was the only thing that could save Busingen. I had little doubt that, despite all its problems, the enclave could (and should) continue to exist, making a good use of the multiple loopholes in both Swiss and German legislation.

I was probably the last person to be giving advice as to how to save the whole German village, yet the Mayor made notes as I spoke, which gave me hope there was some sense in what I was saying.

I wanted to believe that eventually the inventiveness and practicality of Busingers – those specifically German qualities which had helped them survive through the ages – would keep their beautifully idiosyncratic village intact.

It was late afternoon and tractors, returning from the fields, were blocking Busingen's main (and only) street. The air smelled of manure. In a small square outside *gemeindehaus*, two young German *polizei* in green parkas were teaching local schoolboys to ride bicycles. They led the way around the square, with the fascinated little Busingers following them unsteadily on their bikes.

It looked like a good real-life metaphor for Busingen, in tow behind its Big German Brother – wobbly, unsteady and not sure where to turn.

* * *

VERENAHOF

Border Stones Turned Flower Beds

The plight of Busingen made me think of Verenahof – the only European enclave to lose its status in the second half of the twentieth century.

I knew that Verenahof – a tiny bit of Germany that used to belong to Switzerland until 1964 – was now part of the Swiss village of Buttenhardt somewhere near Schaffhausen. It would have been a shame not to visit it while being so close.

The problem was that – just like Busingen – I had failed to locate either Verenahof or Buttenhardt on any maps. My only hope of finding it was therefore in the hands of Gunnar Lang, the Mayor of Busingen, who had mentioned attending the disenclavement ceremony there in 1967 – three years after the enclave's handover to Switzerland was officially agreed upon. Herr Lang was kind enough to offer me a lift to Verenahof the day after our meeting. He also promised to try and find some local contacts for me to talk to.

As for the ex-enclave's (or, from a German perspective, ex-exclave's) history, I was lucky to have found a couple of pages on Verenahof in *The Exclave Problem of Western Europe* by my fellow rootless cosmopolitan Honore M. Catudal, Jr. – the book that I had come to call my "Enclavian Bible". (I – or rather "Sally" – carried it all through the journey.)

According to the omniscient Dr. Catudal, Verenahof – a patch of farmland, approximately eighteen acres in area, used to be part of the German commune Wiechs am Randen near Buttenhardt, about five hundred yards away from the German border. Its origins go back to the Middle Ages, when the Verena church (or nunnery, according to another source) owned this portion of uncultivated land.

Verenahof's highly unusual status was the product of the extreme irregularity (if not to say madness) of the German-Swiss border, which – unlike most "normal" frontiers – does not seem to follow the features of the landscape, but bends and zigzags at unexpected intervals. (Isn't it ironic that two most "regular" and meticulous nations in Europe should share the continent's most deviant border?) Through the ages, there were numerous futile attempts by both countries to straighten it up somehow, and it was at one such moment that the status of Verenahof inevitably became an issue.

Schaffhausen had two chances to acquire Verenahof – in 1516 and in 1522, when Count Christoph von Tengen offered to sell it at a bargain price. But on both occasions the city elders, "for reasons which are now unclear" (*pace* Dr. Catudal), refused his offers. As often happens, when they changed their minds several years later, the train had already gone, to use the jargon of Russian market traders: the von Tengen family was no longer keen on selling.

In the aftermath of the Napoleonic wars, when Talleyrand – one of Napoleon's most trusted lieutenants – pressurised the fragmented German states to merge into the Confederation of the Rhine in 1806, Verenahof fell under the jurisdiction of the Grand Duchy of Baden. With the creation of a united Germany in 1871, it became an outlying part of the German Reich, whilst being completely owned by its Swiss residents (farmers), who were required by the Swiss authorities to register as "overseas Swiss" at the Swiss consulate in Freiburg (Germany), despite the fact that the "overseas" territory in question was, in actual fact, part of the small Swiss village of Buttenhardt in the centre of the Swiss canton Schaffhausen!

Since 1854, when Verenahof was excluded from the German Customs area and up until its disenclavement in 1964, its status was not dissimilar to that of modern Busingen: its residents – three families of farmers – paid high German taxes on their Swiss franc earnings. The main difference was that, being Swiss – not German – citizens, Verenahof farmers and their family members could not vote in German elections. On the other hand, as "overseas Swiss", they were not allowed to participate in Swiss municipal elections or to be elected to local (village and/or town) councils.

Also, due to the endless red tape required for arranging a routine German police visit to Verenahof, the minuscule German exclave ended up being *de facto* administered by the village authorities of Buttenhardt. (Hard-to-obtain permissions from the Swiss authorities had to be obtained for armed "foreign" policemen to cross Swiss territory, even if only a couple of hundred yards of it: the Swiss have always been extremely touchy about foreigners with weapons on their neutral terrain.)

By November 1964, when, after eight years of painstaking negotiations, Germany and Switzerland finally signed a treaty providing for Verenahof's absorption by Switzerland (the treaty went into effect in 1967), its dwellers had come to refer to themselves as neither German nor Swiss, but as "Buttenhardters"!

As I myself later learned, for the disenclavement to come into effect, a swap had to be agreed between Germany and Switzerland, whereby the latter donated eighteen acres of its precious territory to Germany in exchange for Verenahof. After years of deliberation, an unpopulated, infertile and rock-strewn patch, directly adjoining the German border, was offered. The Germans, naturally, were not happy with such an exchange, and the difference in the quality of land had to be compensated with the sum of six hundred thousand Swiss francs, reluctantly coughed up by the Swiss government.

This little-known peaceful "annexation" signified the first and only (even if ever so slight) redrawing of Germany's border since World War II.

At the time of Dr. Catudal's visit in the early 1970s, Verenahof was "owned and inhabited by some twenty Swiss nationals" and consisted of "merely three farms and adjacent forest land".

"I keep missing the right turn," the visibly embarrassed Mayor of Busingen was mumbling from behind the wheel. "It's been a long time . . ."

By any standards, thirty-five years was long enough to forget directions to a tiny unmapped (and un-signposted) former enclave. I didn't blame Gunnar Lang for getting lost while driving me to Verenahof, where, as I have said already, he had been only once before – in 1967.

To find the ex-enclave, we had to locate Buttenhardt first. That was proving unexpectedly difficult. There were no signs (in more than one sense) of Buttenhardt in the area, where, according to Gunnar's vague recollections, the village had to be located. Having circled around all the suburbs of Schaffhausen, we kept finding ourselves in the same haunted spot we had already driven through at least twice.

At last, having despaired of applying any logic to his search (a situation of real anguish for a German), Gunnar – in the best tradition of London black cab drivers – randomly dived into some barely visible forest path – and we saw the sought-after sign for Buttenhardt, nailed to a semi-rotten wooden pole.

It was the most amazing road sign I had ever come across, with arrows to "Buttenhardt" pointing in two opposite directions!

As you will understand, the sign did little to facilitate our search for the elusive little village. To cut a long story (or rather journey) short, we did find Buttenhardt in the end – quite by accident.

It was a totally unremarkable one-shop village, which looked clinically dead on that early Friday afternoon. We stopped near the tiny and permanently shut village post office. As if to underline the smallness of the place, a minuscule yellow post motorbike (a "post-moto"?), a baby brother of the famous Swiss "post-auto", was parked at its entrance. A plastic tray for mail was secured to the motorbike's leathery back seat.

Gunnar made his apologies and drove away. The trip took much longer than he had expected, and he was now running late for a meeting. He was the Mayor, after all. And a Mayor, even if only of Busingen, was supposed to keep himself busy.

As a true German, however, he had carried out his promise of putting me in touch with the locals – a lovely elderly couple of retired schoolteachers by the name of Gertrude and Werner Brutsch. Married for thirty-eight years and well into their sixties, the Brutschs were slim, active and, judging by the affectionate looks they would furtively exchange from time to time, still very much in love. A living proof that mature age could still be fun, they were a pleasure to be with.

The only problem was that their English was not much better than my non-existent German; although whenever Gertrude uttered an English word, I couldn't help feeling she did it with a slight Scottish accent. In the end, we managed to get along by discovering that all three of us could speak some basic French.

The Brutschs, who had spent all their lives in Buttenhardt, took me on a tour of their deserted and sleepy village, with Verenahof as a starting point.

The last disenclaved bit of Europe was hiding at the end of the village's main street, behind the school which doubled as Buttenhardt's community hall. It was marked by a modest signpost in the middle of the school playground saying simply "Verenahof" and pointing at a cluster of solid freshly-painted farm houses across the playground. These were, in fact, Verenahof.

"Prior to the disenclavement, the border ran along the edge of the playground, so that the school itself was in Switzerland and the playground in Verenahof that was Germany," said Gertrude.

"It was an ideal place for committing an offence, for Swiss police were barred from accessing the playground," her husband added.

I snapped a couple of shots of the unremarkable ex-German playground and of the even less remarkable farm-houses, and Gertrude took a picture of me looking up at the "Verenahof" sign in feigned excitement.

To be absolutely fair, I *was* rather excited to have finally located this virtually unknown European curio, even if Buttenhardt felt like the most unlikely place on earth where any sort of discovery could be made.

"Is there any memorable story connected with Verenahof?" I asked my escorts.

As it turned out, there was.

In April 1945, three German soldiers, led by *Oberst* (Colonel) von Hartlein – a senior SS officer – took refuge in Verenahof and claimed they were in Germany (which they were indeed!) and hence out of reach of the French occupational forces, stationed across the German border several hundred yards away. A mini-diplomatic crisis ensued. The Swiss authorities in Berne were tipped off, and they alerted the French, who quickly realised that they had no power to extract the Germans, for to "occupy" Verenahof they had to cross the territory of neutral Switzerland. To make matters worse, the Swiss farmers of Verenahof did not mind harbouring the Germans at all and were staunchly refusing all demands from

Berne to extradite them or, at least, to stop giving them food – a request that clashed with their notion of hospitality. "We are farmers, and we will always feed our guests, no matter where they come from," they were reported as saying.

In the end, an agreement was reached between the French and the Swiss, whereby the French would allow a small contingent of Swiss policemen to enter German Verenahof (of which the French were theoretically in control, although they couldn't set foot in it) to arrest the Nazis and to frogmarch them across five hundred yards of Swiss territory to the German border, where they would be handed over to the French occupational forces. And that was precisely what happened. The locals later reminisced that the farmers were not at all pleased with the incursion. The Nazis, naturally, were pleased even less, and the well-groomed Colonel von Hertlein was, allegedly, rather pissed off by the fact that his Swiss police escort was of a lower rank than he was. Indeed, how very irregular and insubordinate!

We retraced our footsteps to the school/village-hall building along the deserted village street that once used to mark the Swiss-German border. In the schoolyard, I spotted a couple of withered flowerbeds. They were framed with moss-covered grey stones, carved with faded, yet still clearly visible letters and numbers: "S", "D", "CS", "1935" and so on. I recalled seeing similar old stones lining the Swiss-German border outside Busingen.

"These stones used to mark the border near the school and went all around the playground," confirmed Gertrude, explaining that "S" stood for *Schweiz* (Switzerland), "D" for *Deutschland* (Germany), and "CS", as I already knew – for *Canton Schaffhausen*.

"Rammed into the ground and nailed to it by special wedge-like 'witness stones', the border posts were very hard to excavate in 1967," added Weiner.

True, the old European borders were supposed to be impregnable and everlasting. Yet too many of them, as I had discovered during my travels in Enclavia, were unnecessary, superfluous and at times totally ridiculous. It was good to see at least some old border posts turned into flowerbed linings – a sight that alone made my short visit to Buttenhardt worthwhile. It gave me hope that one day all the world's borders would be scrapped and their solid and silent markers recycled and put to a more meaningful use.

Gertrude pointed to a nearby lawn, where the big tent erected for the disenclavement celebrations of 1967 once stood.

"It was a very windy day in November," she recalled. "The wind was so strong that it eventually blew the tent away, but this did not spoil the villagers' festive mood."

From my point of view, there was a lot to celebrate for both Germany and Switzerland on that day, for the 1967 Disenclavement had proved not just that European borders could be redrawn without military conflict, but also that age-old territorial disputes between countries could be resolved peacefully and to mutual satisfaction – an important lesson, taught to Europe and the world by the tiny patch of farmland called Verenahof.

It was purely coincidental that my visit to Buttenhardt fell on one of the three days during which Switzerland was facing another momentous choice: whether or not to join the UN. It was a very "comfortist" and unmistakably Swiss decision to extend the Referendum over three days (Friday, Saturday and Sunday) to make sure everybody who so wished could go to the polls at his/her own convenience. (The Swiss "comfortist" voting regulations also provide for filling in the ballots at home and then dropping them at the station, if one so wishes.) Incidentally, the previous 1986 referendum had rejected UN membership by three to one, but it had been held at a time when the Cold War was still raging, and every Swiss household was required by law to have a nuclear bomb shelter. Now, as opinion polls indicated, there were grounds to believe that the traditional Swiss "isolationism" (it was the world's only UN non-member country, except for Vatican City) was coming to an end.

The "No" campaigners, however, were still strong.

We went inside Buttenhardt's own polling station, conveniently situated in . . . the village school building, where else? A "*NEIN*" poster on one of the walls depicted Wilhelm Tell, a legendary fourteenth-century Swiss patriot and the country's defender against foreign invaders, embracing a blond (and, no doubt, Swiss) boy, as if indeed protecting him from all corruptive "foreign" influences. (Or the boy could just as well have been the Austrian governor's son on whose head, as the legend goes, Tell put an apple to be shot through with his crossbow.) On the opposite wall – in truly pluralistic fashion – there hung a "*JA*" poster, only instead of the hooded, wild-looking Wilhelm, with a crossbow on his shoulder, it carried a boring photo of some bespectacled Swiss MP.

Apart from the Brutschs and myself, the polling station was totally deserted – if you didn't count Wilhelm Tell, the boy and the boring bureaucrat on the posters.

"Are you going to cast your ballots?" I asked Gertrude and Weiner.

"We have voted already," they replied in chorus.

I didn't ask them whether they voted "*JA*" or "*NEIN*", but one thing was certain: whatever their votes were, they were definitely the same.

I picked up a clean ballot paper from an unattended stack on an equally unattended table. It was a neatly bound brochure, with twenty-four (!) pages of text, the actual removable voting paper modestly occupying pages 22 and 23. The remaining twenty-two pages were thickly covered with small print describing some mysterious rules and regulations (probably explaining how to mark your option correctly and how to fold the ballot before dropping it into an urn). I thought I could understand a certain lack of enthusiasm towards the referendum: the poor Swiss voters, with their high sense of civic duty, would no doubt feel obliged to read through every page before casting their votes. (A couple of days before I had read in a Swiss newspaper about a train driver who gave three passengers a lift back home in his car after he forgot to stop at their station. "He made a mistake and felt it his duty to amend it," a Swiss railways spokesman said.)

The Brutschs then invited me for a quick cup of tea in their house at 1 Dorfstrasse (One Village Street) – a charming rural address. Weiner showed me a souvenir Disenclavement board, with two original "witness stones" – brown (German) and green (Swiss) –

glued to it. It was revealing to see that the wedge-like stone nails, never intended to be seen above the ground, were nevertheless not only differently coloured, but also clearly marked with small letters "S" and "D" – a testimony to a shared Swiss-German obsession with old frontiers.

The couple talked about their village, which had just one shop, open for one hour a day and selling mostly milk, bread and butter. Buttenhardt didn't have a church, but had a church choir (!), of which both Gertrude and Weiner were members.

"Do you know that Buttenhardt is the highest village in canton Schaffhausen?" Gertrude asked me.

I confessed my complete ignorance about this truly distinctive feature of Buttenhardt, which brought about recollections of my travels in America, where some small Midwest towns liked to advertise themselves to passing motorists in clumsy road-sign doggerels of the type "Climate best by government test!" or by claiming to be "The Biggest Small Town in the United States". The Brutschs' "European" patriotism, however, was different: un-rhymed, quiet (almost subdued) and totally devoid of a small-town conceit, better known as inferiority complex.

Gertrude was throwing frequent glances at her watch. To me, it was unthinkable that anyone could ever be in a hurry in Buttenhardt, but she said she had to drive to Schaffhausen to baby-sit for her daughter and offered me a lift. "Post-buses are rare guests in Buttenhardt," she remarked.

The couple kissed goodbye, and for as long as it took us to drive to the end of the wind-swept Village Street, Weiner stood outside the house and waved to his wife. Well, possibly, to me, too . . .

On the way to Schaffhausen, Gertrude told me she was learning Swedish – for no particular reason, just for fun. It was a good moment to question her about her apparent Scottish accent. It turned out that I was right: a long time ago, she had spent a year learning English in Berwick-upon-Tweed – another geopolitical curio and one of my favourite places in Britain, partly due to its unending English-Scottish duality, partly because, as I had been repeatedly assured by some of my London friends, the town was still officially at war with Russia. Just as when living in London I used to go to Ely Place in search of "displacement", during my one year in Edinburgh I would often escape to Berwick-upon-Tweed – largely for the same reason. The fact of its (alleged) ongoing military confrontation with Russia – curiously – only added to its "neither-here-nor-there" appeal.

No wonder Gertrude enjoyed her time there: her truly European soul would always be willing to embrace dichotomy.

As we drove through some grim industrial outskirts of Schaffhausen, I remembered my recent visit to the displaced English-Scottish town on the banks of the Tweed. It was to Berwick that I would drive "for solace at moments of sadness and indecision", of which there had been many – far too many – during my one year in Edinburgh.

Scottish Power ran a sign on top of an electric goods store in Berwick's main street. An agreeable shop assistant explained that the English town of Berwick was getting its electricity supplies through Scotland's Electricity Board.

Berwick's electricity of ambivalence seemed limitless. The town was pasted with posters announcing a forthcoming game of Berwick Rangers, the local soccer team, which, for some reason, was part of the Scottish Football League. Books on Scotland were on sale in Local History sections of all Berwick's bookshops. Wandering past the beautifully preserved Elizabethan Walls, I spotted the still-functioning headquarters of the Scottish Borderers Legion.

The only conspicuously un-Scottish presence in town (apart from my own that is) was an old Russian cannon, a trophy from the Crimean War, on one of the ramparts – showing that Berwick was not doing too badly in its (alleged) on-going military confrontation with Russia, whose hands were probably too tied up with Chechnya to give sufficient attention to the obscure and remote Berwick Front.

Lest the locals should mistake me for an enemy scout (*à la guerre comme à la guerre!*), I retreated to the town's Public Library. And this is what I learnt there:

Berwick's dual status was a direct result of its chequered history. A thriving Scottish international port, it was plunged into decline when taken by Edward I of England in 1296 – a decline from which it has never fully recovered.

In the next two hundred years, the town changed hands at least thirteen times. After it fell for the last time to the English in 1482, it was still not regarded as a proper English town, but rather as a foreign outpost, like Calais. In a treaty of 1502, Berwick was acknowledged as a neutral or independent state of the Kingdom of England, but not within it. It was only in 1836 that the town was legally incorporated into England, but only *de jure*, for it kept being regarded as a separate entity and continued to print its own banknotes. The last formal traces of Berwick's distinct identity disappeared as recently as 1974, with the formation of the Town Council and the extension of Berwick borough boundaries deep into North Northumberland. Yet even now it still enjoyed the rare status of a royal borough, which, among other perks, allowed Berwick to have a Sheriff, to run its own Records Office and to send two representatives to the Parliament, while the Mayor of Berwick, dressed in traditional purple (!) Scottish ceremonial robes, took the coveted third place next to the Queen (after the Mayors of London and York) in royal processions and at state banquets.

The mystery of Berwick's war with Russia proved simpler than I thought. Throughout the nineteenth century (even after its official incorporation into England) Berwick used to be mentioned in treaties and Acts of Parliament as a separate part of the Queen's (or the King's) realm. As such, it was included in the declaration of hostilities at the outbreak of the Crimean War in 1854, but was forgotten and omitted from the peace treaty two years later. A similar mishap once befell the Principality of Monaco, which, due to its miniscule size, was overlooked and removed from the redrawn map of Europe in the aftermath of the Napoleonic wars. Luckily, Monaco was later remembered, whereas Berwick wasn't.

This uncalled-for reminiscence underlined the simple fact that, after weeks of travelling around Enclavia, I was missing my home country. Not Ukraine or Russia, but Britain.

I felt lonely and out of place in Schaffhausen on the last evening of my long Enclavian journey. Even a large group of embittered-looking Russian tourists, staying at my Hotel Kronenhof, failed to cheer me up. All they were prepared to talk about was what a lovely Swiss Army knife (or cuckoo clock), they had managed to *dostat* – a Sovietism meaning "to get with difficulty", which they still kept using, purely out of habit, I assumed.

There was certainly no difficulty involved in "getting" Swiss Army knives in Schaffhausen, as I made sure of during my brisk rainy walk towards the Rhine: hundreds of them were displayed in every other window of every other closed shop.

Having reached the Rhine, I stood there for a while watching a flock of stubborn Swiss (or, possibly, German) ducks trying to swim against the current and therefore not moving at all, despite working their little pink legs frantically under the water, struggling for all they were worth to get ahead and yet not progressing an inch – it was not a very inspirational scene.

As I walked back to the hotel – dodging the ubiquitous Swiss Army knife-like blades of cold rain – it occurred to me that it was not just Swiss hotels that were "suicidal". Swiss towns on a rainy autumn night could feel pretty suicidal, too.

Eager to get in touch with anyone I knew, I went to the hotel's computer room, but then remembered that the coin-operated, yet malfunctioning, PC there typed "z" instead of "y" and "y" instead of "z". Not wanting to send my friends e-mails ending "Bze!" instead of "Bye!", I returned to my room and spent the rest of the evening watching a German (or, possibly, Austrian) version of *Who Wants to be a Millionaire*, with a good-looking female version of Chris Tarrant as presenter and a jackpot of one million Euros – a clear indication that the programme was German or Austrian, but not Swiss.

I fell asleep feeling more like a "one-person human enclave" than ever before.

My last morning in Schaffhausen was unexpectedly sunny. Pushing "Sally" along the cobbles towards the station, I bumped into an official from the Schaffhausen Tourism Bureau, whom I had met briefly the day before. I was clearly adjusting to the town (a scary realisation) and therefore had to get out of there fast.

There was still an hour to go before my train to Zurich, from where I was flying back to London. It was fairly early in the morning, and I was worried that the Aperto café might have temporarily altered its name to "Chiuso", but it was already *aperto* – thank God.

Just as I had a couple of days before, I sat in the café's "conservatory" on Platform One – an enclave of quiet and cosiness amidst the helter-skelter of a busy railway station – nursing an espresso and watching the trains.

An SBB Zurich-Milan pulled up to the platform. The double-edged emblem of Swiss Railways adorned its every coach:

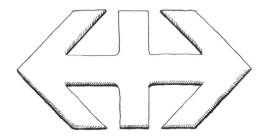

It was a timely reminder of the road sign for "Buttenhardt", with two arrows pointing in two opposite directions. Philosophically speaking, it could pass for a fairly precise representation of my peripatetic existence, fluctuating between a growing desire to settle down and the irrepressible itch to keep travelling – with one arrow pointing to my non-existent home, and the other – to an equally non-existent, illusionary "destination". It could also serve as a schematic representation of an enclave (or, in a broader sense, of the whole of modern Europe), with its life and daily routine per-manently torn apart – and yet, curiously, also kept together! – by two (or, in the case of Europe, many more) different, and often mutually exclusive, sets of rules, attitudes, customs, dialects, banknotes and lifestyles.

If I were to suggest a design for Enclavia's national flag, the "Buttenhardt" road sign would suit it well – both in shape and message. As for Enclavia's state emblem, I had already found one: the double-edged Dutch-Belgian fire-hose connector from Baarle.

Sitting there, in the Platform One café, I was also thinking that, as indicated by the uncertain road sign, I myself might have somewhat lost direction, that it was time for me to unpack "Sally" permanently and to exile "her" – deflated and empty-bellied – to the nearest "waste park".

A shiny Italian *Cisalpino* express came to a stop in front of me for a couple of minutes. It was soon replaced by a blue DB train from Baden. Then by a grey-and-red Swiss SBB one, with special coaches for cyclists. Whenever a train blocked my view from the café, the world would look impenetrable and claustrophobic. Yet, the moment it moved away, I would invariably get a much better perspective of things to come. It was like playing hide-and-seek with my own future.

A young buxom waitress approached my table and asked me to pay for my drink. She was probably worried I would jump on board a passing train without settling my bill – not an unreasonable precaution for a small station café.

I shrugged, put my last Swiss francs onto the tray and stood up to meet my train, which was just pulling into the station.

Bye-bye for now, Enclavia.

Or rather: "Bze-bze!"

* * *

6. Frain (France and Spain)

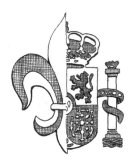

LLIVIA

A "Mini Adventure" in the Pyrenees

"*C'est pas normale . . . Très chaud . . . Je ne mange pas beaucoup quand c'est chaud . . .*" muttered the waitress, plopping down a steaming plate of *saucisses de Toulouse* in front of me.

I was having an *al fresco* lunch outside an unremarkable brasserie near *Galeries Lafayette*. It was so hot that a tiny chocolate, served with my habitual "starter" – a cup of espresso, was melting slowly on the saucer.

Why did I order *saucisses de Toulouse* and not something a bit more refreshing then, you might ask?

The answer is simple: because I WAS in Toulouse, and trying a world-famous local delicacy in its natural habitat, so to speak, has always been one of my travelling hobbies.

I had managed to taste Chicken Kiev in Kiev, where – for some obscure reason – it is called "Chicken Moscow", as well as Chicken

Moscow in Moscow, where, as you might have guessed, it is known as Chicken Kiev. I had eaten Viennese schnitzels in Vienna, Irish stews in Dublin and New York bagels in New York – as well as in "New York" (a Melbourne delicatessen). I had eaten crispy Peking Duck in Beijing and been surprised to discover that it (the Duck) had not been renamed accordingly. And, of course, I used to consume and to cook mountains of Russian salads in Russia, where, incidentally, they were never called "Russian salads", but "Salads Olivier".

Shakespeare's famous "What's in a name?" it seemed applied not just to people, but to food too: both Moscow-cooked "Chicken Kiev" and Kiev-produced "Chicken Moscow" tasted roughly the same – pretty lousy.

It is important to realise that it is not only people, countries, towns and cabs, but also dishes that have their own peculiar identity, having little to do with what they are habitually called. More often than not, that "identity" is also rather uncertain.

The French city of Toulouse on the banks of the Garonne River was in itself a good example of this eclectic mix.

To begin with, historically and architecturally it looked more Spanish Colonial than French. Indeed, during the Franco years, some local hotheads had even tried to establish a breakaway Spanish republic there. Toulouse's two most popular nicknames were the mutually exclusive "Pink City" (due to its unique architectural atmosphere of many hues of red) and "Pastel City" (pastel – the blue paint "that never fades" was the city's main produce in the Middle Ages). Less popular ones were: "The French Seattle", "The Space City" and "The Concorde City"[10], for Toulouse was also Europe's largest centre of space exploration and aircraft building.

To me, however, the Pink-Blue Toulouse was but a short stop on the way to Llivia – a small Spanish (or Catalan, to be more exact)

---

10. *The latter, I was told, was officially dropped after the notorious Concorde accident in Paris and hastily replaced with "The Airbus City".*

town, "surrounded and landlocked" by France, and one of Europe's four remaining "full-scale" enclaves.

If you look at my imaginary map of Enclavia, you will understand why the visit to Llivia had to be undertaken as a separate trip: whereas all other West European enclaves and semi-enclaves are situated roughly along the irregular (and no less imaginary) semi-circle along the borders of Austria, Switzerland, Germany, Holland, Belgium and Italy, Llivia nestles – in proud solitude – hundreds of miles away, in the Pyrenees valley of La Cerdanya. A true "outpost" of Enclavia.

Organising this trip had not been easy. It took my dear friend Oscar Hinterreger – the head of the Austrian Tourism Board's London office, who heroically and selflessly took upon himself the duties of my Enclavia Project Coordinator – many weeks to try and persuade his Spanish colleagues that, although Llivia lay in the French Pyrenees and was surrounded by the French *Département des Pyrénées Orientales*, it was actually part of Spain, and not of France, as they kept asserting. Having failed to convince them, he had little choice but to approach the French tourism authorities, who proved more cooperative. This explains why I had to travel to Llivia via Toulouse rather than via Barcelona, which was nearer.

My *saucisses de Toulouse* were a disappointment. They were charred and wrinkly, and were bashfully balancing on the very edge of a huge and otherwise empty plate (if you ignored – as I did – a tiny hillock of blue-ish, pastel-coloured, mashed potatoes). They resembled dog turds (excuse my French), swept away to the road curb by a not-too-diligent street cleaner. In both appearance and taste, they were much inferior to "Toulouse Sausages" – their London namesakes that I often used to order in my favourite little French bistro on the Grays Inn Road.

In search of a gourmet experience (I was in France, after all!), I looked around at my fellow lunchers, or rather diners, for – just as in Germany, Austria and all over Central and Eastern Europe – lunch in France was the day's main meal and was called "*le dîner*". An elderly couple next to me were unhurriedly consuming their substantial and appetising portions of ducks' hearts – a truly heart-breaking sight, especially for someone stuck with a handful of dog turds on his plate. No one was in a hurry, particularly the waiters, who were behaving like second-rate actors in slow motion. I had noticed a long time before that French lunch (sorry, dinner) was sacrosanct and any outbreak of impatience towards a waiter could only slow him down even further.

My unfortunate choice of lunch had largely marred my impressions of Toulouse. Even the numerous newly-built planes, doing their non-stop trial circles above the city, looked very much like giant Toulouse sausages on the pastel-blue dinner plate of the sky.

* * *

The slow train ride to La Tour de Carole was over five hours long. I couldn't help feeling that my battered, graffiti-covered coach – a challenge to the super-fast TGV-inspired stereotype of French railways – was puffing uphill. This impression, by the way, was absolutely correct, for it was the Pyrenees that the train was heading for.

It was late afternoon, but still very hot, and the coach had no air-conditioning or ventilation. Only when the asthmatic train dived into one of the route's countless tunnels was it briefly swept with a whiff of fresh air from the open windows.

I thought it was good I had left "Sally" at home: she wouldn't have survived the heat. After Merens le Val (altitude 1057m), snow-capped peaks came into view. For over an hour the train chugged along the Spanish border, and at one point I spotted a sign pointing to *Hospitalitet d'Andorra*. This reminded me of my previous trip to the area in 1993, when I was researching a book on the mini-states of Europe, of which Andorra was the oldest and the most peculiar one. Then, of course, I had no idea that – a mere twenty kilometres east of the tiny independent republic – lay another little known European absurdity: a small (thirteen square kilometres) Spanish exclave called Llivia.

In his 1891 *Handbook to Southern France*, Karl Baedeker – somewhat disdainfully – referred to Llivia as "a dirty village of ancient origin with some ruins remaining". It is a pity that the great guidebook writer overlooked the most interesting feature of Llivia – the oldest enclave in Europe.

Founded by the ancient Romans, Llivia had been a pawn in Franco-Spanish struggles up until 1659, when the Peace of the Pyrenees treaty gave thirty-three "villages" in the Cerdagne Plain to Louis XIV of France. The French thought that Llivia was included in the transfer, but the Spanish regarded the territory not as a village (*pueblo*), but as a town (*villa*). Having spotted the discrepancy, the patriotic residents of Llivia, who wanted to remain Spanish, claimed that the treaty had nothing to do with them, and eventually the French had to agree. Yet it was not until 1866 that France and Spain signed a treaty finalising the enclave's boundaries. The present-day enclave of Llivia is the result of a little historical cock-up.

One substantial difference from Campione d'Italia and Busingen, both of which are part of their host country's (Switzerland's) economic and financial system, is that Llivia has always been (and still remains) fully Spanish in its law, taxes, justice and economy – no matter how insignificant the latter may appear – and fiercely Catalan in its politics, language and ethnicity. Despite this, even before the EU came into existence, the French authorities did not levy taxes on French goods "imported" into Llivia – a stark contrast to Busingen.

Also, unlike in Campione, there has never been a problem with access to Llivia from France, not even for ten armed Spanish policemen – the whole of Llivia's police force – arriving for duty from the nearest sizeable Spanish (Catalan) town of Puigcerda, across the French territory. In actual fact, they travel along the so-called "neutral road" (*chemin neutre*) – one thousand six hundred metres long and eight metres wide – which, although built and maintained by the French, is popularly known as the "Spanish Road".

In exchange for Spain's promise never to fortify Llivia, the French had even permitted a small garrison of Spanish troops to quarter in the enclave – something that "neutral" Switzerland would never agree to. All these little "concessions" give enough proof of the fact that the political flexibility of the French is much greater than that of the Swiss.

The most fascinating thing I had learned about Llivia (prior to visiting it that is), came from my "Enclavian Bible", penned by Honore M. Catudal, Jr.

In the Acknowledgements section of the book, the lucky Honore M. Catudal, Jr. spares no effort to thank all those who helped him "at various stages of the research and writing": scholars, ambassadors, editors, diplomats, his wife ("who through her faith, devotion and indefatigable labour kept a difficult husband happy and her family afloat through the trials and tribulations of eight years of student life" – I wonder where people get wives like that!), his mother-in-law (who "generously sheltered my family during my escapades" – what can I say? Like mother, like daughter . . .) and his father, Honore M. Catudal, Sr. But there is one paragraph that stands out in this munificent outpouring of appreciation:

"I owe a unique debt of gratitude to the unknown British sailor who agreed to risk arrest [!] and imprisonment [!!] by Spanish and French border guards in accompanying me to Llivia without passports, which we had forgotten to pick up when leaving our hotel in Barcelona."

This sentence could not fail to elevate (or downgrade) Señor Catudal's scholastic research trip to the level of Stevenson's *Treasure Island* or a thriller by John Le Carré. It also gave the learned author a couple of essential human characteristics: a) he was forgetful; b) he was not quite a daredevil. I could easily associate myself with both: not only had I managed to forget my portable cigarette factory at the Austrian station of Landeck, but, while in Toulouse, I had chucked my hotel key-card into a rubbish bin by mistake and not dared to start rummaging in search of it in full view of a cheerful crowd.

I wonder whether these two qualities can – among others – be classified as peculiar traits of "European-ness"?

The train was approaching La Tour de Carole. Having closed Señor Catudal's book, I patted my breast pocket to make sure my brand-new British passport was still there. Not out of fear of "arrest" and/or "imprisonment", but purely out of habit, for in my previous Soviet life one was supposed to carry a passport at all times.

Due to my friend Oscar's failure to persuade the Spanish tourism authorities that Llivia was part of their domain, I had to be accommodated in France – in the mountain hamlet of Varcebollere, a couple of miles from the Spanish border and about ten miles from Llivia. To get there I had to take a taxi from La Tour de Carole.

The village was tiny, ancient and secluded: a cluster of old huts, a permanently shut stone shed, *La Mairie*, and next to it my Auberge des Ecureuils *(Squirrels' Inn)*, a solid medieval country house, built into the rock. The village made me think of a little old lady, who had strayed into the Pyrenees and dozed off forever while resting on the bank of a mountain stream.

Owned by a French-English couple, Etienne and Patricia Lafitte, "Squirrels' Inn" should really have been named "Bees' Inn", for Etienne's father was a renowned beekeeper and kept a little museum of bees and honey as well as plenty of beehives. It could also have been renamed "Bats' Inn", for the myriads of bats which kept me awake at night with their piercing baby-like squeals outside the open window of my room. Incidentally, I didn't spot a single squirrel during my stay.

Today's Llivia was much less "dirty" than it had, allegedly, been in 1891 *(pace* Herr Baedeker), and its per capita rate of recycling bins must have been one of the highest in both France and Spain. Yet, despite this seemingly un-Spanish obsession with cleanliness, the hooray-patriotism of its one thousand inhabitants remained unchanged and the town stayed fiercely – even ostentatiously – Catalan, to the extent that hearing French spoken in Llivia's cobbled streets was as unlikely as being exposed to the sounds of a techno beat in the middle of a Roman Catholic funeral liturgy.

When I tried to order a beer in a Llivia bar in French, the owner replied in broken English. And although I could well understand the underlying reasons for such unyielding nationalism, I was saddened to see that, unlike other enclaves, which managed to combine the best (and often the worst) features of both mother country and host state, Llivia was totally devoid of dichotomy.

In short, to my considerable chagrin, the town struck me as both uninteresting and lacklustre. Yes, Llivia was dead. And not just from noon to 4pm, when its narrow cobbled streets would become totally deserted, and elaborately carved wooden shutters would fall upon the windows of rustic stone cottages, as if the houses themselves had shut their eyes for a *siesta* – a Spanish tradition, not observed in the nearby French towns. (In Toulouse, some shops would also close down between noon and 4pm, but it was rather a "*siesta* by stealth", for there were no provisions for it under French legislation.) One could be forgiven for thinking that *siesta* in Llivia lasted twenty-four hours a day.

That soporific feeling could probably be partly explained by the proliferation of pharmacies, selling all sorts of herbal cures made from the Pyrenees plants and wild flowers – Llivia's main "industry". As we know, most herbal remedies are used to solve sleep problems. So could it be that the pungent smells of natural tranquillisers from the pharmacies, mingling with the faint odours of alpine flowers, not yet picked to become "remedies", kept all Llivia's residents (including the kind-eyed friendly dogs) in a constant semi-comatose sleepwalking state?

Characteristically, the town's main attraction was a pharmacy – *Farmacia de Esteva,* founded (allegedly) in 1594 and advertising itself as "Europe's oldest" (I could recall at least one other pharmacy – in Tallinn – claiming to be "Europe's oldest", too). The pharmacy-related exhibits constituted ninety percent of the stock at the local Municipal Museum and included glass jars for medicines, special furniture for cordials, medieval laboratory equipment, portraits of renowned "herb collectors" and an ancient prescription book, with almost two thousand entries. I could not quite grasp the meaning of the effigy of a mountain goat at the Museum entrance. Was it supposed to represent the healing qualities of goat milk? Or could the effigy's glassy bulging eyes be a warning against overindulging in drugs, even if natural?

Paradoxically, this multitude of chemists was Llivia's only trait that could pass for being distinctly French, for the French are known as world champion pill-poppers, consuming more prescription drugs per capita that any other nation. "The French now consume between two and four times more tranquillisers and antidepressants than the British, Italians and the Germans," according to *Le Figaro* newspaper.

Walking through the sunlit and ever-empty squares and streets of Llivia, I couldn't help drawing comparisons with the fictitious "regional centre of N." from *The Twelve Chairs* – my favourite Russian satirical novel – in which "there were so many hairdressing establishments and funeral homes . . . that the inhabitants seemed to be born merely in order to have a shave, get their hair cut, freshen up their heads with toilet water and then die." I was tempted to conclude that the inhabitants of Llivia were born "merely in order" to pop several thousand pills, aimed at prolonging their existence, and then happily kick the bucket.

Even the ads for the forthcoming annual "international" music festival in the town's main square near the Castle Hill did little to dispel the monotony. For some reason, they featured mostly East European performers and ensembles: Lithuania's State Symphony Orchestra, bands from the Czech Republic and Slovakia and the Choir of Moscow Patriarchy – all of which somehow brought Llivia an inch closer to the provincial Russian "regional centre of N.".

A huge red-and-yellow *Senyera* – Catalonia's national flag – stood in the corner of the modest office of Josep Alcalde, the chain-smoking thirty-six-year-old Mayor of Llivia. A member of the United Catalonia Party, which he himself described as "moderately nationalistic", he was also an hotelier and the president of the local ice-hockey club.

He started by telling me of a letter he had received the day before from the nearby French village a couple of miles away. The letter had taken fifteen days to arrive, for according to some bizarre EC regulations, all inter-EU mail had to go though a sorting office in Amsterdam. "I could have walked there myself in half an hour and picked it up," he shrugged. The Mayor also complained that to call the same French village from Llivia he would have to dial an international code – an irritating discrepancy that I had experienced myself when a local public phone rejected my France Telecom phone card.

These remarks by the Mayor were timely in the sense that they reminded me of Llivia's enclave status – which I had almost forgotten about by then.

I asked Senor Alcalde about Llivia's relations with its French neighbours.

"We used to have more contacts with the French some time ago, when France was much richer than Spain," he said, putting out one cigarette and immediately lighting up another. "We used to go to France to shop, to gamble and to watch porn movies . . . Now, when Spain is experiencing an unprecedented economic boom, it is the other way around: the French come here for bargains. Even French wine and French cheese are cheaper here than in France itself, and the currency is now the same – the Euro."

I wanted to say that – in my several hours in Llivia – I had failed to spot a single gambling joint, blue-movie theatre or a French person, for that matter, but I thought better of it.

Despite his distinctively Catalan attitudes, the Mayor sounded very pro-Euro and pro-EU – he was the first Enclavian official I had met who adhered to the idea of European unification. Was it because Llivia itself was so unremarkable and homogeneous?

"Our main asset is the climate," the Mayor went on. "We have the highest number of sunshine days in Europe. [Haven't I heard this before?] Our air is good for asthma and TB. Otherwise, there's nothing much here: tourism, farming and a tiny dairy factory, staffed and owned by one person."

Nothing much indeed. Not even a library, as I had discovered to my considerable surprise: it is hard to find a library-less town anywhere in Europe these days.

A native of Llivia, Josep was an economist "with unfinished education", as he himself put it. He had been elected Mayor two years before. The position was unpaid, but as the owner of the town's biggest hotel – The Llivia – he probably did not need a salary.

I asked the Mayor why no one spoke French in Llivia.

"Only less than one percent of the town's population are French citizens," he replied, inhaling deeply, with the tip of his cigarette pointing at the portrait of Jordi Pujol, the President of Catalonia, looking down at me sternly from the wall. "We are becoming more and more aware of our Catalan identity. Very few people are willing to speak French – they would rather talk to you in English. I don't even know what political parties are in power in France, and I don't care: I'd rather stay friendly with the French than play politics with them."

This "moderately nationalistic" approach could be partly explained by the sad history of the Catalan Republic, created in the early 1930s only to be crushed by Franco in the closing months of the Spanish Civil War – a takeover that was followed by thirty-six years of linguistic, cultural and political repression. And yet, to me, the multi-lingual and multi-cultural mini melting pots of Baarle, Campione and Busingen felt much more appealing – and much more "European", if you know what I mean.

The Mayor suggested I went for a meal at Llivia's "oldest and best" restaurant, Can Ventura, owned and run by his brother Jordi. It was 11am, and I had to hurry before Can Ventura – like everything else in Llivia – shut its doors for *siesta*.

Can Ventura was a gingerbread-style two-storey house, built in the late eighteenth century. The main dining hall, with a high vaulted ceiling, was dark and empty. The sleep-inducing sounds of Beethoven's *Moonlight Sonata* forced me to suppress a huge yawn.

Jordi – a look-alike of his brother – greeted me at the entrance.

"We specialise in a *mélange* of Spanish and Catalan cuisine," he explained.

"What's the difference between the two?"

"Catalan cuisine is less filling and more sophisticated than Spanish, and *tapas* are not as common."

He showed me the impressive wine list – where, significantly, only five (!) wines out of several hundred were French – and then the menu. The first item I spotted there was *saucisses de Llivia* (!), with wild mushrooms, green beans and grilled asparagus. It was plain they were not as free from French influence in Llivia as they pretended to be.

My s*aucisses de Llivia* tasted much better than the s*aucisses de Toulouse* I had tried in Toulouse, yet still not half as good as the "Toulouse sausages" from the bistro on the Grays Inn Road, London.

I was soon joined by an elderly couple from New Zealand, whom I took at first for fellow Australians. Their visit to Llivia had been spurred by an article in the *Press of Christchurch* newspaper, of which they showed me a copy. The piece, intriguingly entitled "France's Spanish Island", referred to Llivia as "one of Europe's strangest anomalies". The author had obviously never been to Baarle.

The article ended on a rather dramatic, almost Kafka-esque, note:

"I mentally start tearing my hair out. Perhaps it has all been a dream. Maybe Llivia doesn't even exist, or maybe the date is September 31. Whatever, you'll have to go and find the place for yourself."

No wonder, my fellow diners (sorry, lunchers) had not been able to resist the journalist's desperate call. Before they could start tearing their hair out, even if only "mentally", I paid my bill and went out into the blazing midday sunlight.

Llivia was in the grips of *siesta*. As I stood outside the restaurant, smoking and squinting at the sun, the burning ash of my cigarette was the only thing that moved in the whole town.

I walked past the houses, with their elaborately carved doors and shutters firmly closed. I thought I could hear muffled snoring sounds from behind them.

The town was spotlessly clean, yet the tops of the green Spanish postboxes were covered with a thin layer of dust. Or was it pollen from all the as yet unpicked alpine flowers brought here by the wind?

I stood at the window of a closed estate agent displaying a grandiose-looking model of Llivia's future: modern high-rise buildings, wide thoroughfares etc. – and hoped that those far-reaching architectural fantasies would never come to fruition. Looking away from the window at the motionless townscape, I realised with relief that there was little chance of these plans ever being carried out. (A friend of mine who visited Llivia recently assures me that it has changed a lot of late, and the "model" that I saw has become reality.)

The air was thick and muggy. It felt as if a thunderstorm was approaching.

At times, a warm stateless breeze brought a faint duty-free fragrance of wild flowers across the border from France.

I kept trudging the streets purposelessly – a lonely figure amongst sturdy buildings, shiny recycling bins and dusty post-boxes – and didn't notice how I had fallen asleep, without stopping walking.

I was sleepwalking through Llivia's centuries-long slumber . . .

I woke up with a start when I reached the ugly multi-storey concrete box of Hotel Llivia, owned by the Mayor. One look at the monstrous 1970s building was enough to galvanise my worries about the town's would-be architectural development.

There were still three hours before Josep Alcalde was due to drive me to La Tour de Carole station, from where I was to catch a train back to Toulouse (the Mayor had kindly offered me a lift after our morning conversation in the Town Hall).

I lowered myself into a battered leather armchair in the empty hotel lobby, decorated with fake "marble" columns with peeling stucco. On the table in front of me was a pile of dog-eared English paperbacks, a soiled backgammon set, a couple of old copies of *The Sun* and some printed sheets of paper. Viewed together, these objects added up to one distinct image: the British holidaymaker. Or the bored British holidaymaker, to be more exact. I remembered the Mayor saying that Hotel Llivia was used as base for a UK tour operator, specialising in holidays for the elderly.

I picked up one A4-size sheet of paper. In its right corner, there was a drawing of a puzzled, yet cheerful, elderly couple, both sporting Union Jack panama hats. They stood near a road sign and held an open map. "MINI ADVENTURE NO. 1: Valley Walk. Duration approximately 1½ hours; distance approximately 3.5 miles" ran large clear letters at the top of the sheet. It was a gripping read:

> 1. Leave the hotel and cross over the main road up to the right on Carrer de Puigcerda. Take first road on the left, Carrer bell Lloc, passing lovely holiday homes and gardens . . .

And so on. Every foot of the walk was clearly explained and signposted:

> 4. Now you are behind the ancient fortified hill of pre-Roman Llivia. Continue straight ahead and when you cross the river you are in France . . . Cross over the main road and head back to Spain and Llivia!

I was very pleased to find yet another reminder of Llivia's enclave status: even old-age pensioners here could limp between Spain and France on a routine and unhurried afternoon stroll.

> 5. Follow the winding road past the cows [!] down to the main road between Estavar and Llivia. Then turn right, cross the rickety footbridge and there you will find a bench. Enjoy the break!

True, all these border-crossings could prove rather tiring in the end.

I wish I could have a chat with one of the intrepid venerable adventurers, targeted by the anonymous tour operator. But there was no sign of them (or anyone else) around: the hikers were probably enjoying their well-deserved after-lunch sleep somewhere on a bench near the rickety footbridge by the cows . . .

My attention was then grabbed by point eight of the "MINI ADVENTURE":

> Carry straight on and then turn left to the Forum of Llivia and the football field where part of the 1992 Summer Olympics was held.

I had no idea that Llivia had been a venue for the 1992 Barcelona Olympics. Why weren't they called the "Llivia Olympics" then?

And precisely which "part" had been held here, I wondered? Could it be that some of the athletes had come here to unwind and to get a good shut-eye after losing the competition?

I addressed these questions to Josep Alcalde, the Mayor of Llivia, when he finally came to pick me up in his jeep.

"This is a slight exaggeration," he grinned from behind the wheel. "Our stadium was briefly used as a training base for one African football team during the pre-Olympic week in 1991."

The days of Llivia's Olympic glory had been brief indeed.

We drove past the bridge, past the bench and past the cows. "Now we are in France," the Mayor muttered with barely-concealed irritation. It was the first and only time when I was pleased to leave an enclave and to be back in the real world.

It felt as if – like the British pensioners – I had just experienced a slow "mini adventure". Like my learned predecessor, Honore M. Catudal, Jr., I had managed to avoid arrest and/or imprisonment while in Llivia, yet I hadn't quite escaped an even bigger danger: tedium.

Waiting for my train, I had a beer on the platform at La Tour de Carole. The tiny station was "totally surrounded and land-locked" by the Pyrenees. Heavy black clouds above the mountains were pregnant with rain, and curved flashes of lightning – like God's own ECG – would momentarily bridge together two randomly chosen distant peaks.

The skies finally opened up, and torrents of warm, long-awaited rain flooded the station in no time.

The rain pounded the ground forcefully, as if trying to flatten the Pyrenees themselves.

Unlike the other waiting passengers, I did not run inside, but kept sitting there, on the platform, getting drenched and breathing in the intoxicating scent of mountain flowers, enhanced by the rain and mixed with the sweet odour of railway tar – the overpowering smell of happiness, freedom and new MEGA-adventures to come.

* * *

7. Belmany (Belgium and Germany)

VENNBAHN

Balabka's Germany

When a taxi driver (or a waiter) starts telling you about his family, it is a sure sign that you are about to be ripped off.

The Turkish driver, who was taking us – me and my four-year-old son Andrei – from Aachen to Raeren, kept talking non-stop about the plight of his numerous relatives as we rode towards the German-Belgian border. For all I knew, we could have already been in Belgium, for the roadside towns and villages were signposted in two languages – German and French – as if each of them had two different personalities: Aachen/La Chapelle, Monzen/Lomliers, Kettems/Eupen. The owner of our hotel in Raeren, with whom I had spoken on the phone from London, had assured me that the journey from Aachen should not take more than ten minutes (the distance on the map was ten kilometres). And yet we had already been on the road for over half an hour.

We passed a mysterious-looking supermarket-like structure with thoroughly curtained windows and a huge sign – "Amnesia" – on its roof. It was probably a brothel, where the customers were likely to forget what "services" they had actually paid for. I thought that the same sign would look appropriate on the roof of our taxi, for it was definitely a severe case of forgetfulness that our gregarious family-oriented driver was suffering from. He seemed totally oblivious as to where he was going and would stop at every petrol station to ask for directions.

Our destination was Vennbahn – a little Belgian railway line, cutting into German territory to form five Belgian pockets (enclaves) inside it. These were the only remaining West European enclaves that I had not visited.

Vennbahn was supposed to have been the very first destination of my travels in Enclavia. My friend Michael Hellmerich from the London office of the German Tourism Board, who had kindly agreed to help me organise this part of my journey (despite the fact that it was Belgium, not Germany, I was heading for), had been unable to find anyone sober enough to talk to me, the reason being the annual Carnival. So my visit had to be postponed for a month or so, by which time it was my turn to look after Andrei – nicknamed Balabka for the bubbling sounds he used to make as a baby – and there was little choice but take him with me.

I don't quite remember how it happened, but Andrei had been a Germanophile almost from the moment of his birth. It was probably because I often travelled to Germany and would bring him shiny and seemingly unbreakable German toys. I would also tell him stories about the country's beauty, its cleanliness and its wonderfully efficient trains. He must have overheard the name "Busingen", which I often repeated in conversations. Not long after learning to talk he began saying that he was German (!), that he worked (!) in Germany and had an office in a town called "Misbisingen". To little Andrei, everything German was an archetype of absolute perfection, and I would sometimes mislead him by saying that this or that particular food (like an apple or a bowl of chicken soup) came from Germany, in order to persuade him to eat it.

By far the highest point of Balabka's life had been when I took him (aged three) on an assignment to Cologne – a city which he absorbed greedily while sitting (and at times nodding off) on my shoulders as I dashed around gathering material for an article.

No wonder he was absolutely delighted when I told him I was taking him to . . . well, there was a small problem here, for it was actually the small Belgian town of Raeren that we were supposed to be based in. In any case, I said we were going to Germany, my little lie being somewhat mitigated by the fact that even the London-based Belgian tourism official, from whom I tried to get our hotel's phone number, was dead sure that Raeren *was* in Germany. "How can a hotel called Zum Onkel Jonathan and with the address '1, Hauptstrasse, Raeren', be anywhere else but in Germany?" she insisted.

The phone number I had finally got hold of had the Belgian country code "32" in front of it.

To be fair, this confusion could be easily explained. The majority of Europeans (including myself – until my visit to Vennbahn that is) know from school that the kingdom of Belgium incorporates two autonomous parts: Flemish-speaking Flanders and French-speaking Wallonia – and tend to ignore the existence of the German-speaking region of Belgium (*Deutchsprachige Gemenschaft Belgiens*), which has a population of over seventy thousand, its own parliament and its own capital (Eupen). The reality is that, contrary to what is asserted by many a reference source, Belgium has not two, but three official languages: French, Flemish and German.

So, telling my Germanophile son that we were going to Germany was not such an outright fabrication, after all.

The garrulous amnesiac driver finally disgorged us in the deserted main street of Raeren, which had two official names: Hauptstrasse and Rue Principale. He asked me for forty Euros while sticking out all FIVE fingers on his right hand. I gave him forty, not fifty, of course – the right thing to do, bearing in mind that the normal price of a cab ride from Aachen, as I found out later, was fourteen Euros!

Zum Onkel Jonathan was a two-storey whitewashed cottage with a little restaurant at the front. We were met by a quiet and matter-of-fact young lad called Arndt – the eldest son of the hotel owners, Dieter and Erna Creutz. "Raeren is not a tourist area," he told us (as if we hadn't noticed this already), and he explained that the hotel had been opened by his granddad ("No, his name was not Jonathan") and named "after a popular German song" – the last comment brought a smile to Andrei's little face, for he was now in no doubt whatsoever that we were in Germany.

Arndt was genuinely surprised that we had come to see Vennbahn. "It is having many financial problems and is not working," he noted, with that peculiar, somewhat bored, "know-it-all" grimace characteristic of teenagers all over the world. He happened to be a *Dynamo Kiev* fan and asked me what I thought of Andrei Shevchenko – probably one of their players. "Not much," I said honestly. "You'd better ask me about Andrei Vitaliev." My joke fell on deaf ears.

We were the hotel's only guests. Arndt soon left, having locked the house from the outside (we were given the keys to the front doors). Our visit to Vennbahn was scheduled for the following morning, and we had the best part of a dreary Sunday afternoon to kill.

From the flimsy hotel brochure, I discovered that Raeren was "the ideal starting point for such things as hiking, cycling or excursions to interesting cultural places in the EUREGIO Maas-Rhein." It was the second time during my travels in Enclavia that I had been confronted with that mysterious roaring word "Euregio" (I had first heard it from the ex-butcher Mayor of Kleinwalsertal).

We didn't feel like cycling for the simple reason that we had no bikes, nor did we feel like going on an excursion. The only thing left was "hiking" along Raeren's main – and pretty much only – street, to the accompaniment of the screams of some mad roosters who had obviously lost all track of time.

The invisible roosters seemed to be the only creatures alive in Raeren on that Sunday afternoon. All the main street shops were shut. A strong smell of manure was reaching us from nearby fields. The town looked neither German nor French nor Belgian, but something in between. A semi-torn previous-year's poster on one of the walls announced a one-off Raeren gig of Die Prinzen – probably a rock group – as part of their *Deutschland Tour* (sic). "What country is this, after all?" I wondered silently.

At the very end of Hauptstrasse, we stumbled upon a playground, but to Balabka's dismay it was enclosed by an iron fence, topped with barbed wire, its gates locked.

"What are we going to do here, Dad?" my son asked me.

I wished I knew.

As we were retracing our steps back to the hotel, Andrei picked up something from the ground.

"What is it, Daddy?"

He was holding a black garter of the type worn by strippers and table dancers (at least, the guys who had actually *seen* them strip and table-dance, and had even tucked rumpled banknotes under similar garters, had told me so). How could I explain to him what it was? And how had the garter ended up there – in the gutter – at the road curb in Raeren? Had it been dropped by a forgetful staffer from the nearby Amnesia brothel? "Just drop it, will you?" I said parentally and, having grabbed Andrei's hand, led him away. I could see he was slightly disappointed with rural Raeren, which looked nothing like his imaginary German dream town of Misbisingen.

Raeren was still recovering after the recent Carnival. Photos of ridiculously dressed locals adorned the walls of the tiny restaurant of our hotel, where we dined that evening. At one point, a white-faced and red-nosed man in a pointed hat fell into the bar and ordered a Pastis. He was evidently reluctant to part with his Carnival costume of Pierrot – a French pantomime character (and a very "un-German" one).

"This man was the master of the Carnival," explained Dieter Creutz, the hotel owner, who was waiting on us. He proceeded to show us his own Carnival dress – that of an elf.

Not to confuse my son any further, I felt it my duty to open his eyes to the fact that we were actually NOT in Germany, but in Belgium. Very close to Germany, but not quite in it. Andrei took the truth with unexpected calm.

The restaurant's menu was unmistakably French, and featured *légumes*, *plât du jour*, *vins de la maison* and over a hundred other French wines. As the evening progressed and the bar filled up with locals, I could see that its *ambience* was unmistakably French too: loud voices, lots of laughter and friendly *badinage*. I also noticed that most patrons were drinking wine, not beer. The only disharmony was that everyone spoke German.

Andrei, who was overindulging in *jus d'orange*, had soon to be taken to the restaurant's toilet, where he unexpectedly made an amazing discovery.

"Look, this is Germany!" he cried happily, entering a neat and sterile toilet cabin, with a *Gebemit* electronic flushing device. "And this is Belgium!" he added, pointing at a battered (and not very clean) "street-style" open urinal next to it.

He was clearly coming to grips with the town's dichotomy.

Vennbahn was tired. More than that. It was clinically dead. The only trains at Raeren station that were actually moving were those on the screen-saver of an old computer in the office of Edgar Hungs, the newly appointed Vennbahn manager.

"The phone cables at the station are so old that we cannot even have an Internet connection," he complained, sucking on a charred and stinky cigar butt, which must have been lit for the last time in the middle of the previous century, when Vennbahn was still up and running.

Herr Hungs was Vennbahn's only employee (and employer). His German company, with the tongue-breaking name Eisenbahn-Bau-Betriebs-Satisfizierung A.G. had just taken over the troubled historic railway. A couple of months prior to our visit, Vennbahn, then a state-run Belgian enterprise, had gone bust, and its entire staff – both German and Belgian – had been made redundant. Herr Hung was now facing the difficult task of turning the railway around by hiring a new workforce, finding new investors and changing Vennbahn's whole image.

"We have developed a seven-year-long reconstruction program," he was saying. "In future, we are planning to combine tourist trains with some commercial traffic, to rent trains out for parties and so on. But first, tracks need to be changed and rolling stock renovated . . ."

While we were talking, Andrei was dashing around the office sporting the saucepan-shaped peaked cap of a Belgian station-master, lent to him by Herr Hungs. The hat was too big for him and kept sliding down his face. It made him look like a little caricature of Charles de Gaulle.

We left the station building, which, although on Belgian territory, was typically Prussian in its design and architecture – a reminder of Vennbahn's "enclave-forming" nature, the very thing that had brought us there. A couple of trains without locomotives were "parked" on rusty tracks, overgrown with brown railway weeds. It was clear they had been stationary for many months. Had they been motorcars, not railway carriages, they could have been easily classified as "dumped" and removed. Some of them could even have featured in the *Folkestone Herald*'s weekly column "Dumped Car of the Week".

"Our trains consist mostly of 1935 Belgian carriages and Mitropa cars, built in East Germany," Herr Hungs said without much enthusiasm.

I noticed a faded chalk inscription on one of the cargo trucks, which was tucked away in a sideline: "Not in common use: Return to Harwich."

Just like the forgotten Harwich-bound cargo truck, Vennbahn itself was no longer "in common use" – a great shame for the world's only railway that belonged to one country and ran across another. Built in 1889 as a fully German railroad, it was given to Belgium by the Treaty of Versailles[11] in the aftermath of the WWI. A special international commission agreed – after several years of deliberation – that part of Vennbahn, namely "the track bed, with its buildings between Raeren and Kalterherbert", was to be ceded to Belgium, whereas the resulting five enclaves were to "remain part

---

11. *The same treaty, incidentally, ceded to Belgium the very part of Germany that now constituted Deutchsprachige Gemenschaft Belgiens – the German-speaking area of Belgium.*

of Germany". The German names of all five stations on the stretch were retained, freight charges and fares could be paid in either German or Belgian currency, and countless strict German regulations about ticket-offices, waiting rooms, notice boards, left luggage, etc. were all accepted by the Belgians. Both countries ran customs controls for both German and Belgian passengers at both ends of the section. And whereas conductors, pointsmen and other "minor" railway workers could be either Belgian or German, the train drivers had to be exclusively Belgian nationals!

On 18 May 1940, Adolf Hitler ordered that Belgium's *cantons de l'Est* be re-annexed, and Vennbahn was triumphantly returned to service as a fully German railway line. During WWII, it was in much use supplying the German army until it was all but destroyed by the Allied offensive in the winter of 1944–45. Scarcely a viaduct was spared, and it was not until 1947 that Vennbahn was partially reopened under its previous – Belgian – ownership. By 1990, the railway had become commercially unviable, and the local community was trying to raise money to transform it into a tourist attraction.

"The grant from the local Euregio, however, was not sufficient to sustain the railway, and the whole tourist venture was allowed to die," Herr Hungs concluded with a sigh.

"What IS a Euregio?" I asked.

"It is one of the ninety-two branches of the European Regional Development Fund, with headquarters in Brussels . . ."

I had heard a similar explanation (which didn't explain a lot) from the Mayor of Kleinwalsertal. Whatever it meant, one thing was certain: it was the "Euregio" that stood behind Vennbahn's near-terminal decline.

We were trudging along the empty tracks, with Andrei running excitedly ahead of us, like a miniature human steam engine. Herr Hungs explained that, by international regulations, not just the track, but five metres of land on both sides of it, belonged to the country that owned the railway. That was why German police could not deal with any offences on Vennbahn, even though it ran through the German territory, but had to contact their Belgian colleagues instead.

Running in zigzags, my London-born half-Ukrainian-half-Australian boy was repeatedly trespassing from Belgium into his beloved Germany and back again, which made him a true little European. At least, in his father's eyes.

Our escort pointed out other signs of dichotomy in Vennbahn, like a grey Deutsche Telecom cabin in front of the Belgian station building. The railway used German signals, but with Belgian colours. Despite being German, the signals were situated on the right side of the track – Belgian-style – whereas in Germany they would belong strictly on the left.

We passed by a deserted pointsman's hut next to what Herr Hungs called "the last manual-change point in Germany". I wanted to point out that, since the point was actually part of the track, he should have called it "the last manual-change point in Belgium", but I didn't, having noticed that the hut itself stood several metres away from the rails – in what could be Germany.

Before leaving Raeren station, we popped into the engine shed, where disused Belgian and German-made diesels and steam locomotives – looking equally tired and forlorn – stood next to each other, like exhibits in a transport museum.

"Look, Daddy, these engines are asleep!" exclaimed Andrei, who was then still in the *Thomas and Friends* stage of his development (soon to be followed by the *Harry Potter* period).

I wanted to believe that he was right, and that the Raeren depot was indeed an engine dormitory – not an engine mortuary.

With Vennbahn at a standstill, it was impossible to take a train through the five nameless mini-enclaves which it formed. Instead, Herr Hungs kindly offered to drive us to them. We drove past the former Customs hut, from where the first American soldier stepped onto German territory in 1944. We stopped for a Diet Coke for adults ("Daddy, this bad drink will turn you into a donkey!") and a glass of orange juice for my health-conscious son at the Freihaus restaurant, which, although on Belgian territory, had a German phone line and a number in the local (Belgian) phone directory preceded by Germany's international dialling code: "49".

We then crawled through the "schizophrenic" village of Liechtenbuch, dissected by the border into two "sub-villages": Liechtenbuch Raeren (Belgian) and Liechtenbuch Stadt (German). The difference between the two was not that striking, yet it was noticeable: the Belgian "sub-village" had lots of shoddy and rather old redbrick structures, whereas the German one consisted almost exclusively of neat modern cottages.

The truth of the matter was that the border here did not represent a linguistic or even a cultural divide, unlike the frontier between France and Spain in Llivia, or between Switzerland and Italy in Campione. There was no huge idiosyncrasy in the redbrick Belgian school next to a gleaming German superstore, where they sold, among other things, only *Deutsche Telecom* international phone cards – totally useless across the road in Belgium. Or, maybe, having visited so many enclaves, I was simply getting used to their all-permeating uncertainty?

"Daddy, what is a cemetery?"

For lack of a park, we were taking an evening stroll across the graveyard of Raeren parish church – only marginally more exciting than Hauptstrasse, with its garters in the gutter and barbed wire playgrounds.

"This is the place where people go after they die."

"You mean this is heaven?"

During our several days in Raeren, Andrei took to the typically French "continental" breakfast at our hotel: baguettes, croissants, jam, sausages, ham, cheese and – importantly (for him) – no "yucky" cereals. The fact that, on that particular morning, he fell asleep two minutes after we entered the pleasantly untidy office of Hubert Aussems, the Mayor of Raeren, may have been due to having consumed too many breakfast croissants. While we were talking, I could hear my son's gentle snores from under the Mayor's massive desk, where he had found himself a cosy shelter.

I asked the Mayor about the area's apparent dualism.

"You are right: here we have German working mentality and Belgian lifestyle," said the Mayor.

"What exactly do you mean by 'Belgian lifestyle'?"

"Well, it is a certain ease of living. You see, here we like to work, but we also like good food and are very sociable and informal – much more so than in Germany. So we have a nice mixture of German punctiliousness and Wallonian hedonism, so to speak."

Indeed, the Mayor himself was wearing a casual striped polo shirt under his jacket – an unthinkable piece of office attire for an average German *Burgmeister*. From under his desk, I could hear the heavy breathing of one little victim of that very "Wallonian hedonism".

"Are there any downsides?"

"Yes. Forty-five percent of the Raeren population are German citizens, and many travel to Germany for work every morning. But, based in Belgium, they also have to pay Belgian taxes, which are much higher than German ones, and when they retire, they often have problems with their German health insurance that does not cover foreign residents."

It sounded like the typical "Busingen scenario" that I had observed in so many enclaves – which Raeren, incidentally, wasn't.

"The situation should get better when Belgian and German taxes are due to be equalised," the Mayor went on. "We can't wait for this to happen, for most of our townsfolk have a dual mentality, open both to Germany and to France."

He obviously meant "to Germany and to Belgium" but, having myself experienced Raeren's indisputable "French-ness", I chose not to correct the Mayor's Freudian slip.

Before saying goodbye, the Mayor advised us (Andrei was awake by then, squinting at me sleepily from under the table) to take a bus to Eupen, the capital of German-speaking Belgium and the seat of its Parliament. He offered to call the Parliament to forewarn them of our visit, and it took him almost ten minutes to find the phone directory on his disorderly desk, piled up with newspapers, folders and empty bottles of mineral water. "Wallonian bureaucracy," he mumbled apologetically, having finally ferreted the directory from under a hillock of papers.

I was not so sure about the bureaucracy, but this German-speaking office was definitely affected by a touch of "WALFRELGIAN" (Wallonian-French-Belgian) charismatic mess.

"*Bienvenue à Eupen – La Capital Secret de la Belgique Allemande*!" was written on a motorway billboard. For some obscure reason, in French . . .

I liked the "secret capital" bit of the message, although the main "secret" I was hoping to uncover in Eupen was that of the evasive "Euregios".

The German Region of Belgium's Parliament (its official name) was located in the very centre of Eupen, in a deceptively small late-baroque house. The Mayor of Raeren had managed to get through to Roger Hilgers, the Parliament's communications officer – an extremely young man, only a fraction older than Andrei, or so it seemed.

He started by telling us that there were two German-speaking regions of Belgium – Northern and Southern, and to get from one to another, one had to pass through Wallonia. According to him, the German-Belgian Parliament had more powers than that of Wallonia; it could even sign its own international treaties on matters of culture and education, as it had recently with France and Luxembourg. As he himself put it: "We have more competence than Wallonia."

The building was all but deserted, for all the MPs were on holiday. We descended a carpeted staircase to have a look at the room, where the Parliament would normally sit.

The "house" was the size of an average classroom in a British state school, only much neater. A full bottle of Spa mineral water stood in the middle of each of the twenty-five desks (the total number of MPs). Three further seats were on a small podium in the corner. They were reserved for the region's Ministers: Minister for Culture and Education, Minister for Social and Health Affairs and Minister President, who was also responsible for the area's economy. The Ministers shared one larger desk, with three bottles of water on it. In the absence of the politicians it was easy to imagine the bottles conducting their own bubbly and clinky debates.

Mr. Hilgers named each of the six political parties represented in the Parliament – from the ruling Socialist Christian Party to the Party of German-Speaking Belgium, which, he assured us, was not so much pro-independence as pro-German-culture and stood for little more than increased "competence" for the Parliament.

The role of the virtual "head of state" belonged to the so-called President of the Community, whose separate office, with a portrait of the Belgian royal couple above the fireplace, was next door.

"The people of the region feel more Belgian than German," young Mr. Hilgers told us when we returned to his tiny cubicle of an office. "We all support the Belgian football team, despite watching German television."

He then uttered the sentence I had been half-expecting to hear: "We see ourselves as a laboratory of united Europe, yet no one in Brussels wants to know about our achievements and our problems."

"How about a Euregio?" I probed tentatively, feeling rather as though I was offering Mr. Hilgers some exotic Italian drink.

"Yes, they have made us part of the Maas-Rhein Euregio, but the only project they have so far been willing to support is Vennbahn."

"Which is why it is now on its last legs – or rather wheels," I wanted to add, but didn't.

According to Mr. Hilgers, the Maas-Rhein Euregio incorporated bits of Germany, Belgium and the Netherlands and had its headquarters in Maastricht. I made up my mind to pay a visit, if only to find out *what* on earth it was about.

It was time for us to leave: two official meetings in one day was more than enough for Andrei. Mr. Hilgers rewarded him for his patience with a paper flag of the German-speaking part of Belgium, or "Belmany" as I had come to call it for the sake of brevity. It depicted a regulation dragon underneath a no-less-regulation crown.

As my own reward for Andrei, I took him for an ice cream in a *pâtisserie* near the bus station.

While he was eating, I looked at an orderly and tidy German-style bus shelter through the window, now "sheltering" two Belgian teenagers – a boy and girl – sealed together in a seemingly endless *French* kiss.

I suddenly realised that, having completed my exploration of Vennbahn, I had become the first person (after Honore M. Catudal) to have visited *all* existing enclaves of Western Europe. Did this "achievement" bring me closer to understanding the nature of "European-ness"? I was not sure about that, but in any case – to celebrate the occasion – I ordered an ice-cream for myself, too.

All the way back to Raeren, Andrei was waving his new German-Belgian flag from the back seat of the bus.

*   *   *

8. EU-SSR

MAASTRICHT

A handwritten note, prominently displayed in the window of a kiosk on Platform Two of Amsterdam Centraal station, was categorical: "We don't accept banknotes over fifty Euros" it said underneath a drawing of a crossed out one hundred Euro banknote, which I had not yet seen in reality.

I thought that spotting that angry note while waiting for a train to Maastricht, the birthplace of the Euro (and of the EU, for that matter) was symbolic: ten odd years after the agreement on the European political and monetary union was reached in that Dutch town, things were not quite right in EU-SSR, bogged down in red tape, chronic inefficiency and never-ending corruption scandals. Even the much-publicised new Euro banknotes, with windows and gateways on the front designed to symbolise "the spirit of openness and co-operation", seemed to be in short supply.

The level of "openness", too, left much to be desired – as demonstrated by my numerous futile attempts to make an appointment with a single Brussels bureaucrat to discuss the problems of the enclaves. "By enclaves you mean 'enlargement', don't you?" was the most common response of the countless secretaries and anonymous PAs I had managed to contact by phone. When I explained what the enclaves actually were, they would normally advise me to talk to either "Mr. Schmidt", or "Mr. Jacque", both of whom were "unfortunately away in Strasbourg". By the time I tried to trace them down in Strasbourg, they (Mr. Schmaque or Mr. Jidt) had invariably gone back to Brussels, or occasionally to Luxembourg. Or they would be "away for the weekend", which – as I discovered – for most EU bureaucrats began at 3pm on Friday and ended on Tuesday morning.

Even fixing an appointment with a fairly insignificant (by Brussels standards) official from "Euregio Maas-Rhein", where I was heading, proved impossible. "We do not make appointments by phone," I was rebuffed by another Personal Assistant to no person in particular. "If you turn up here, you might be able to speak to somebody."

It would have made sense to go to Maastricht straight from the Vennbahn area, but Andrei needed to be taken back to London first. So I had to try and uncover the mystery of "Euregio" by undertaking a separate trip to Maastricht.

"Can you give me one Euro?" one of the smartly dressed and multi-lingual Amsterdam station beggars whined behind my back. I was tempted to ask him whether he accepted hundred-Euro banknotes.

I did not realise that Holland was – relatively speaking – so large. It took me over three hours to get to Maastricht. About an hour after leaving Amsterdam, the train stopped at Utrecht station. It was there that I had first stepped out onto Western soil from my Moscow–Hook of Holland carriage during my first ever journey abroad in 1988. The stop in Utrecht was only about five minutes long, and I was the only passenger brave enough to venture onto the empty platform – only to be shooed back in by the ever-vigilant KGB train steward. "A small step for a man", it went completely unnoticed by "mankind". Yet for me, it was no less important than Neil Armstrong's "giant leap" onto the rough surface of the Moon.

The platform looked exactly the same as it had in 1988. It was I who was different and no longer besotted with the West. In fact, the more I learned about the ways, methods and aspirations of the EU bureaucrats, the more similarities I was finding with their Soviet counterparts. Travelling inside the European Union, I often could not help the feeling of being back in the USSR.

I spent the rest of the journey looking through the window at the neat cubes of compressed rubbish along the track, ready for further recycling, and leafing through a stack of Euregio brochures, sent to me from Maastricht on request. They did little to lift the lid on the mystery.

To begin with, the exact definition of a Euregio was nowhere to be found[12]. The glossy German-published A4-size pamphlet "Cross-border Cooperation Initiative INTERREG" ("not to be made use of by political parties, election candidates or their assisting election officers for canvassing purposes during the course of an election campaign") started with the following, somewhat German-accented, statement: "The aim of drawing Europe's peoples into an even closer union is also one that has practical and everyday relevance in Europe's border regions." So far so good . . . Against this background, the EU has been supporting internal and exterior cross-border co-operation since 1990 through its largest Community Initiative – INTERREG.

The pamphlet spoke of the mystifying "INTERREG I", "INTERREG II", even "INTERREG II A", but all my attempts to grasp what INTERREG, let alone "Euregio", actually stood for proved futile. This made me wonder what "political party" would seriously want to use this pamphlet "during the course of an election campaign", unless it was bent on losing by a huge margin.

---

12. My Dictionary of the European Communities, *which has entries on any number of European concepts, also stays mum.*

In despair, I opened a much smaller document – "PROQUA. Euregio Meuse–Rhine". At least it explained straight away that "PROQUA" was "the project for qualifications and the labour market". What followed this pretty evasive explanation was a quotation.

Look, I hate doing this to you, but will nevertheless have to reproduce it in full:

> In providing Community assistance under this initiative to border areas, the Commission will accord priority to proposals which ... include the establishment or development of shared institutional or administrative structures intended to widen and deepen cross-border co-operation between public agencies, private organisations and voluntary bodies; where possible, these shared institutional or administrative structures should have the competence to implement jointly determined projects.

The source of this inspiring quotation was duly indicated underneath it:

> COMMISSION NOTICE TO THE MEMBER STATES laying down guidelines for operational programmes which Member States are invited to establish in the framework of a Community initiative concerning ... cross border co-operation ...
> (INTERREG II 94/94/C 180/13)

This reminded me of a caption I once saw under a photo in *Korea Today* magazine: "Happy workers listening to Great Leader Kim II Sung's favourite opera *The Great Leader's Five-Paragraph Programme of Modernising the Country's Agriculture*".

With nostalgia, I remembered Baarle's double-edged "international" fire-hose connector – an example of a true "cross-border co-operation", made by people who had never heard of Euregios or INTERREGs, to say nothing of PROQUAs.

I felt like immediately implementing the disposal of the brochure through the framework of the train window. As I was about to do so, I spotted the words "Euregio Structures" on page three:

> The PROQUA networks are the creative laboratory of PROQUA
> Phase I. The Euregio structures ensure that project lead times are
> long enough for users and providers to get to know one another's
> core competences . . .

It was hopeless . . .

There were only two pamphlets left (patience, my dear readers), and I had somewhat better luck with them. From the first one I learned that "The Euregional Council" for Euregio Maas-Rhein consisted of eighty-one (!) members sitting in two chambers, five Commissions and a "joint presidium". The pamphlet also – at long last – made a feeble attempt to provide a definition for the INTERREG programme, which was apparently "a community initiative of the European Commission, aimed at combating under-development in the border regions of the member states". Not particularly helpful, but at least comprehensible . . .

The last pamphlet was in German, yet with an English (just about) title, *Fun For Family & Co*. It was advertising a travel card which allowed its holder to use all types of public transport within the Euregio, where, according to the previous brochure, "Europe was taking concrete shape". The travel card, at least, was something concrete . . .

In short, looking through all those "documents" hardly brought me any closer to solving the mystery of the Euregios. Amazingly, even their overall number in Europe remained uncertain: one brochure claimed there were fifty-six, another ninety, and a third one ninety-two. And each of them employed hundreds of well-paid (by European taxpayers) bureaucrats! This astonishing mess gave a new meaning to the claim by the "PROQUA" pamphlet that Euregio Meuse-Rhine was "like a miniature EU". Out of everything I had read on the train, this was the only statement that made perfect sense.

By the end of the journey, I had nodded off. Any wonder?

The first thing I saw on the platform at Maastricht station was an unattended black toilet seat, propped against a lamp post – an object as baffling and unlikely as the stripper's garter Andrei had picked up in Raeren. (The only reason it had not been "removed" and "destroyed" was probably that it looked nothing like a potential terrorist bomb.)

The toilet seat enigma reminded me of the reason for my Maastricht visit – to locate the no-less-enigmatic Euregio Maas-Rhein headquarters. Not being a Euregio travelcard holder, I had to walk there, of course. Following arrows to "Belgium" and with a map in my hand, I marched purposefully towards the town suburb, where the offices were located.

Soon, I stood in front of the Limburg Province Government Complex – a drab 1980s building where the first EU Treaty, the so-called Treaty of Maastricht, had been signed in February 1992. Architecturally the complex reminded me of the former STASI head-quarters in Berlin. The building's interior – low ceilings, long dark corridors, and massive staircases – only enhanced the resemblance.

It was 11:30am (I had started my journey early), but there was only one person inside the spacious Euregio offices on the third floor. He was a lean, pale youngster, with watery-blue eyes, full of ennui and world-weariness. His name was Bernard, and his position, as his business card put it, was the equivocal "INTERREG Management". Sitting behind an empty desk, he was staring at the ceiling.

"You have come at a bad moment," he muttered, not even trying to conceal his annoyance at the appearance of an unexpected and uncalled-for visitor. "I am about to go downstairs for lunch."

"I won't keep you long," I promised. "I just wanted to ask you what Euregio is."

"There are ninety of them in Europe, and they are all administered by a Directorate General in Brussels."

It was like asking someone what time it was and hearing in reply: "Yes, but the post-office is just round the corner."

Knowing the Eurocrats' inherent dislike of direct questions (and answers), I re-phrased my query:

"What is the purpose of this Euregio?"

"To stimulate cross-border co-operation," he mumbled and, having thrown a furtive look at his watch, added: "Look, I really have to go: our canteen closes in 30 minutes, and there won't be anything left."

"What do you do yourself?"

"I distribute European money – formerly ECUs, now Euros."

I had to restrain myself from asking Bernard to "distribute" some to me.

"Can you give me some examples of the ventures you are supporting?" I persisted.

"Look, you are talking to the wrong person. I only DISTRIBUTE money . . . Go to our website, if you want to know the details."

"But surely you must be aware of what projects you are financing."

He went into a sulking mode and muttered something that sounded like "cross-border involvement for small businesses" (probably quoting one of the soporific pamphlets I had read on the train) and then added resolutely: "I told you, you're talking to the wrong person. Go to our website!"

His last remark sounded like a barely camouflaged version of "Go to hell!"

"OK," said I, about to give up. "What's your website address?"

He didn't know it, of course.

As a last resort, I decided to fake softening up a little.

"I appreciate that you are in a hurry," I lied. "I would have gladly talked to the *right* person instead, but you seem to be the only one here. Where are all the other staff?"

"They are all away supervising projects in the field."

"Which projects?"

"Go to our website."

"Listen, don't you think our conversation is going in circles?" I started losing my *sang-froid*.

"They arrange meetings to implement cross-border activities."

"But don't cross-border activities happen anyway, without meetings to implement them, as I have seen from having visited a number of West European enclaves which you, I suspect, have never heard about?" I was almost yelling now, ready to pounce on him with my fists clenched.

A piercing ring from his mobile saved Bernard from grievous bodily harm – and me from an unplanned holiday inside a comfortable Dutch (or Belgian) prison cell. "It's about lunch," he announced triumphantly. "I really have to run."

He dashed out of the room, but I followed him. As we were running down the stairs, Bernard – visibly cheered by the impending meal and probably eager to somewhat alter the impression of an uncooperative ignoramus he must have felt (rightly) he had made – decided to offer me an olive branch.

"I can give you one bit of information that might interest you," he puffed out as we were racing the corridors towards the canteen. "The budget of our Euregio has risen from thirty-three million ECUs in 1994 to fifty-two million Euros in 2002!"

The information was indeed invaluable. I could now understand why all sorts of taxes and prices in the EU countries (including Britain, which, incidentally, had no Euregios of its own) kept rising year after year: someone had to pay for the maintenance of this voracious ninety-headed Euregio Hydra.

As Bernard was about to open the door to the canteen, I held him by the sleeve and asked for directions to the town centre. Needless to say, he didn't know that either.

I let go of Bernard and wished him *bon appétit*.

Maastricht struck me as a small town with a big nose. The layout of its narrow medieval lanes was as puzzling and chaotic as the structure of the EU itself. The streets ran in circles (like my conversation with Bernard) and semi-circles, so that you would inevitably return to the same place you had started from – it was a grid that spoke of hopelessness.

I soon discovered that, apart from the "New" Limburg Government Complex I had visited, the town boasted another – Old – Government building in its centre. It was also home to such obscure EU institutions as the European Centre for Development Policy Management, the European Documentation Centre (which sounded like an ideal place for treating insomniacs), the European Institute of Public Administration, the European Journalism Centre and a number of others – all of which gave it the peculiar bureaucratic appeal, if not of Brussels or Strasbourg, then definitely of Kirchberg – the Eurocrats' small-ish haven in Luxembourg.

I realised why they were always eager to give you receipts for any purchase – no matter how small – in Maastricht (I had been given an unasked-for receipt, the size of a British tabloid, when buying a battery for my camera): it was a town of bureaucrats, and bureaucrats (particularly the European variety) have generous expense accounts, enabling them to claim back almost everything.

With lots of expenses and no expense account, I found Maastricht restaurants forbidding to the point that I had to flee from a Turkish café in the central square after just a quick glimpse at its menu. I sincerely regretted not having joined Bernard for lunch (not that he had invited me) in the Government Building canteen, heavily subsidised by European taxpayers (and that included myself). Maastricht was also rather mercenary. At the VVV tourism office they charged me €1.25 for a promotional brochure *Maastricht: The Art of Fine Living* (they should have added "for Euro-bureaucrats") – as no other tourism office in the world would have done. They demanded fifty cents for the use of a railway station public toilet – by far the most expensive establishment of its kind that I had ever come across. The moment I dropped a coin into a slot and the door opened, two desperate men rushed in quickly after me – for free! The significance of the black toilet seat on the platform – the first thing I had seen in Maastricht – was now more or less clear to me. Unlike that of the Euregios, I hasten to add.

My return journey to Amsterdam was disastrous. The train departed Maastricht one hour behind schedule. "They are experiencing slight technical problems," a Dutch girl, sitting next to me, explained, having listened to a crackling intercom announcement in Dutch. It was a bad omen: from my sad British Rail experience, I knew that whenever they mentioned "slight problems", it meant really big trouble. I was right.

"The locomotive is defective and needs to be replaced" was the next translation I was offered, when the train got stuck again – this time in Roermond.

We all had to disembark and board "replacement buses" to Eindhoven. At times I felt like pinching myself to make sure I was *not* in Britain. The situation was made worse by the fact that my elder son Mitya was waiting for me at Amsterdam Centraal station, and I had no mobile to warn him that I was running several hours late.

The last leg of my protracted return journey – from Eindhoven to Amsterdam – went without incident. The translator girl was singing to the rhythm of the train wheels. A Portuguese youngster with curly hair was reading Dante's *Inferno* in Dutch (I felt I could write my own version of *Inferno* after this trip). A tall grey man across the aisle was smoking a pipe. They were my fellow European travellers, and I felt at ease among them.

The sun was setting behind the windows, its bright red disc rolling after the train, as if willing to be our travel companion too.

The train's progress was smooth and noiseless, and I suddenly thought that it could pass for an on-wheels metaphor for the whole of the EU: there was nothing wrong with the passengers, the carriages, the track or the rolling stock – it was the *locomotive* that was defective and in need of being scrapped.

* * *

BRUSSELS

The European Council of heads of governments meets privately two or three times a year and delegates most decisions to Councils of the European Ministers of the various departments. These also conduct their affairs in secret, in effect decide policies, and pass these decisions to the European Commission . . . Under them are over twenty thousand bureaucrats (with tax-free salaries) who manufacture regulations. Several hundred standing committees meet daily. There is virtually no public responsibility all through this apparatus . . . The whole structure is repugnant to both democracy and common sense.

Robert Conquest, *Reflections on a Ravaged Century*

> In the distant future, one could perhaps imagine a new association of nations, composed of individual states of superior national quality that could challenge the imminent overpowering of the world by the American union.
>
> From Adolf Hitler's second book, unearthed by the Jewish scholar Gerhard Weinberg

Having failed to make an appointment with any Euro-bureaucrats in Brussels, I was nevertheless keen to find out at least something about their vision, if not of the West European enclaves they had never heard about, then at least of Europe in general.

One sympathetic EU Headquarters PA-to-no-person-in-particular, who was clearly keen to mitigate my disappointment at not being able to interview her elusive bosses, suggested I went and saw "Mini-Europe" – a theme park in the outskirts of Brussels, which, in her words, "embodied the EC's vision" of our continent. She even volunteered to make an appointment with one of the Mini-Europe officials to show me around. At that point, I remembered that many enclave dwellers had referred to their towns or villages as a mini-Europe. Since I was already in Brussels and had no better offers for the day, I decided to give it a shot.

At the tourist information office at Bruxelles-Midi train station, the same terminal from which my travels in Enclavia had started, I picked up a leaflet headlined "Welcome to Brussels, the capital of Europe!" and a couple of glossy Mini-Europe pamphlets. They gave me directions to the Bruparck area, where Mini-Europe was located.

During the forty-minute-long Metro ride, I had plenty of time to study the brochures. According to them, Mini-Europe was a two and a half hectare park featuring "350 monuments and miniature working models of the most important European sites and monuments". Built in 1989 "under the auspices of the EU" at the cost of fifteen million Belgian francs (out of the EU taxpayers' uncomplaining pockets, of course), it was "a window on Europe" and "an exciting voyage through Europe" – all at the same time.

"Cheer on the matador at the Corrida in Seville, watch the launch of Ariane V, follow the Thalys train from Paris to the other end of France, let Mount Vesuvius explode and feel the earthquake!" goaded one brochure, explaining that all those events could be achieved by "activating pushbuttons in the neighbourhood of the monuments". Another pamphlet invited would-be visitors to "break down the Berlin Wall!" – by pressing other pushbuttons, no doubt.

To me, whose whole life had been cruelly fractured by the Berlin Wall, it sounded tactless.

The Bruparck exhibition area was dominated by the Atomium, a giant sculpture representing an iron molecule (enlarged one hundred and sixty-five billion times – well, allegedly, for how could one check?), built for the 1958 World Fair. Contemplating its proximity to the miniaturised "Europe", I couldn't help remembering a remark by Ilya Ilf and Evgeny Petrov to the effect that bureaucrats had always been fascinated with utterly useless models of enormous fountain pens and minuscule steam engines.

"Eat the rich!" ran an angry graffiti on a concrete fence near the Atomium. I thought that in its peremptory tone it somehow echoed the slogan of "Mini-Europe": "Discover Europe's nicest places!"

To get to Mini-Europe, I had to walk through a fun fair lined with neat redbrick buildings – a set which reminded me of the approach to a Disneyland-style theme park.

The Mini-Europe official was to meet me near the ticket office. Waiting for him, I watched the people about to enter the exhibition grounds. There were not too many of them, and very few bothered to buy tickets (€11 per person). Instead, they flashed some VIP passes and official letters in the face of a guard at the turnstile, and he would wave them through. Could it be that free entry to Mini-Europe was just another of the EU employees' multiple perks? Whatever it was, one thing was clear – there were far too many VIPs in Brussels. As the same Ilf and Petrov once wrote about getting into a popular Moscow theatre, "only courting couples and wealthy heirs go to the box office. The other citizens (they make up the majority, you may observe) go straight to the manager . . ."

Associations with the Soviet Union were all but unavoidable in Brussels . . .

The Mini-Europe official was late. I knew he would be (Euro-bureaucrats always are). Yet, being a "mini-Eurocrat", he was not terribly late – a mere fifteen minutes.

We went through the gates, decorated with a large plastic "Euro-Turtle" – the official mascot of Mini-Europe (was there a hint of the notoriously slow pace of Brussels bureaucracy?) and found ourselves in the "Central Square".

I felt like Gulliver in Euro-Lilliputia. On my right was a toy-like version of Dover Castle. Next to it a P&O Ferry *The Pride of Dover* – the size of a large water rat – was chugging noiselessly across the puddle of the English Channel towards the smallish Eiffel Tower, around which a model Thalys train was circling.

"Do you have little TGV trains too?" I asked my escort – just for the sake of it.

"We used to," he replied. "But then we replaced them with Thalys who are one of our sponsors."

It was good to know that one could actually pay to become part of the "Mini-Europe" scene.

"All models here are one-twenty-fifth of their normal size, except for the Vesuvius volcano which is one thousand times smaller," the mini-official carried on.

In the distance, I could see the shrunk Vesuvius spit out mini-fire at the press of a button, like an oversized cigarette lighter, and could hear it make some hoarse coughing sounds, like an inveterate smoker after his first morning fag.

"What is the purpose of it all?" I asked him.

He looked puzzled: "To learn about Europe, of course . . ." And then he added after a pause: "It is handy for the Americans who can do the whole of Europe in two hours."

This last comment was probably meant as a joke.

"The whole of Europe?" I exclaimed in disbelief. "I can't wait to see a little Moscow, where I haven't been since defecting. Imagine: a tiny Kremlin. Or better: a miniature KGB building in

Lubyanka Street. The very thought of it makes me nostalgic. And how about my native Ukraine, say?"

He cut me short: "We only have the EU member countries here."

"Then why do you call it 'Mini-Europe' and not 'Mini-EU'?"

He couldn't answer that, and looked at his watch.

"I am afraid I have an important meeting in five minutes. In any case, everything here is self-explanatory. Enjoy yourself."

He stepped over the English Channel and vanished from view.

The minion was right: it *was* all pretty self-explanatory. Only not in the way he would have wanted. Judging from the scale of Mini-Europe, by far the largest country on the continent was . . . Belgium. Proportionally, it was about ten times bigger than Italy. And the model of Brussels' baroque Market Square was the grandest one of all. To my sheer consternation, I discovered that Amsterdam, my favourite European city – which I have branded "the people's capital of Europe" – was actually located on Belgian territory! Having opened the theme park's catalogue, kindly left behind by the mini-official, I saw that Amsterdam was listed as part of the Belgian section there, too!

That finding shocked me so much that I didn't notice I had wandered into Spain and was standing in the middle of Seville's Plaza de Toroz staring at a sign which read: "Say '*Olé*' in the microphone." I did, but nothing happened.

I then walked past the hedge marking Spain's border with France, hoping against hope to stumble upon Llivia. But the enclaves, of course, had no place in that Brusselised version of Europe. Nor had Turkey, Russia, Ukraine, Norway or even Switzerland, for none of them were members of the EU.

It has to be said that some of the EU member-countries were pretty hard-done-by, too – compared to Belgium that is. A single model of the Adolph Bridge represented Luxembourg; Greece consisted of just two buildings, one of which was the Acropolis. And poor Austria had nothing but an eighteenth-century abbey in the town of Melk. Yet Belgium incorporated twenty-two different structures – two of which were, incidentally, in Amsterdam – and a disproportionately huge chunk of territory.

"What is Europe? A geographical entity? A community of peoples who share history, culture and humanistic values – Greek gods, Roman law and Judeo-Christian heritage? Or is it merely an abstraction, a sort of mythic identity, like Europa herself, the princess abducted by Zeus disguised as a snow-white bull?" John Vinocur (incidentally, himself an American of Jewish/Ukrainian descent) questioned rhetorically in March 2004.

Brussels tries to portray itself as the only place where the answers to all these questions are known – and have been known for donkey's years. Indeed, in 1985, the leaders of the EU nations officially subscribed to a strategy "to create a European identity" – a project that didn't go further than introducing a European Union passport, the starry EU flag, the equally starry EU car licence plates and – then – the Euro. I find it hard to understand how one can artificially "create" an identity – a category that, by definition, appears by itself and staunchly resists outside influences? Uniform passports, flags, licence plates etc. can only be offshoots of a common identity that is already in existence, rather than factors helping to mould it. Just as a common currency should stem naturally from already harmonised national economies, rather than represent an attempt to forge this harmonisation from above – a classic case of putting the cart before the horse. And a fine example of an imperial (British? Russian? EU-an?) psyche too.

One thing is certain: a European identity, if there is such a thing, has little, if anything, in common with the cheerful crowds of self-satisfied (yet far from self-sufficient) EU bureaucrats, so preoccupied with creating a European super-state with themselves at the helm. In the words of Conservative MEP Daniel Hannan, "the reason that we feel closer to our nations than to the EU is not simply that the EU often does things badly. It is also because the nations are able to draw on a deep well of sentiment; of poetry and literature, of national heroes, of history. The EU offers us the trappings of statehood with no underlying sense of common identity."

His MEP colleague Louise Weiss put it even more bluntly: "European community institutions have produced European beets, butter, cheese, wine, veal and even pigs. But they have not produced Europeans." I wonder whether the EC's decision to provide its own civil servants with free Viagra (as reported in *The Times*) had something to do with this apparent lack of productivity? Or was it prompted by the stream of complaints from Germany claiming that ten Euro notes in men's pockets could cause impotence?

Despite the Euro-bureaucrats' apparent infertility, however, Europeans do exist. And their existence has nothing to do with Viagra. I know it for sure, simply because I consider myself a European and because, as far as I know, Viagra was not used very widely in the Stalinist Soviet Union in 1953 – the year of my conception.

Standing on top of the miniature Montmartre hillock and listening to a crackling recording of singing nightingales played out from some hidden loudspeakers, I felt uneasy. It was precisely the feeling I had experienced once in Las Vegas, after getting lost in its new Paris Casino.

I had come to Las Vegas in the middle of my six-month-long American journey. In a way, I liked the place for its boisterous and unadulterated Kitsch – Las Vegas' euphemism for "culture", spelt with a capital "K" – and for its total lack of pretence, as if the city was constantly taking the mickey out of itself. "Mechanic on duty. Free aspirin and tender sympathy," ran a sign on top of a city garage. One certainly needed a lot of aspirin, and even more "tender sympathy", to cope with Las Vegas.

One evening I was walking along Las Vegas Boulevard, known locally as The Strip, on my way to the New York-New York Casino – not to gamble, but simply curious as to how Las Vegas' city fathers could seriously claim to have "recreated" the seemingly inimitable Big Apple inside it. "We have saved you a lot of airfare," I had heard one of them saying earlier on local radio.

I never made it to "New York". Blinded by The Strip's epileptic lights (anything without moving lights had no right to be there) and deafened by the din of traffic, I felt a desperate need for an aspirin, when my attention was distracted by a brightly-lit and somewhat downsized Eiffel Tower. Squeaky "Victorian" lifts were taking tourists to the top and back down – straight to the entrance of a smaller replica of the famous Paris opera house Le Grand Opera. I deduced it was the façade of the brand new Las Vegas–Paris hotel-casino. After many months in the States, my nostalgia for Europe was such that I decided to pop in.

I dived under the replicated Arc de Triomphe and, having passed through a huge and windowless gambling hall, found myself . . . in an old Paris street. In fact, it was not just one street, but a whole Paris quarter, with cobbled narrow lanes, cafes, shops (Le Tabac, La Pâtisserie, La Boulangerie), platans and even Parisians themselves (!) – sitting on benches, queuing for baguettes and kissing under the trees. A street busker, sporting a traditional French beret cap of the early 1960s, stood on the corner with his accordion.

The power of illusion was so strong that it took me a while to realise that everything in that fake Paris quarter – the shops, the cobbles, the houses, the trees, the street signs (*Les Toilettes*) and even the "Parisians" – was made of plastic. The sultry blue sky above my head was but a vast painted canvas (or was it a tarpaulin?) and the recorded whingeing sounds of the plastic busker's plastic accordion were mixing with the non-stop hungry bleating of the voracious fruit machines from a gambling hall behind the wall.

I popped into La Boulangerie, attracted by the appetizing displays of freshly baked baguettes and croissants in its window. I hadn't had proper "European" bread – as opposed to its cotton-wool American variety – for many weeks. Inside, they were selling nothing but muffins and waffles, and all the croissants and baguettes on display were purely "decorative" and made of plastic.

Feeling claustrophobic, I could not wait to get out of this plastic world of well-crafted make-believe.

One sign you won't find easily in Las Vegas casinos, however, is "Exit". I didn't notice how I got lost in the cobweb of plastic streets. Exhausted and dizzy, I lowered myself onto a plastic chair outside a "Bistro" and ordered *un café noir*, which proved to be of the wishy-washy American variety.

Sipping the tepid drink and making notes on my memo pad, I was suddenly blinded by a bright camera flash, then another one, then yet another.

I looked up. A flock of Japanese tourists on the opposite side of the plastic "street" were aiming the gaping barrels of their Nikons at me. Ready to shoot.

My first thought was that they had mistaken me for some obscure Hollywood star, but it didn't take me long to realise that they simply viewed me as part of the "Paris" set: a writer scribbling away at a Paris café ... Perhaps they even thought that – like all the other mannequins in the quarter – I, too, was made of plastic ...

"Stop it! I am not plastic! I am real!!!" I wanted to scream – but didn't, for a treacherous thought flashed through my aspirin-hungry brain: what if they were right and – after many months in the USA – *I had become plastic indeed*?

I ducked, then jumped up from my seat and, having overturned the plastic table and the chair, took to my heels, not stopping until I was back on The Strip. Even now, I have no idea how I found the exit.

The feverish lights of Las Vegas Boulevard kept blinking tirelessly, as if searching for something they were never meant to find.

Just like Las Vegas, Mini-Europe's plastic "Paris"[13] had nothing to do with the real Paris. And "Mini-Europe" itself had nothing to do with Europe as such, nor even with a "model of Europe", as it claimed to be. It was rather an Americanised model of the European superstate, with its centre in Brussels.

This impression was strengthened by a quick visit to the "EuroShop" on the fringe of the theme park.

The choice of "European" souvenirs there seemed very American: EU flags, "Brussels is the Heart of Europe" tea mugs, playing cards with Euro-banknote jackets, Euro-erasers, Euro-key-holders ...

---

13. *They had a plastic Venice in Las Vegas, too: in the "Venetian" Casino they "recreated" – among other things – Venice's St Marco's Square and a bit of The Grand Canal with plastic gondolas and imitation gondoliers.*

The item that annoyed me most, however, was the giveaway "Map of Europe", where only the EU member countries were printed in different colours and all others in pale pink, like some uninhabited parts of Antarctica that hadn't been properly explored – or even discovered. It was a clear indication that, from Brussels' point of view, those other countries did not matter at all.

This brought to memory a casual remark made by the former French President Jacques Chirac, one of the main architects of the EU in its present form. The comment was made during Chirac's brief visit to Britain in November 2003, when, visibly annoyed by the British reluctance to wholeheartedly approve the draft European Constitution, he tried to lecture Tony Blair on how to be a good European: "The key, he said, was to show respect to those who really mattered, and they were the original founder members of the European Community – a team of six which includes France, but not Britain."[14]

I felt really sorry for the new EU members, who were then about to join the EU. It was clear that they would never "really matter" from the "good European" Chirac's point of view.

* * *

---

14. *Quotation taken from* The Daily Telegraph.

European Uncertainty

(INSTEAD OF AN EPILOGUE)

Once, in Liechtenstein, I was shown an extraordinary brochure under the title "The Nation's Culturgram". Produced and distributed by the Mormon-run Brigham Young University in Utah, USA, it was one of a series of brief "cultural identity" descriptions for every single country in the world.

From the "Culturgram" on Liechtenstein, one of Europe's most peculiar mini-states, an inquisitive reader could learn that, in the tiny principality, "a handshake is usually the appropriate form of greeting"; that "both men and women may sit with legs crossed with one knee over the other", and that "to wave or nod to somebody across the street is acceptable".

It also listed such bizarre and clearly endemic local customs as "hands are not used much during conversation, but it is impolite to talk with hands in the pockets". It provided a would-be foreign visitor with useful behavioural tips of the type: "gloves are removed before shaking hands"; "pointing the index finger to one's head is an insult"; "any acts of personal hygiene, such as cleaning one's fingernails, are not appropriate in public"; and, to crown it all, "if a yawn cannot be suppressed, hand covers the open mouth".

Browsing through the brochure, I felt an urge to point my index finger to my head – in a brazen breach of Liechtenstein's unique rules of etiquette.

And although I haven't yet come across a "Culturgram" on Britain, it is not hard to imagine how it might read.

It would probably say that in Britain it is customary to appear in public with one's private parts covered with tailored pieces of cloth, locally known as shirts, skirts and pants; that while consuming food, it is advisable to do so with the help of one's mouth rather than nose, eyes or ears; and that spitting into someone else's mug of beer in a pub – as well as hitting a Brit on the front side of his head, which the locals call a "face" – can be taken as an insult.

Just like the unfortunate "Mini Europe" theme park in Brussels, the "Culturgram" was but an outrageous trivialisation of the very concept it was trying to represent. "Cultural identities . . . were never monolithic and are becoming much less so," – in the words of Professor Paul Gifford, Director of the Institute of European Cultural Identity Studies at St. Andrews University.

Significantly, Prof. Gifford's introductory lecture to his series of seminars on a European Identity focused on Julia Kristeva, a Bulgarian-born and Sorbonne-educated French writer and scholar, who famously referred to herself and her fellow Europeans as "strangers to ourselves".

I was invited to the Institute to talk about my travels to the enclaves of Europe. And on my own vision of a European identity, too. They might have thought that, with my complicated background – both culturally and ethnically – I could pass for an adequate walking (and talking) learning aid on the subject of European Identity, and they were probably right.

However, those students and lecturers, who expected me to come up with a definition of a "European identity", or that of a "true European", must have been disappointed, for my travels in Enclavia had not brought me an inch closer to defining either of them. On the contrary, they had left me feeling even more uncertain about the meaning of "European-ness". Incidentally, I have always believed that being a writer is not about providing answers and definitions, but rather about getting increasingly – almost childishly – puzzled by reality and therefore posing more and more questions. Defining and categorising are the realms of scientists, scholars and reference books, and in the case of a "European identity" none of those has yet been able to come up with anything even distantly coherent.

I would happily agree with Felipe Fernandez-Armesto, who noted in the Introduction to *The Times Guide to the Peoples of Europe*: "Today's search for a European identity is hampered by the difficulty of saying what it is and recognising what it means."

Or with Pascal Couchepin, the Swiss Economics Minister, who wrote in his book *I Believe in Political Action*: "There is no strong European identity and it is not desirable there should be one."

Or with Theodore Zeldin's caution, voiced in his excellent book *The French*: "To describe a nation of 54 million [the French], still less one of 220 million [the whole of Europe], in a single phrase, to attribute to all its inhabitants identical moral qualities, that in any case are hard enough to be certain about when dealing with one individual or family, is a natural reaction in the face of the complexity of the world, but it is a habit born of despair, which persists because there seems no obvious way of avoiding it."

"A habit born of despair" could serve as a good epigraph, or rather epitaph, to all stereotyping "Culturgrams" and their like.

And yet, as you may have noticed, at the beginning of my travels in the few remaining enclaves of Europe – these real-life laboratories of natural European integration – I could not help ticking off some common ("European"?) qualities and traits, characteristic of nearly all of them.

Firstly, it seemed to me that by their all-permeating ambivalence, most of the enclaves themselves defied national stereotypes – read nationalism as such.

Secondly, I found the enclaves' residents (except perhaps for those of Llivia) thoroughly uncertain as to their cultural and national allegiances, routinely split between a host country and a historic motherland. "Strangers to themselves" indeed!

This uncertainty was equally typical of their perception by others (read identity) who were always tempted to label the "Enclavians" as rootless aliens, who belonged "neither here nor there" (*pace* Bill Bryson).

Among other possible "Enclavian" (European?) qualities, I would name adaptability, tolerance, flexibility, practicality, resilience and ingenuity (born out of necessity) in the face of international bureaucracy.

The further I travelled, however, the more vague, inconclusive and, yes, uncertain, those characteristics appeared. So, in the end, I gave up focusing on similarities and concentrated on differences instead.

If I were to draw one conclusion in the aftermath of my travels, it would be that there's no such concept as a "European identity", but there is definitely a notion of "European uncertainty". It is the willingness to accept the latter as a substitute for an "identity" that, to my mind, defines "true Europeans" (I mean, first and foremost, the residents of the enclaves themselves) and makes them different from Americans, or, say, Australians, who are not yet ready to do so, and hence are busy trying to bestow various fictitious identities upon themselves.

This beautiful and diverse "European uncertainty" is a direct challenge to the EU-inspired idea of federalist pan-European-ness, achieved "by stealth and gradualism" (Mark Leonard) and so cynically summed up by Valery Giscard d'Estaing in his address to the Convention on the Future of Europe, held in Brussels (where else?) in March, 2002: "The world would feel better if Europe spoke with a single voice."

The mere thought of this "single-voiced Europe" of the future is enough to give me the creeps. Such a "voice", by the way, is most likely to be a tireless drone from Brussels on "cross-border co-operation", "transnational dissemination of culture" and the like. How very dispiriting!

It must have been this scary vision of a thoroughly homogenised Brussels-controlled Europe that prompted Tim Parks to remark in the *New Statesman*: "Rather than postulating an identity against the rest of the world, the EU invites the surrounding world, country by country, to surrender identity and collapse into its amorphous embrace."

If so, the much-publicised recent EU enlargement will, sooner or later, inevitably backfire, and will become the very bone the EU will eventually choke upon – for the post-communist countries of Eastern and Central Europe won't be in a hurry to "surrender" their treasured "identities", for which they fought so bravely and persistently throughout many decades of Soviet domination. Could this become the ultimate crisis that will herald the end of the EU, as foreseen by the above-mentioned Pascal Couchepin, who wrote: "I am convinced that in the long term, in not more than several decades, the European Union will disappear."

I certainly hope that he was right, and that Europe's multiple, diverse and inimitable solo voices won't merge into one standard EU-conducted choir.

With "uncertainty" as the main and, it seems, pretty much the only component of European-ness, your archetypal European individual is bound to be hard to describe. Each enclave resident could perhaps pass as one, to a degree, and claim his or her "Passport to Enclavia" – my imaginary ID of "European-ness".

I could also offer myself – a one-person human enclave, unsure of his identity – as an example. Yet, for reasons of modesty (even if false), I'd like to nominate instead my good friend Mel Huang – a US-based political scientist of Chinese origins and a self-confessed Estonian (not to be confused with an Etonian!).

Conceived in Ithaca, NY, but born in Taiwan, Mel grew up in Hawaii and in California. His early years were fully bilingual (English/Chinese), yet by the age of six he had become exclusively English. Mel's teens were mostly spent in a poverty-ridden Chinese quarter of San Francisco. His father drank himself to death in front of him at the age of forty-one. Yet his deprived childhood did not deter Mel from pursuing an academic career. Having graduated from Cornell University, where he majored in Russian and East European studies, Mel became fascinated with the Baltic republics of the former USSR, particularly, for some reason, with Estonia. He taught himself the little country's tongue-breaking Finno-Ugric language, with its fourteen case endings, two different infinitives, and yet just one word for "he" and "she"; no future tense, and, to cap it all, something called the "partitive plural" – not to mention the ubiquitous double vowels and consonants, which make it seem as if the alphabet itself suffers from a chronic stutter. By the time Mel went to live there in 1996–98, working as a consultant for the Estonian government and later as Editor of the Tallinn-based *City Paper*, his command of Estonian was such that, had it not been for his distinctly Chinese appearance, he could have easily passed for a native Tallinner.

Back in the USA, Mel was soon hailed as the country's top expert on the Baltics. In addition to Estonian, he can now operate in Russian, Polish, Ukrainian, Italian, Latvian, Lithuanian (another extremely complicated language), German and Welsh (!). Like me, he seems unable to stay put for too long and keeps commuting between America and Europe.

"I feel legally an American, but spiritually European," he told me. "I don't believe in the European superstate, but I do believe in Europe as a spiritual and cultural unit. I feel much more comfortable in any corner of Europe than in the heart of Manhattan or Washington, DC, and if I could pick a home, it would be Tallinn, but that doesn't always work: I carry an American passport, and a ninety-day visa does not make a home."

I am sure my friend Mel (who, incidentally, cancelled his membership of the Republican Party on the day Dubya Bush became President) would gladly exchange his US passport for that of Enclavia.

Just like my eldest son, Mitya – now based in Canada with his French-speaking Québéquoise girlfriend, carrying an Australian passport and leading a global, peripatetic existence, yet still considering himself a European. European-ness, in his view, is "feeling both a victor and a victim of history". A tellingly "uncertain" definition . . .

While I was talking to students and teachers at the Institute of European Cultural Identity Studies, my five-year-old London-born and Edinburgh-based Australian-Ukrainian-English-Russian-Italian-Scottish Germanophile son Andrei, alias Balabka, was sleeping peacefully on the sofa in Prof. Gifford's office next door.

Having woken up by the very end of my talk, he timidly entered the lecture-hall.

I introduced Andrei as a true little European, and the audience burst into applause.

Looking at him, I remembered the words of Professor Norman Davies, the author of best-selling *Europe: A History*, at the Edinburgh Book Festival a couple of months earlier: "Multiple identity is the key to Europe's future."

My darling boy stood there, blinking bashfully under the lights and clearly embarrassed by all the attention. In one of his little hands was the key to Europe's future. In the other – a freshly issued Passport to Enclavia.

London – Melbourne – Edinburgh – Folkestone

DONATION

Part of the proceeds of *Passport to Enclavia* go to The Foundation for Endangered Languages – as Vitali Vitaliev writes, "because I am a linguist by education, love languages and think they shouldn't be allowed to die." The aims of the Foundation are:

- to raise awareness of endangered languages, both inside and outside the communities where they are spoken, through all channels and media;
- to support the use of endangered languages in all contexts: at home, in education, in the media, and in social, cultural and economic life;
- to monitor linguistic policies and practices, and to seek to influence the appropriate authorities where necessary;
- to support the documentation of endangered languages, by offering financial assistance, training, or facilities for the publication of results;
- to collect together and make available information of use in the preservation of endangered languages; to disseminate information on all of the above activities as widely as possible.

For further information please visit their website: www.ogmios.org

REPORTAGE PRESS

REPORTAGE PRESS is a new publishing house specialising in books on foreign affairs or set in foreign countries: non-fiction, fiction, essays, travel books or just books written from a stranger's viewpoint. Good books like this are now hard to come by – largely because British publishers have become frightened of publishing books that will not guarantee massive sales.

At REPORTAGE PRESS we are not averse to taking risks in order to bring to our readers the books they want to read. Visit our website: www.reportagepress.com. Five percent of the profits from our books go to charity.

You can buy further copies of *Passport to Enclavia* directly from the website, where you can find out more about our authors and upcoming titles.

REPORTAGE PRESS